Chris

Merry Christmas
To my Daddy.
Love
Brandy

THE COMPLETE
BOXER

Milo G. Denlinger
Anne F. Paramoure
Alfred Putnam
Gerda Umlauff
Robert W. Leach

Third Edition

Eighth Printing

HOWELL BOOK HOUSE INC.

845 Third Avenue, New York, N.Y. 10022

1972

Foreword

FOR some time there has been need of a new and complete book on the Boxer. Bearing this fact in mind, this volume is submitted to Boxer fanciers and to the public in general.

I have gone to great pains in tracing the German bloodlines, and while I can appreciate that this information will not be of interest to the novice, it should appeal to the advanced fancier in establishing his breeding program.

If the expert should find in it some little fact of record that even he did not know, or if his memory is refreshed, then I will have been repaid for my efforts.

In conclusion, I should like to thank all those who have given me information at various times, and in particular to express my gratitude to Mrs. Anne Fitzgerald Paramoure for her translation of the German, to Mr. Alfred Putnam for writing the chapter on the temperament of the Boxer, and to the many fanciers who so kindly allowed me to reproduce pictures of their outstanding dogs.

MILO G. DENLINGER

Second Edition

In this, the second edition, we have included information on the Boxer from fifteen countries around the world, together with many new photographs, in order to bring the book up to date and give the reader information heretofore unobtainable.

MILO G. DENLINGER

Third Edition

In this, the third edition, we have been fortunate in being able to include a chapter on West Coast Boxers by Mr. Robert W. Leach, of West Coast fame.

MILO G. DENLINGER

3

CHAMPION BANG AWAY OF SIRRAH CREST

Owned by Dr. and Mrs. R. C. Harris

**TOP WINNING BOXER OF ALL TIME
WITH 121 ALL-BREED BESTS IN SHOW**

4

Table of Contents

From Painting by Rauberhauptmann (1738-1771)
National Museum, Munich

6

CHAPTER I

The Personal Element

UNLESS a man has a natural love of dogs he will never make a success of keeping them, for he must be willing to sacrifice cheerfully his comfort and leisure hours doing what is necessary for them. He must see in them something more than simply a means to an end. The best animals in the world have always been bred for the love of them or the love of breeding and caring for them, rather than purely for the profit they bring; and the person who does not like dogs had better not attempt to keep them at all. Kindness is as important in the kennel as it is anywhere else. While a natural love of dogs will make the work lighter, the beginner should also have some idea of what to do for their welfare. He should not go into the kennel business, but should grow into it. Success depends less upon the way he keeps it—the food, the care, and the faithful performance of many little details of management; trained thinking is as necessary as wise working, and the prospective breeder must study the laws of breeding and learn its theoretical side, just as he would learn the rudiments of any other business before undertaking to manage it. Perseverance, too, is essential with dogs; and the more earnest and persistent the effort, the greater as a rule is the permanent improvement achieved.

Though we do not lack good types in most breeds, breeding dogs means more than the mere reproduction of the species. It means the development and mating of animals that will produce progeny of greater merit than the parents; and the test or any breeder's skill lies in his young stock showing improvement over the old along the directions he desires.

The beginner setting out to breed the best should adopt as his ideal the recognized standard of excellence of the variety, should select his breeding stock from the families most uniformly producing the type of dog nearest his ideal, and should choose thence the best available individuals—those most highly endowed with the typical characteristics and with the power of transmitting them. He must learn to mate like with like, generation after generation, thus condensing the good qualities of many into individuals, and increasing the prepotency of these excellences by selection rather than by in-breeding and he must bear always in mind the general principle that the road to permanent improvement lies through animals that exhibit unmistakable evidence of perfect health and constitutional vigor and that are well developed before they produce progeny intended for further breeding. Briefly, he must breed for what he wants, and remembering that "like begets like," systematically breed from the best.

Without a "good bringing up," involving complete nutrition, the possibilities of perfection inherited from the parents are at best only partially realized. Every improvement in feed and sanitation means less illness, stronger puppies, and—other things equal—a healthier and so better type in the next generation, for the results of good nourishment are transmitted to the offspring in the form of constitutional vigor.

It is only by continuous selection for his ideal upon the lines already laid down, by so far as possible avoiding consanguinity with its attendant risks, and by providing the best possible environment that the breeder can reasonably hope, while gradually and step by step attaining his goal, to increase the beauty, health and fruitfulness of the breed in which he is interested, and so confer lasting good on his fellow dog-owners and breeders.

The question of food is at the root of all life-conditions, for without food even existence would be impossible; and the animal body is built up of the chemical compounds composing the foods which nourish it, so that the growth and develop-

8

ment of an animal depends upon the character of the foods consumed by it, and the composition of its body is noticeably affected by the composition of its food. Put very simply, according to the kind of food supplied, so to some extent the character of the body varies, for the whole animal is made up directly and solely from the chemical elements in its food, and cannot of itself originate either matter or energy. Growth is not a miraculous dispensation of Providence. A dog, whether well or ill bred, cannot make growth out of nothing, or good growth out of poor and stinted food. Its growth comes directly out of the food; and flesh and bone must go in at the mouth in the form of good and proper food before they appear in the animal body. Accordingly as we furnish suitable or inadequate foods, so in proportion are the bodies of our dogs healthy, sound, well-developed, firm-fleshed and muscular or the reverse. They are as we build them . . . neither more nor less.

But though this general statement is true, it by no means follows that a dog may be regarded as a mechanical apparatus into which foods of definite chemical composition can be fed with the certainty of producing specific results. The vital element must be considered, for a dog is more than a mere machine; it has individuality and personal idiosyncrasy; it has individual likes and dislikes; it has a nervous system exercising great influence on nutrition and so upon growth; and it has high mental faculty, the right development and use of which depends largely on the proper nourishment of its body.

Broadly speaking, the best families of our various breeds have been raised to their present state of superiority by continued attention to feeding and breeding, and it cannot be said that either of these agencies has played the more important role in amelioration, since both are equally necessary to produce and maintain improvement.

Digestion and assimilation, like other functions, are certainly more or less hereditary; and our finest strains of dogs, having for generations enjoyed the liberal nutrition so necessary to their best development, have acquired a digestive habit craving ample and well-balanced feeding. We occasion-

9

ally see a highly bred dog in unthrifty condition where ordinary individuals seem to do tolerably well; and careless owners too often attribute such cases to the superior animal being naturally a bad doer; without giving thought to the fact that it inherits from its lines of well-fed ancestors an assimilative system calling for good and plentiful fare, and that it cannot therefore reasonably be expected to thrive on a ration barely sufficing for dogs of strains hereditarily inured to indifferent feeding.

The value of highly bred dogs lies largely in the fact that liberal feeding and good care, continued for generations, have produced an organization capable of responding to proper feeding and care, and of turning them to good account; and to keep the vital powers of such animals at the maximum by liberal nutrition and a generally high standard of living must be the principal aim of the breeder who seeks to maintain unimpaired the racial characters for which he values his improved stock.

Food has always been an important factor in producing and maintaining improvement in all useful kinds of animals, and the owner who invests in highly bred stock and gives it the same food and treatment usually meted out to indifferent animals will find succeeding generations deteriorate until the superior strain reaches the standard of the common stock ordinarily kept under such conditions, for the development of an organism is limited by its environment, and common, every-day stock represents the highest standard which can be attained under ordinary, every-day management. Hence, the familiar saying that highly bred animals which are good for anything should prove superior to ordinary stock under ordinary as well as under improved life conditions is as absurd as it is misleading. Improved breeding involves improved feeding; and to say that "it costs no more to keep a good dog than a poor one" is to state what is not true. It costs considerably more to properly maintain highly bred animals than common ones, but the profits are proportionately greater, for well bred dogs undoubtedly pay better and give more satisfaction than ordinary ones if proper food and care be given; but their superiority is due to their having enjoyed superior advantages over ordinary stock in the way of food and management, and if they are to remain superior they must continue to enjoy these advantages.

It has been said that "many persons do not know what a good animal is, even though they raise animals all their lives," and it is certainly a fact that the perfectly developed, healthy, firm-fleshed, active, intelligent and contented dog is an exception rather than the rule. Such an animal is not an accident. It is the product of understanding and solicitous care— the ample reward of the owner who really loves his stock and will at any time sacrifice his own comfort for its well-being.

Good feeding and good breeding go together. Both have shared in producing our present-day dogs; and it is only by the most judicious care in feeding as well as in breeding that the standard of excellence thus reached can be maintained. Without good food all improved strains of animals, no matter how highly bred, deteriorate or run out; and it is only when the conditions of feeding and management remain unchanged that valued characteristics owing their existence to these conditions are transmitted from generation to generation. Thus, the familiar adage that "the breed goes in at the mouth" is, like so many old breeding maxims, not without reasonable foundation.

LITTER OF BOXER PUPS
Berolina Kennels, Hatfield, Pa.
Mr. and Mrs. Herbert A. Brauer

A BOXER
From Painting in National Museum, Munich

CHAPTER II

Early Boxer History

THE earlier history of the Boxer breed, like that of many other breeds of dogs, is somewhat vague, as it extends back through centuries of unrecorded ancestry. The first German standard for the Boxer was not adopted until January 14, 1902, with the first studbook published some two years later, and before those events details of Boxer lore are few.

The Germans were scornful of dog breeding until it was established in England and elsewhere as an industry, and even after they had begun breeding seriously and scientifically in the latter years of the nineteenth century, they gave only slow and reluctant recognition to their own native varieties, neglecting them in favor of fashionable foreign breeds, particularly those of English origin.

One difficulty in tracing the descent of any breed of dogs from early times is that, not only were no accurate records kept but names were used very loosely. Substantially the same stock bore different names in different countries and at different periods. On the other hand, the same name might be used at various times and places to describe quite different animals. Varieties and species were confused with whole groups of breeds while a writer's description, if based on direct observation, might easily have been taken from local variants or atypical specimens. Then too, it is likely enough that fashions shifted as they do today and cross-breeding must have occurred with considerable frequency. Prior to

13

the beginning of scientific breeding in the nineteenth century little attempt could have been made to do more than follow the general principle that like begets like, although some efforts were doubtless made to secure puppies from individuals which had proved outstanding as hunters or workers, as the case might be.

As far back as the time of the ancient Assyrians, more than 2000 B.C., a strain of dogs with powerful build, heavy head and great courage was bred and used in war. Centuries later the name of Molossian was given to dogs of this type, named from the city of Molossis in Epirus, beyond the limits of modern Greece in what is today Albania. From here presumably they spread with the migration of primitive tribes and were in common use among the Celtic and Teutonic peoples, as fighters and protectors. They extended as far as the British Isles, whence specimens were exported to Rome in the second century A.D. Even at this early date the British dogs through selective breeding, appear to have been superior to their continental relations. They resembled the English Mastiffs of today and this breed has kept the original type intact through countless generations. The earlier specimens were valuable animals, highly esteemed by their masters and heavy penalties were provided by Teutonic tribal law for maiming or killing them.

During the Middle Ages the basic stock developed into three principal types. In England the original Mastiff type remained more watchdog than hunting dog. Crossed with dogs which were probably the ancestors of the modern Scottish Deerhounds, Irish Wolfhounds and Great Danes, a faster, lighter built breed, with some of the refinement of the sight hounds, was produced. Introduced into Germany in the sixteenth century, where they were known as Englische Dogge, they became very popular and were raised in great numbers. They were the ancestors of the modern Great Dane, or Deutsche Dogge and were carefully bred by the aristocracy for hunting bears, wild boars and the like. The third type, called Bullenbeisser (bull-biter) or Bärenbeisser (bear-biter) can be traced in Germany through pictures, hunting handbooks and literary sources from about the sixteenth century.

14

The woodcuts of Jost Ammon, 1539-1591, show clearly recognizable specimens with characteristic head and cropped ears although the tails are left long as in the modern Dane. Hans Friederich von Flemming in 1719 described the Bullbeisser as of medium size but heavy build, with clipped ears and tail. Through selection a smaller type was developed, known as the Brabanter, which is illustrated by J. E. L. Riedinger of Augsburg, 1698-1767. They were hunters and fighters, fierce looking and hence employed as yard and chain dogs as they made good watchdogs.

During the middle ages the Bullenbeisser were the only hunting hounds in Germany, in contrast to England where the sight hounds were commonly used, and this was doubtless a factor in the great popularity of the Englische Dogge in Germany after the sixteenth century. Wagner states that the main portion of most of the old German hunting packs was made up of "Rueden", described as coarse-haired dogs with wolfish heads and bushy tails, which were freely bred by the peasants. This description leads us to assume that the dogs in question were the ancestors of the modern German Shepherd which was certainly used to protect the flocks from attack by wolves and other predatory animals. "Rüde" is still the usual term for a male dog or stud among German fanciers of the Shepherd Dog.

These "Rueden" are said to have suffered great losses during the hunts due to their style of fighting. For this reason, or because they were peasant owned and bred (or perhaps for both reasons) they seem to have been regarded as highly expendable and little effort was taken in their breeding. The Bullenbeisser and Doggen however, secured hold on the nose or ears in such a way as generally to avoid serious injury while giving the hunters time to reach the kill. Their value was accordingly much greater and they were highly prized and carefully bred. Being kept for a particular purpose, the Bullenbeisser was peculiarly subject to any change in environment, taste or custom which affected his specific usefulness. The larger type of Bären or Bullenbeisser with his tremendous strength and courage and ancient lineage, was gradually replaced by the faster and more elegant Englische Dogge in

15

the favor of the aristocracy in Germany even as the Mastiff largely disappeared in England. In both countries therefore, a smaller and lighter dog of the original stock was developed. In England where bull baiting, bear baiting and other animal fights were very popular at least as early as Elizabethan times the Bulldog eventually evolved, but the modern extreme type of this latter breed did not appear until well into the nineteenth century. Earlier specimens resembled the small Bullenbeisser in type and size although the presence of whites and parti-colors characterized the English breed only.

In Germany the small Bullenbeisser continued to be used, along with the Englische Dogge at the courts and hunting lodges. As the population increased and the hunts gradually dwindled however, they became comparatively rare. By the end of the eighteenth century and the Napoleonic wars which largely did away with the ducal estates, only a few boarhunts were still maintained. Perhaps the breed was continued through the descendants of such court dogs, dispersed into private hands when the hunts were broken up. The last such occasion is said to have been held at the Kurhesser Court in 1865. However, the statements of many writers indicate that the Boxer was a domestic dog as early as 1800, so it is likely that much of the breeding stock was already in private hands by that date.

The small Bullenbeisser or Brabanter had been bred and trained to hold in check the most fiery bull and to obtain a grip on the nose which he held, regardless of the animal's efforts. When social conditions eliminated his function in the court hunts, the transition to a cattle dealer's dog must have been easy. If his prestige suffered a social eclipse, the employment thus provided doubtless served to prevent the small Bullenbeisser from disappearing altogether.

During the first decade of the nineteenth century the Bullenbeisser was described as an intelligent dog, being readily taught tricks as well as being easily trained for hunting. His intelligence and tractability led to popularity with theater and circus people. This had the beneficent effect of perpetuating the breed during the lean years. His personality combining watchfulness and intelligence has remained little changed

BOSKO IMMERGRUN 24
and
DON JUAN IMMERGRUN 74

CH. BLANKA v. ANGERTOR
NO. 4

BULLENBEISSER
From Painting by Reidinger (1698-1767)

17

down to modern times and he has proved himself eminently suitable for his modern role as house dog and companion.

During the middle and latter part of the nineteenth century the Bullenbeisser, having ceased to be bred for hunting by the courts and having become associated in the public mind with butchers, cattlemen and actors, was not highly regarded. In addition he suffered from the German tendency at that period to disregard all the native breeds in favor of foreign importations, particularly from England. Among such importations were the English Bulldogs and Bullterriers of that day, which were then crossed with Bullenbeisser stock. This had less effect upon general body type than might be supposed, for the modern English Bulldog with his wide front, tremendous head and comparatively light hindquarters has been obtained by selective breeding and is very different from his ancestors. The early nineteenth century Bulldog was a close relative of the Bullenbeisser and was a square-built, long-legged dog of great activity. Even as late as 1895, this type was still being eliminated from the Bulldog breed in England, by selection.

In Germany an opposite process took place. Here the older, more active type which had existed for generations remained the ideal and those individuals which approached the low-to-the-ground cloddiness of the Bulldog, were in their turn bred out. For a period of years however, the Bullenbeisser's progress remained at a low ebb. No club for his promotion and improvement yet existed and consequently no records were kept. The butchers and countrymen into whose hands the breed had now passed, had probably never heard of such things. Indeed, the whole modern conception of the dog fancy, with its thoroughly organized shows, detailed pedigrees and hundreds of breeders, handlers and judges, many of them professionals, was a thing of the future.

By about 1880 then, the Bullenbeisser had lost his aristocratic connections and had become a butcher's dog, useful around slaughter houses for rounding up cattle and popular with students and actors for his tractability and good disposition. His undershot jaw gave so strong a grip that he was often unable to let go of his own volition. The teeth locked together and the grip had to be broken by inserting a sheathed hunting-knife and twisting it. Because of this proclivity, a popular animal act on the stage showed the dog being lifted to the roof by his grip on a rope and lowered again.

The name "Boxer" is comparatively modern, apparently dating from about 1890. It must have won general acceptance by 1896 when the first specialty club was formed at Munich under the name, "Boxer Klub". It has been claimed that the name "Boxer" was jokingly applied by an English traveler who noted a tendency of the dog to use its paws in fighting. This seems improbable. Any such action would likely result in a badly bitten if not broken leg. On the other hand, a German breeder of forty years' experience states positively that the Boxer does *not* use his feet, except to try to extinguish a small flame such as a burning match. But the Boxer does box with his head. He will hit (not bite) a cat with his muzzle hard enough to knock it out and he will box a ball with his nose. Or perhaps, since the German dictionary translates "boxer" as "prize-fighter" the name was bestowed in appreciation of the fighting qualities of the breed rather than its technique.

Prior to 1830 it is claimed that the Bullenbeisser was usually fawn or brindle in color with a black mask. White was introduced through the use of imported stock from England. From photographs of dogs just before the turn of the century, it is clear that some were almost pure white. Bulldogs, bull-terriers, in fact anything that resembled a Boxer to any appreciable degree was used for breeding at that time. There was little demand for puppies however, and it was not until the breed began to be exhibited at shows and was actively supported by a group of determined fanciers, that its status gradually improved. A Boxer class was first offered in Munich in 1895 but a real demand for the breed was not evident until the 1920's, after years of showing and selection to improve the stock.

Among the early breeders and exhibitors who played an important part in Boxer affairs were Herr Joseph Widman (first president of the club and owner of Ch. Rigo v. Angertor), Jakob Dauer (father of the noted photographer of dogs), Joseph Frey (whose Meta v.d. Passage has been termed the mother of the breed), George Alt and Georg Lechner of Mu-

19

nich (both active before 1890), A. Kolb of St. Salvator Kennels, Hans Maier, also of Munich, Albert Schmoeger and Grenz of Stuttgart (the first show held in Munich since the War, on June 1, 1947, was a memorial to Schmoeger), Otto Roth of Pfalzgau Kennels in Mannheim, Stuerzer of the Deutenkofen Kennels who bred Ch. Rolf v. Vogelsberg and Haunstaedter of Biederstein Kennels. Schmoeger's sons still continue his kennel. Dr. Julius Schuelein of Treuherz, one-time owner of Ch. Rolf v. Vogelsberg, has been interested in Boxers since about 1906. He now lives in New York and has shown us the courtesy of furnishing a photograph of the bronze statue of Rolf which stands in his office. A reproduction of this bronze is found in this volume. Mr. Valentine Martin, another German fancier of the early 1900's and the owner of the Stuttgarter Kennels of New Jersey, died late in 1947.

Although many of the early recorded breeders were in Munich, Emil Ilgner wrote in 1902 that the breed was especially numerous in Württemberg and that in the south of Germany, the breed was customarily called "Boxeln". At that time, after having been pushed into the background by the popularity of foreign breeds such as the English Bulldog and the Bullterrier, the Boxer was beginning to come to the fore again. Ilgner's book, "Gebrauchs-und-Luxushunde" portrays a Boxer named Bosko owned by Gustav de Boss of Bonn, which resembles a Boston Terrier in appearance and markings. The resemblance is so striking that it is not surprising that Ilgner, a Dachshund fancier, was misled by it. He actually states that at a period when the Germans were dazzled by foreign importations and took little interest in home products, the Americans were more discerning. "To them", he says, "our Boxers were very pleasing. They called them simply Boston Terriers, because the first fanciers happened to be in that city. Now the Boston Terrier is all the fashion on the other side of the water"!

The first years of the Boxer Club in Germany must have been fairly stormy ones. Although a few members favored the English Bulldog type, most of them opposed this strongly and the first standard was devised with a view to eliminating foreign types. Arguments resulted in the formation of a

OLD TYPE BOXER
From Book by Emil Ilgner-1902

second club, the Deutscher Boxer Klub, and others were founded in various parts of Germany as well as in Switzerland and Holland. The first two clubs soon united but there were further schisms before the final agreement in May, 1910. The "Boxer Klub mit dem Sitz in Munich" was the eventual outcome and remained the parent club although there were numerous local units.

The first Boxer Studbook was not published until 1904 and in the same year the "Boxer Blätter" was issued under Dr. Neumann. Later it was edited by Dr. Schuelein and after the first World War, by Philip Stockmann.

Considering the vigorous efforts made to rid the breed of foreign strains, it is interesting to note that No. 1 in the Studbook, Flocki, was sired by Dr. Toenniessen's Tom, a bulldog, out of Alt's Schecken No. 50, a white (or more probably from her name, a parti-color). Flocki proved to be of no ultimate importance as a producer but a full sister, Ch. Blanka v. Angertor No. 4 (whelped in 1895) was very important indeed for she became the dam of Meta v.d. Passage No. 30, one of the outstanding bitches of the breed. Incidentally, Meta was the own granddam of Arnulf Grandenz AKC 78043, the first Boxer registered with the American Kennel Club. Flocki resembled Bosko, being marked like a Boston Terrier, with white blaze, collar and front legs.

The Boxers of the 1890's and early 1900's were heavy, slow animals with tremendous heads, as compared to their modern descendants. Moritz v. Pfalzgau No. 104, Maier's Lord No. 13 and Hugo v. Pfalzgau No. 85 differ but little from studies made by the artist, J. E. L. Riedinger of Augsburg who died in 1767. Nor do they differ greatly from such early specimens of the English Bulldog as Crib and Rosa, painted in 1817. Ch. Rolf v. Vogelsberg No. 113 however, whelped in 1908, had the quality and refinement of the best modern dogs if we may judge by the bronze model made of him by his owner. The pendulum has swung to such an extent nevertheless, that we are warned today against allowing the Boxer to become too fine in bone but to select heavy bitches for breeding.

Another valuable reminder comes from Dr. Leon F. Whitney in his "Salute to the Boxer" printed in Boxer Briefs, May

1947. Dr. Whitney, a veterinarian, as well as a widely known student of genetics and breeding problems, has had years of experience with many breeds. He praises the Boxer as being free from many common skin diseases, an easy keeper on diets simple to feed, a natural mother and easy to raise. Moreover, he ranks the breed at the top in resistance to contagious diseases such as true distemper and housedog disease. Finally, Dr. Whitney praises the Boxer's disposition which he says is 90% excellent, but points out the vital importance of continuing to turn out only representative dispositions.

It is an interesting fact that when a breed is selected and inbred over a period of years for either type or performance, certain bloodlines tend gradually to oust all others. Eventually all the important winners and producers come to be descended in male line from two or three prepotent sires, or even from a single one. This is true of the English race horse which now traces in male line to three stallions in the late 17th or early 18th century. It is true of the Scottish Terrier, a breed in which all champions for a number of years have traced to two half-brothers sired by Rambler. Standard Schnauzers trace to Seppel and Schnauzer; German Shepherds, to Horand v. Grafrath.

In the case of Boxers, the present day winners apparently all trace in male line to Box St. Salvator No. 59, a wheaten male who when mated to Mary v. Nymphenburg No. 65, produced Flock St. Salvator No. 14 in 1894. Both Box and Mary, though subsequently registered, were of unknown breeding and have carried on only through Flock.

A handful of other dogs appear at the back of all modern champion pedigrees. Nero Aschenbrenner, unregistered, sired Wotan No. 46, a golden brindle who ranks after Flock St. Salvator in importance, although it is through his daughters and granddaughters that he carried on. Maier's Sultan bred to Frey's Nelly (both unregistered) produced Weber's Ella No. 108, who was Wotan's dam. Moreau No. 72 (whose name suggests a French origin) bred to Meta No. 73 produced Bosko Immergrun No. 24, a red brindle marked like a Boston Terrier. Bosko sired Rose of Graudenz, dam of the first Boxer registered by the American Kennel Club and herself the first Amer-

23

ican-owned Boxer whose name has come down to us. Bosko carried on however, solely through his fawn daughter, Mucki v. Vogelsberg, the dam of Siegerin Frigga v. Vogelsberg, a brindle. Dr. Toenniessen's Tom, the Bulldog, has already been mentioned. The other notable sire of the early days was Lechner's Box No. 48, a fawn and white whelped in 1887.

The dam of Lechner's Box was a French bitch imported by George Alt of Munich and afterwards registered as Alt's Flora No. 49. She was a dark brindle and was mated to a local dog whose name, color, owner and breeding are unrecorded. The puppies were just another Boxer litter, considered of no particular importance. A year or two later Alt's Flora was bred to her son Box, who passed into the hands of Georg Lechner of Munich. From this mating came two important bitches, the brindle Alt's Flora II No. 11 and the fawn and white Alt's Schecken No. 50. When Lechner's Box was three years old, in 1890 he was mated to his daughter, Alt's Flora II, who was also his half-sister, and produced Maier's Lord No. 13 (a brindle like his dam and granddam) who carried three crosses of Alt's Flora I.

Maier's Lord was a golden brindle, strongly inbred and a powerful influence on the breed. It was not however, until he was about seven years old that he sired Piccolo v. Angertor No. 17, an almost pure white, whelped in 1897 out of Maier's Flora No. 47. Maier's Flora, a fawn and white said to have been of French ancestry, was also whelped in 1897. A year and a half later, in June, 1899, she produced a litter by Lord (then close to nine years old) which contained the red fawn bitch, Mirzl No. 44. Mirzl at the age of two was bred to Wotan and whelped the fawn Ella Dauer No. 103, dam of the great Ch. Rigo v. Angertor, and Moritz v. Pfalzgau No. 104, a fawn, who sired Else v. Pfalzgau (a double Wotan granddaughter), the dam of Ch. Kurt v. Pfalzgau who carried the male line of Box St. Salvator down to the present day.

Piccolo v. Angertor, the white brother of the dark fawn Mirzl, was mated to another white, Ch. Blanka v. Angertor No. 4, a daughter of the bulldog, Dr. Toenniessen's Tom and Alt's Schecken No. 50, a fawn and white sister to Piccolo's granddam, Alt's Flora II. This mating continued the inbreed-

24

MUHLBAUERS FLOCKI NO. 1
First entry in the Stud Book

META v.d. PASSAGE NO. 30

ing to Alt's Flora and Lechner's Box and produced Meta v.d. Passage No. 30, whelped November 2, 1898. This bitch has been called the mother of the breed. She produced at least three litters containing six important individuals, five of them, sons. In 1900 the fawn male Hugo v. Pfalzgau No. 85 was whelped by the six year old Flock St. Salvator and about 1905 passed into the hands of Otto Roth of Mannheim. Hugo left four important sons—all fawns, Hockstein's Nazi No. 175 whelped in 1903; Hans v. Pfalzgau No. 540 whelped in 1906; Ch. Kurt v. Pfalzgau whelped in the same year and from whom all the important male lines of today are derived; and Ch. Remus v. Pfalzgau whelped in 1907, who sired the extraordinary show winner Ch. Milo v. Eigelstein. Here again it is interesting to note that Hugo was a mature animal of six or seven when he sired his most notable winners and producers, Kurt and Remus.

So far as the pedigrees show, the mating which produced Hugo was an outcross and his parents were not related. However, since the grandparents of Flock St. Salvator are all unknown, it is impossible to be certain. There may have been a relationship farther back. Meta's picture, evidently taken when she had nursed many puppies, appears heavy set and somewhat low to the ground. Hugo is the old-fashioned type. His sire, Flock, is described as a forerunner of the modern dog, combining strength with elegance though too light in color and suffering in expression from a flat skull. Flock doubtless contributed his stylish build, and to him and Wotan may be due the suppression of the large amount of white found in the earlier descendants of Lechner's Box, for neither Flock nor Wotan has white recorded in his ancestry. Hugo v. Pfalzgau's picture strongly resembles Moritz v. Pfalzgau No. 104, whose dam Mirzl was a full sister to Piccolo v. Angertor. Moritz was a Wotan son and when mated to Busecker's Loni, a Wotan daughter out of Meta v.d. Passage, produced Else v. Pfalzgau. Hugo and Else, son and granddaughter of Meta v.d. Passage with additional line breeding through Mirzl, produced Ch. Kurt v. Pfalzgau, a truly great fawn who is described as faultless in build and body though somewhat lacking in head. Withal he was a wonderful sire. His greatest son, Ch. Rolf v.

Vogelsberg was the result of further line breeding for he was out of Venus v. Vogelsberg by Kurt's half-brother, Hockstein's Nazi from a daughter of Ch. Gigerl and a bitch whose dam was inbred to Maier's Lord through a mating of the latter to his daughter, Mucki v. Isartal, a full sister to Mirzl.

Going back to Meta v.d. Passage, we find that she whelped two more sons by Flock St. Salvator, Schlag Bitru No. 111, a brindle of quality in the same year as Hugo v. Pfalzgau and Ch. Schani v.d. Passage No. 128 two years later, in 1902. Schani, like his sire Flock and grandsire Box St. Salvator, was a very light fawn or wheaten. Mated to Ella Dauer (by Wotan out of Mirzl and so a full sister to Moritz v. Pfalzgau), Schani produced Ch. Rigo v. Angertor. Rigo, a deep red fawn, despite his light sire (a fact which corroborates the theory that Wotan strongly affected the color of the breed), approached the modern type and proved a phenomenal show dog. At the age of two he won first in a class of 32 outstanding males at Frankfurt in 1906 and was the first Boxer to sell for the then noteworthy price of 1,000 marks. His success brought the fawns to the front and they soon far surpassed brindles in popularity. None of Rigo's older sons equalled his sire in quality however, nor did they attain any great importance as producers. His daughters were another story. Dora v. Vogelsberg became the dam of Ch. Rolf Walhall; Lutti v. Eigelstein became the dam of Ch. Milo v. Eigelstein; Siegerin Lotti v. Lindenfels, the dam (by her sire Rigo) of Sieger Tango Hermes; a granddaughter, Siegerin Liesel v. Deutenkofen, the dam of Ch. Cäsar v. Deutenkofen. Liesel was sired by Ch. Rino II v.d. Elbe, Rigo's best son, one of a litter whelped when he was seven years old, out of Ella v. Osterland, which contained three outstanding males. Cäsar was doubly descended from Rigo, since his sire, Ch. Moritz v. Goldrain was a Rigo great-grandson through Ch. Rolf Walhall's dam.

In 1901, between her two litters by Flock St. Salvator, Meta v.d. Passage whelped two sons by Wotan. The daughter, Busecker's Loni No. 382, dam of Else v. Pfalzgau, may have been from this same litter. The sons by Wotan were Prinz Mark v. Graudenz No. 118 and Ch. Gigerl No. 113. All three were brindle like their sire, Ch. Gigerl. Although very popu-

27

lar at stud and prepotent in transmitting his solid brindle color, Gigerl left only one important producer, Siegerin **Frigga v. Vogelsberg.** Frigga's daughter, Venus v. Vogelsberg (by Hockstein's Nazi) was the dam of Ch. Rolf v. Vogelsberg. Dora v. Vogelsberg, out of Frigga by Rigo v. Angertor, was bred to Rolf v. Vogelsberg and produced Ch. Rolf v. Walhall, who consequently was inbred to Frigga. It is through the latter's dam, Mucki v. Vogelsberg, that Bosko v. Immergrun appears in modern pedigrees. I think it is wrong to state that Gigerl represents Wotan's greatest influence on Boxer history. Moritz v. Pfalzgau, Else v. Pfalzgau (his double **granddaughter**) and Ella Dauer, dam of Rigo v. Angertor, would seem at least equally important.

During the first decade of the 19th century fawns predominated. Except for Wotan and Gigerl there were few brindles of consequence. Then in 1908 came Rolf v. Vogelsberg who began his show career at the age of two and did much to stimulate public interest in the brindles. A little later, about 1912, classes were divided by color, with fawns and brindles shown separately.

Rolf stood nearly 24 inches at the shoulder, one of the largest Boxers of his time and the bronze made of him by F. v. Miram-Stockmann shows a truly outstanding individual who could compete against the best today. Rolf was outstanding in head and neck, shoulders, hindquarters and feet. His chief fault, like Gigerl's, was a slightly arched back. Descended in male line from four generations of fawns—Box St. Salvator, Flock St. Salvator, Hugo v. Pfalzgau and Kurt v. Pfalzgau, Rolf took his color from his dam's side and his prominent winners were all brindle males.

The inheritance of color in dogs has been most thoroughly discussed in the second edition of "How to Breed Dogs", by Leon F. Whitney, published in 1947. Widely known as a geneticist and student of breeding problems, Dr. Whitney has carried on many experiments of his own as well as summarizing the findings of other writers. Coat color in Boxers belongs to the same series which is found in Great Danes, Greyhounds, Bulldogs and Bullterriers. Earlier writers have warned against continually breeding fawn to fawn for genera-

28

Wen dieses Paar erst mal bewacht, der sag' der
Freiheit Gute Nacht.
He, who is guarded by this pair can say goodbye
to freedom for the time being.

tion after generation, on the ground that it results in a pale, washed-out color. The same is said to be true of Danes, although some breeders claim success. Probably a careful selection of fawn individuals which were not only strongly colored themselves but coming from strongly colored stock would be successful in maintaining a desirable fawn.

In Boxers, the basic color is fawn, which may vary from a deep red to light yellow. The variations are caused by dilution factors which are recessive and so may be carried by dogs which do not show the characteristic themselves. When such a dog is mated to a dog carrying the same recessive modifier, the light color will show up in some of the puppies. Brindle is produced by a dominant modifying factor acting upon the fawn color. Brindle, like fawn, can vary widely both in the number and intensity of the stripes and in the color of the background. The same recessive modifiers which affect fawn alone can affect the fawn background upon which the brindling factor acts. In actual practice some brindles are almost black while others are so light that they might also pass for fawns with a few dark tickings. The latter might be due to the effect of dilution factors. Some of these very light brindles are no doubt registered as fawns, which can create confusion for anyone attempting to study color inheritance through entries in the Studbook. Properly speaking, two fawns should produce all fawn puppies, but a very light brindle mistakenly registered as a fawn, could produce brindle puppies by a true fawn. Brindles bred to fawns and brindles bred to brindles normally produce both fawn and brindle puppies, for most brindles carry only one gene of the dominant brindle modifier. However, some dogs produce only brindle puppies, indicating that they carry two brindle genes, one derived from each parent. In such a case it would not matter whether the dog were mated to a brindle or a fawn. All of the puppies would be brindles. But the brindle puppies with a fawn parent would carry only a single brindle gene and so might produce fawn puppies, while some of the puppies by a pure dominant brindle out of a brindle might carry two brindle genes like the sire. (The same would of course be true if the dam instead of the sire carried two brindle genes, but it is harder to be sure in the

30

EGON V. GUMBERTUSBRUNEN BZB. 5908
Czechoslovakia, 1938

case of a bitch as she produces comparatively few puppies).
It is tempting to theorize that Rolf v. Vogelsberg may have
been a pure dominant carrying two brindle factors, but the
evidence is against it. Wagner lists five of his get, all brindles,
and declares that he transmitted his qualities almost wholly
through brindle males, whereas his son, Rolf Walhall, was a
successful sire of both sexes and colors. Access to the German
Studbooks should reveal whether Rolf v. Vogelsberg sired any
fawns. However, Gordon lists his son, Siegfried v. Hirschpark, as a red and the Norwegian scientists, Dahl and Quel-
prud, who studied 6,564 entries in the first twenty-one volumes
of the Studbook, thought it doubtful that pure brindles existed.
Whitney, however, is positive that they do and states that he
has found several sires which produce brindles only. Rolf's
pedigree does not support the theory that he carried two brindle factors for his sire, Kurt v. Pfalzgau, is listed as a fawn
from two fawn parents. The only possibility is that, if both
Kurt and his dam, Else v. Pfalzgau, were really very light
brindles, wrongly classified, they handed on a brindle factor
from Else's dam, the Wotan daughter, Busecker's Loni.

Beside the basic fawn color and the brindle modifier, Boxers
carry various combinations of white. Nearly all, in fact, have
at least a few white hairs on the chest or toes. White was
prominent in the small group of prepotent individuals at the
beginning of the Studbook, as has been related. It was severely frowned upon by German breeders and the big winners of
the next few years were solid colored. However, white toes
may be seen in the pictures of such dogs as Gigerl and Rigo v.
Angertor. Kurt v. Pfalzgau had white feet and a white patch
on his chest, as did Rolf v. Vogelsberg. Rolf v. Walhall had
white feet, Moritz v. Goldrain, a white chest patch, as did Cäsar Deutenkofen and his three sons, Check v. Hunenstein,
Granti Struthio and Buko v. Biederstein and the latter's son,
Iwein v. Dom. Thence it reappears in the leading sires of the
past fifteen years. Under the present standard a Boxer may
have white markings which do not exceed a total of one-third
of the body area and the pictures in the Boxer Parade (*Popular Dogs* special Boxer issue, June, 1947) reveal many champions with considerable white on chest, feet and even extended to

EDLER v. ISARSTRAND BZB. 14591
Czechoslovakia, 1938

full white collars and face markings. Still larger areas occur on puppies which do not appear in the show ring and may even be so extensive that the dog is almost entirely white.

Whitney devotes a chapter to the inheritance of what he calls the "white collar color" pattern, which is found in many breeds including several in the series to which Boxers belong. It is the most common of the several different whites which are variously inherited. This white is of three main types, namely: (1) a minimum of white (toes, chest spot, tail tip, etc.) on a solid colored dog; (2) a somewhat larger amount of white with a definite white collar; and finally (3) a dog which is largely white with some patches of color. There are considerable variations within these limits. Boxers are normally of the first or second type. Whitney reports a study of 83 matings containing 608 puppies. A previous study in which only solid colored dogs of type 1 were mated, produced 888 puppies, all solid colored. Accordingly, in the later study this type of mating was omitted. So were matings of two type 3 individuals, which regularly produce offspring of the same type. In the 83 matings studied, the parents were of all three types but none of the type 1 dogs were from two type 1 parents. No pair of white collared dogs produced solid colored puppies. Solid colored dogs which carry type 2 or type 3 as a recessive, produce solid color plus whichever recessive is carried. It becomes clear that we are dealing with a genetic color series in which solid color is dominant over either type 2 or type 3, and type 2 is dominant over type 3, which is recessive to both the others. Consequently, nearly white puppies are likely to occur in any mating where both parents carry the type 3 factor, even though it may have been carried recessively for a number of generations. The result will be the same whether the type 3 factor is carried by a solid colored dog or by one with the full white collar markings. Two type 2 dogs which did not carry the type 3 factor should produce all type 2 like the parents, although Whitney does not record any such matings. Such early individuals as Blanka and Piccolo v. Angertor, Alt's Schecken and Meta v.d. Passage were clearly of type 3. Gigerl, Hugo and Moritz v. Pfalzgau were of type 1, Bosko Immergrun and many modern dogs are of type 2.

Whitney also states that black Boxers were common in Germany but rare in America. Blacks, of course, occur in Danes, Greyhounds and Whippets, which belong to the same color series as Boxers. However, since black is dominant over both fawn and brindle it is necessary that one of the parents be black in order to obtain black puppies. The Harlequin black and white is a special pattern peculiar to Great Danes and does not occur in Boxers. It is quite distinct from the spotting which may result from the white collar pattern of type 3. Blue, a dilute black, is due to a dilution gene which is not found in Boxers.

It has been claimed that Boxers with a great deal of white are inclined to be deaf. Whitney claims that out of some thirty white puppies, he has yet to see one with any hearing difficulty. His studies on deafness indicate that it is color linked in the case of harlequins and merles (neither of which colors are found among Boxers). It also runs in families and is often found in Bullterriers. Since Bullterrier crosses were made in the 19th century, some Boxers may have inherited this type of deafness. It is apparently a recessive, but if it occurs in white the fact is purely accidental. Naturally, where such a fault is carried and white puppies are found, some of the deaf pups would be white as well. Some of Whitney's puppies were totally deaf and some only partially so. And some compensated by their alertness to such an extent that it was some time before their deafness became apparent. Such puppies may appear stubborn or stupid when they are actually partially deaf and particularly, if they die or are sold young the breeder may remain unaware of the fact.

Rolf v. Vogelsberg was one of the slow maturing type which wears well and has great staying powers, in contrast to the quick maturer which, particularly in the larger breeds, often turns out to be a flash in the pan. When nearly two years old, Rolf was purchased by Dr. Julius Schuelein of Munich who saw him on the street and recognized his outstanding quality. He began his show career in 1910 at the age of two and remained undefeated. However, his true value as a sire

35

was not appreciated for many years. Prejudice and undue stress upon the roached back, which was his chief fault, hindered many from breeding to him. Rolf's first important son, Schelm v. Angertor (out of a Rigo v. Angertor bitch, the fawn Ch. Charlotte v. Steinhausen), was whelped in 1910. He was sold to Switzerland but left a daughter, Daisy v. Friedensengel, who became the dam of Ch. Moritz v. Goldrain, as well as a son, Rolf Ismaning, sire of Zwibel v. Dom. In 1911 came Rolf Walhall and in 1912 the first recorded Sieger to go to America, the brindle Dampf v. Dom. Owned by Ex-Governor Lehman, Dampf was the first Boxer to become an A.K.C. champion, finishing in 1915, but if he left any American-bred progeny, they were never registered. Siegerin Rassel v. Dom, the granddam of Iwein v. Dom, sire of Sigurd, was whelped in 1916 and Siegerin Betti v. Goldrain, two years later. Rolf was eight and ten years old respectively when these last two were whelped.

Rolf's stud career was limited by the War. It is claimed that the Boxer was the first breed used by the German Army during World War I. At any rate, some sixty of them entered the service in 1914 although the breed was not officially recognized for police work until 1925. Rolf, at the age of six, formed one of the 1914 contingent and was one of the few survivors of the group. At the age of eleven he won the open class at Munich and was Sieger for the fifth time, surviving until past twelve years old.

Rolf's sons were widely scattered. Schelm v. Angertor and Siegfried v. Hirschpark went to Switzerland, Wotan v. Dom to Sweden, Dampf v. Dom to America. Ch. Rolf v. Walhall remained to carry on the line in Germany. The stud activities of this younger Rolf, whelped in 1911, were severely curtailed by the war. Of his six Sieger sons, the oldest, Ch. Moritz v. Goldrain, was not whelped until 1918. Uli and Uto v.d. Adelegg and Drill v. Gumbertusbrunnen followed in 1920; Illo v. Blankenberg and Egon v. Gumbertusbrunnen in 1921. The latter two were fawns, the other four, brindles. Rolf's Siegerin daughters include Anita v. Rechenberg, Brunsvigas Mirzel, Asta v. Waldfried, Rassel v.d. Adelegg and Cora Tre-

36

BRONZE of ROLF von VOGELSBERG
Courtesy of Dr. Julius Schuelein, New York City

dintafu. He also sired Mira v. Goldrain, the dam of Sieger Buko v. Biederstein.

Ch. Milo v. Eigelstein, whelped in 1911 was the greatest fawn of his day and like Rolf v. Vogelsberg, undefeated. Owing to the separation of classes by color, they never met in the ring except once when Milo won the challenge trophy. Their breeding activities were likewise separated for Milo was at stud in Berlin and Rolf in Munich. Milo was extensively used at stud but left no sons which were his equal. He is said to have transmitted loose shoulders and badly spread paws. Perhaps it was not all Milo's fault that he did not score heavily as a sire, for at three years of age he was retired from competition and died not long afterward. Had Rolf v. Vogelsberg or Rolf Walhall ended their careers at that age they might have left no more impress on the breed than Milo. The Milo blood is still to be found, though not in the male line. His son, Sieger Omar v. Falkenhorst, and grandson, Sieger Pascha Neunberg, occur through Belfine v. Isarstrand, dam of Edler v. Isarstrand. Argo v. Schonbuch, another Milo son, sired Sieger Astor v. Hiltensberg, who carried down in male line to Landa of Mazelaine.

Through Sieger Edler v. Isarstrand there is Milo blood at the back of quite a number of American Boxer pedigrees. Indeed, the second American Boxer champion, Bluecher v. Rosengarten, traced in male line to Milo, through Armin v. Grafeneck, Sieger Tasso v.d. Spree and Sieger Treu v. Kurland, while Bluecher's dam was also by a Milo grandson. Asta v.d. Adelegg, a Milo granddaughter who whelped one of the first Boxer litters in America, came over in whelp to a Milo great grandson, Blitz v. Moosburg. Her son from this litter when subsequently bred to her daughters by Bluecher carried five lines to Milo, and their descendants are still to be found in considerable numbers. Milo stock in general has been criticized as lacking in head. Milo's grandson, Sieger Tasso v.d. Spree, also sired Sieger Harras v. Sachsenhof, said to have been the best of Milo's descendants, who unfortunately died very young leaving few get. Whether through accident or an inherited lack of stamina, longevity does not seem to have characterized the Milo line. Harras v. Sachsenhof does appear

38

in American pedigrees however, for his daughter, Zitta v. Durrenberg, was the granddam of Check v. Hunenstein. Zitta carried two more lines to Milo on her dam's side. Perhaps it was partly the combination of Milo lines which made the mating of Check with Ch. Landa of Mazelaine so successful, for Landa traced to Milo through both sire and dam. Cilly v. Hohenneuffen, a notable German producing bitch who was dam of the still greater Siegerin Gretel v. Hohenneuffen, was also a Milo descendant, though only in the fifth generation. Writing in 1926, only fifteen years after his birth, Herr Phillip Stockmann of the von Dom Kennels declared that the Milo blood had entirely disappeared, as one might say, into the sand, but though he has left no male line still producing he has certainly contributed to an important extent to the breed as it is constituted today.

It has already been stated that Ch. Rolf Walhall carried on the male line of Rolf v. Vogelsberg. From the close of World War I and particularly during the early 1920's, his sons began to dominate the picture. Sieger Egon v. Gumbertusbrunnen, police trained, and Egon's sons, Sieger Hansel v. Stolzenfels and Sieger Edler v. Isarstrand, are still to be found in many pedigrees, but they are becoming rare in male line. A few champions at stud in America today trace to Egon through less known sons, Golf v. Frankonia and Castor v. Hohenneuffen. A Moritz v. Goldrain son, Sieger Alex v.d. Magdalenenquelle, was active during the middle of the decade, but it was Ch. Cäsar v. Deutenkofen who really established the Rolf-Moritz line on a firm footing. Cäsar's impressive list includes the Sieger brothers, Hansel and Hermes v. Biederstein, Ch. Check v. Hunenstein, Sieger Granti Struthio, Ch. Buko v. Biederstein, and the producing daughter Dudel v. Pfarrhaus. Check was the only one who came to America and he was not whelped until 1927. Iwein v. Dom, two years older than Check, was a fawn son of the Austrian Sieger Buko v. Biederstein. Not a champion himself, Iwein sired many excellent Boxers including Siegerin Tea v. Isebeck, but he was supremely important as the sire of Int. Ch. Sigurd v. Dom. Sigurd's influence upon the Boxer of today has been so great that it cannot be exaggerated and he is fully discussed later on. He was whelped in 1929 and since the 1930's marked the real rise of the Boxer in America many of his get and grand-get were imported. Sieger Hermes v. Biederstein, through his grandson, Hermes v.d. Uhlandshöhe, had a number of American descendants, of whom at least one, Ch. Viktor v. Kraichgau, traces in male line. Sieger Hansl v. Biederstein, Check v. Hunenstein and Granti Struthio are also represented, Hansl's great contribution being the Siegerin Gretel v. Hohenneuffen.

It has been claimed that the bitch winners at German Sieger shows are inclined to be somewhat large and doggy in type and that they do not produce title winners themselves. How much truth there may be to this assertion I cannot say, but it must be remembered that the German system provides for only two Siegers and two Siegerins yearly, one each in fawns and one each in brindles. Since a bitch is limited to two litters at most per year, a Siegerin obviously has a mathematically much smaller chance than a Sieger when it comes to producing winners. Stockmann, indeed, says that there are always good stud dogs available and that here a breed warden can give good advice, but that correspondingly good bitches are usually lacking. He adds that the best bitches seldom come from Siegerins. The bitch, however, should be of the best bloodlines, and without careful study of the stud book rational breeding is impossible.

There have however, been a number of Siegerins who did produce title winners. Among them may be mentioned Siegerin Lotti v. Lindenfels, dam of Sieger Tango Hermes, Siegerin Liesel Deutenkofen, dam of Ch. Cäsar Deutenkofen and Sieger Alexander Deutenkofen, Siegerin Gretel v. Hohenneuffen, dam of Siegerin Dina v. Uracher Wasserfall, Siegerin Betti v. Goldrain, dam of Sieger Astor and Siegerin Asta v. Hiltensberg, Siegerin Rassel v. Birkenhain, dam of Sieger Drill v. Gumbertusbrunnen, Siegerin Daisy v. Biederstein, dam of Siegers Hansl and Hermes v. Biederstein.

Ten years ago the American shows were still to a high degree dominated by German-bred dogs and it was not until 1947 that an American-bred achieved the distinction of siring the greatest number of champions by a single sire

40

INT. CH. SIGURD VON DOM OF BARMERE

Sire: Iwein v. Dom   Dam: Belinde Hassia
Bred by von Dom Kennels in Germany; imported, owned and shown
to AKC Ch. in U.S.A. by the late Mrs. William Z. Breed

finished during the year. In spite of lavish importation of the best dogs and bitches available, American breeders did not immediately succeed in producing individuals to equal Germany's best. This may be ascribed to a variety of causes. For one thing, the German system of rearing was generally different. Large kennels staffed by professionals were practically unknown and puppies were frequently farmed out in one's and two's so that they grew up as house dogs, receiving a maximum of freedom and individual attention. Moreover, it was not thought wise to raise too many puppies to a litter. Although litters as large as thirteen were not uncommon, with an average from five to seven, only five, or at most six, were ordinarily raised and since bitches were harder to sell, the puppies selected for disposal were frequently females. Only the most promising puppies from the best dams were kept, so that there was less likelihood of breeding from inferior bitches.

The show system also had an important influence. Titles were awarded only at certain shows, where the best dogs from the local events were exhibited. Distances being comparatively short, most of the outstanding dogs of a given year would compete against each other and the best individuals were not withdrawn from open competition after winning. Rolf v. Vogelsberg, for instance, won the Sieger title five times. In the early days in this country exhibitors were often widely separated. Moreover, breeders here lacked the personal knowledge of the ancestors and close relations of their dogs. They were only names on a pedigree, their faults and virtues for the most part unknown.

After the advent of Hitler, the dog fancy like everything else, came under government control. The independent breed clubs, affiliated with the all-breed association—the Deutsche Kartell für Hundewesen—but having their own stud books and a large share of independence, became subdivisions of a subdivision. The Kartell itself became only the Reichsgruppe Deutsche Hundewesen, a section of the Reichsverband Deutscher Kleintierzüchter (the national association of small animal breeders). Registration rules became more stringent. In at least some of the working breeds it was required that first one and later both parents should have passed at least

INT. CH. LUSTIG VON DOM OF TULGEY WOOD
Owned by Tulgey Wood Kennels
Erwin O. Freund, Chicago, Illinois

the most elementary training test if a litter was to be registered. Non-Aryans were not permitted to belong to the clubs.

Various books and articles on Boxer breeding in Germany stress the importance of the Breed Warden, who was designated to supervise breeding activities and pass upon matings. He had to be consulted by the owners of bitches and only a dog approved by him could be used, if the puppies were to be registered. Hence about fifty per cent of the puppy crop each year was sired by two or three outstanding studs, whose outstanding value soon became apparent when so many matrons visited them. I believe that this matter of the breed warden has been greatly over-emphasized. An oldtime German breeder now in this country, who has known the breed for some forty years, told me that breed wardens were not important in his time. Stockmann (himself a breed warden for a number of years) writes in 1926 advising the selection of a stud dog before the bitch comes in heat, after careful consideration. He recommends that a beginner ask the breed warden for his opinion, but makes no mention of any compulsory feature. Neither do the directions for registration mention it. I know that during the 1920's the German Shepherd Dog Club (Verein für Deutsche Schäferhunde) had an elaborate system of breed inspection. Owners brought their dogs to be examined individually and after study of the dog and his pedigree, those accepted as suitable to improve the breed were entered in a special book, the Körbuch, with breeding recommendations. However, the inspection was not compulsory and I do not think rejection barred a dog or bitch from registration in the stud book if subsequently used for breeding. Any compulsory features of the breed warden system must, I am quite sure, have been introduced under Hitler.

Since 1938 or the first part of 1939 American breeders have been out of touch with Boxer affairs in Germany and communications are only just beginning to be reestablished. During 1937 Boxers had the fourth largest entry at the 23 important shows. German Shepherds came first, Foxterriers second, and Dachshunde third. The largest entry was 109 at the Reichssieger show in Munich. In 1938 the Reichssieger show at Cologne was reported in the Boxer Blätter as having

44

INT. CH. DORIAN VON MARIENHOF OF MAZELAINE
Owned by Mazelaine Kennels,
Mr. and Mrs. John Phelps Wagner, Milwaukee, Wisconsin

entries of high quality and very uniform, with the males, especially the fawns, better than the females. The brindle males were criticized as small compared to the fawns, most of them being hardly of medium size. Heads and eyes were good and hindquarters had improved, but there were many bad pasterns, toed out feet and poor fronts, as well as long backs and falling croups. In spite of the "high quality" asserted this is hardly a bright picture.

What has happened during and since the war seems to be largely a matter of speculation. It seems improbable that the breed suffered heavily during the early years. The bombings would have destroyed some dogs in the cities, no doubt, but until the actual invasion and its aftermath it is probable that country breeders, at least, could manage to care for and feed their dogs. If breeding was restricted to the best specimens it would preserve quality even if quantity was somewhat reduced.

Since the war's end there have been several importations of Boxers which have already become American champions. At least some of these were selected on the spot by fanciers serving in Germany. They may be useful in linebreeding, but the Boxer fancy in this country is now strong enough to stand by itself. Our best American-breds can hold their own in any competition. There may have been and probably will be importations of poor quality and doubtful pedigree palmed off upon ignorant purchasers with no real knowledge of the breed. I have had first-hand reports of a place at Frankfurt where dogs of all sorts were sold with obviously spurious papers. Any prospective purchasers should be careful to deal only with established and reputable breeders.

Boxer breeders in Holland are reported to be active again since the War. Alaska v.d. Hollants Roem, whose American championship was published early in 1948, came to this country by way of England, where breed activity is also reviving. Boxers are likewise reported in India and Palestine. No less than 86 served with troops in the Middle East. Mrs. R. Menzel, whose Ben Satan Kennels at Linz, Austria, were prominent before the War, is now head of the Palestine Canine Research Institute. Quite a number of Boxers bred by her came to this country. Several were owned by Sumbula

46

Kennels, including Ch. Agel bath Satan, who became the dam of two champions. Agel's daughter, Simonetta se Sumbula, was the dam of Ch. Nordhoff Simonetta and the granddam of three champions, including Ch. Beacon Out of Bounds. Another bitch, Ortelma bath Satan, was imported about 1924— probably the first Austrian bitch to come to America.

The modern Boxer has a history of almost sixty years in the stud books. During that period we can trace the individual dogs and bitches and assess their importance to the breed. Back of that time our knowledge is more general. We must depend on a few drawings and paintings which show recognizable Boxers, and upon written descriptions. When all is said there is surprisingly little change, and the Boxer's popularity remains unimpaired. As popular as ever in his homeland, he has now spread not only throughout Europe but to Asia, South America, Hawaii, the West Indies and Canada in addition to the United States.

Photo by Brown
INT. CH. UTZ VON DOM OF MAZELAINE
Owned by Mazelaine Kennels,
Mr. and Mrs. John Phelps Wagner,
Milwaukee, Wisconsin

GERMAN CHAMPION CALO V.D. WUPPERSTADT, 44973
German Boxer, brindle male

CHAPTER III

How German Champions Are Made

CHAMPIONSHIP titles in Germany have varied somewhat at different periods. Judging by the early stud books, around the year 1900, the term "champion" was used for a time, but was apparently superseded by the more native term "Sieger," which means literally a conqueror or victor. The Pinscher-Klub, founded in 1895, at Cologne, published the first volume of its studbook at the end of 1902. This contains minutes of its earliest meetings. At Erfurt on September 15, 1900, a decision was made regarding the awarding of Sieger titles. They were to be conferred on dogs winning three first prizes in the Open class, under three different approved judges at recognized shows and two first prizes in the Sieger class, and non-members of the Klub were eligible. This is the same, requirement as in Volume I of the studbook of the Bayerischer Schnauzer-Klub, founded in 1907, which appeared in 1910. The Cologne and Munich clubs amalgamated in 1922 as the Pinscher-Schnauzer-Klub and their first studbook, published in 1923, states that the title of Sieger (or its feminine equivalent, Siegerin) shall be awarded to dogs winning three first prizes with the rating "excellent" under three different approved judges at recognized shows. The title of "Jahressieger" or Year Champion was to be awarded at the annual specialty show by an approved Klub judge to the best dog in all classes, with a rating of "excellent." The same requirements applied to the "Jahressiegerin" title for bitches. By 1925 the term "Klubsieger" was applied

49

to dogs receiving the first type award. There could be as many of these in a given year as fulfilled the requirements, and the Jahressieger was usually, though not always, a Klubsieger also. By 1925, likewise, Miniature Schnauzers were divided by color, so that a double set of Jahressieger titles was awarded, one for blacks and one for pepper and salts.

In 1902 Oberleutnant Emil Ilgner (retired) published "Gebrauchs-und Luxushunde." In this he lists 17 breed specialty clubs which published their own studbooks, in addition to the D.H.St.B., the all-breed stud book, comparable to the AKC studbook in this country, and the D.G.St.B., the all-breed studbook for working dogs. He does not state when the specialty clubs were founded but the Dachshund Club had already (in 1902) published ten volumes of its studbook, the German Wirehaired Pointers five, the Foxterriers nine, the St. Bernards and Collies three each, while the German Shepherd Dog Club was founded in 1899 and the Pinscher-Klub, as above stated, in 1895. The Deutschen Kartell für Hundewesen was founded by a group of clubs, among which the S.V. was a charter member. It corresponded to the AKC and even though the specialty clubs kept their own studbooks the AKC required the Kartell stamp on all German registrations before German dogs were accepted for registration over here. Probably the various clubs made their own rules for sieger titles, at least in the early days, but Ilgner makes no mention of what they were. The first volume of the Pinscher-Klub records the award of the title of "Champion" in 1899 at Cologne and also at Amsterdam in Holland in 1901. The S.V. for many years awarded only two titles annually, "Sieger" for dogs and "Siegerin" for bitches.

In 1933 the Nazi government muscled in on the dog fancy, as on so many other things. The Kartell became the Reichsverband für das Deutsche Hundewesen, in the Reichsfachgruppe Deutsches Hundewesen (RDH), and the specialty clubs belonging to it each became a Fachschaft or "Section." The Jahressieger title or its equivalent became Reichssieger, and was awarded at the annual Reichssieger show. The Klubsieger title became Fachschaftsieger. In 1937 the RDH became a member of the Reichsverband Deutscher Kleintierzüchter

50

(German Reich Organization of Small Animal Breeders). Orders were given that in breeding both parents should have received the rating of "very good" or "excellent" from a judge approved by the Section. In the case of working breeds at least one parent must also have an "Ausbildungskennzeichen" or training certificate. This rule went into effect July 1, 1937, according to Felix Ebner in his "Schnauzer und Pinscher," published in that year. He also stated beginning January 1, 1938, a working certificate would be required for both parents.

The terms Siegeranwärter and Siegeranwärterin are used for a dog or bitch which has wins toward a title. Such a dog would correspond to a championship certificate winner in England. The title of Weltsieger (world champion) appears to be awarded at one important European show annually, with competition open to qualified dogs from various countries. The August, 1937, issue of the Mitteilungen of the Fachschaft für Schnauzer und Pinscher gives a report of the World Congress of the Fédération Cynologique Internationale (FCI) at Paris in July and in another item lists German Schnauzer winners at Paris, which included five Weltsieger and Weltsiegerin titles. In July, 1938, it was announced that the Antwartschaft for the Internationale Schönheits-Championat (International Bench Championship) as well as the Reichssieger titles would be competed for at Cologne in October. The report of the Paris show in 1937 mentions an Internationale Championats-Anwärterin. This would seem to indicate that these International Championships were awarded on a basis similar to the Fachschaft or Klubsieger titles and were not the same as the Weltsieger titles.

CH. QUALITY OF BARMERE "Cue"
Sire: Int. Ch. Sigurd v. Dom of Barmere
Dam: Ch. Blanka v. Bopserwald of Barmere
Owner: Roger E. Hannaford, Cincinnati, Ohio

CH. QUEST OF TULGEY WOOD
Sire: Int. Ch. Lustig v. Dom of Tulgey Wood
Dam: Alma
Breeder: Tulgey Wood Kennels, Chicago, Ill.
Owner: Keith Merrill, Herndon, Virginia

CH. RIOT OF SIRRAH CREST
Sire: Ch. Utz v. Dom of Mazelaine
Dam: Ch. Kokokreme of Sirrah Crest
Breeder and Owner: Dr. and Mrs. R. C. Harris

CHAPTER IV
A Short Explanation of German Grammar
By Anne FitzGerald Paramoure

THE translation of foreign pedigrees and show reports is not easy, even for one who is well acquainted with the language in its everyday form. Just as the novice finds many English words used in an unfamiliar sense, so there is a special vocabulary employed by German-speaking breeders and exhibitors. To translate them it may be necessary to plow through ten or twenty variations of meaning in the unabridged dictionary, with no certainty that one will select the correct equivalent, even if it is included, while the ordinary abridged dictionary is likely to be no help whatever. Abbreviations are very frequently used, and may be fully as puzzling as an unfamiliar use of a familiar word.

Dogs imported from Germany, Austria, Switzerland or Czechoslovakia may all have German pedigrees, and the breeds in which importations are or have been common are numerous. They range from such extremely popular breeds as Boxers, Dobermans, Dachshunds and German Shepherds through the Schnauzers and Great Danes to such comparative rarities as Weimaraners, German Short-haired Pointers and Miniature Pinschers.

While the following pages will not supply even an elementary course in the German language, they may enable the fancier confronted with the pedigree of an imported dog, a foreign show record or an advertisement of stock for sale to understand the important items without too much difficulty. A few facts which will be useful to anyone without a reading knowledge of ordinary German are also included.

All German nouns are capitalized, not merely proper names. Adjectives are not capitalized, even though they may form part of a kennel name, unless actually used in place of a noun. The formal second person "Sie" (meaning YOU) is also regularly capitalized. When an adjective is attached to the front of a noun so as to make a single word, however, it is capitalized instead of the noun to which it is attached, as in *Kleintierzuchter,* meaning small animal breeder.

German plurals are not formed by adding *S,* but in most cases by adding *er, e* or *en* to the root of the noun. Sometimes the root vowel is changed by the addition of an umlaut (··) over a, o or u, making it ä, ö, or ü. This may be the only change or it may be in addition to the plural endings already mentioned. The umlaut stands for an *e* which is not written. In proper names or in a word beginning with a capital the *e* is often written in place of the umlaut, and where printing is done with type which does not include the umlauts the *e* itself may likewise be used. The umlaut can be important for three reasons: it changes the pronunciation, it may be the only sign that a word is plural and not singular; in a German dictionary or index all names or words which contain an umlaut will be alphabetized as though the letter *e* were printed after the vowel over which it is used. This may mean that a name or word will be found several lines or even pages away from the same name or word without the umlaut. Moreover, the presence or absence of the umlaut may completely change the meaning of a word. For instance, *Mucke* means a whim, while *Mücke* is a gnat. Finally, the feminine of many nouns is formed by adding an umlaut to the vowel and the suffix *in* to the end of the word, so Hund, dog (general or masculine) becomes Hündin, bitch.

Other peculiarities which may confuse those not familiar with the language are: nouns have four cases, nominative, genitive (usually ending in *s* or *es* but sometimes in *e, en* or *ens*), dative and accusative. There are three genders, masculine, feminine and neuter. Adjectives and pronouns also change their endings. All this is too complicated for anyone without some knowledge of German to follow in detail, but is mentioned to make clear the fact that a change in ending may indicate simply a different grammatical form of the same word.

56

Another peculiarity is that the perfect participle of verbs is formed by adding *ge* to the *front* of the verb in most cases. Thus the participle of *decken* (meaning to breed) is *gedeckt* (bred) and the word will be found in a dictionary under *d* and not *g*. Compound verbs with *inseparable* prefixes do not add the augment *ge* for the participle, however. On the other hand, compound verbs with *separable* prefixes insert the *ge* between the prefix and the verb root, the participle of *anfangen* (to begin) being *angefangen*. In certain other tenses the separable prefix of the verb in the main clause comes at the end of the phrase or sentence, as for instance, *ich fang an* (I begin) is a form of *anfangen*. As a compound verb may have quite a different meaning from the simple one from which it is formed, non-Germans unaccustomed to this usage find it extremely confusing to discover at the end of a sentence a prefix which may unexpectedly change the whole meaning. The Teutonic word order which frequently puts the verb at the end of the sentence instead of where other people would expect it is also confusing.

The names of German dogs, which are likely to appear dauntingly long and formidable to those who do not understand the language are much easier to remember if they are broken down into their separate parts. Most of them consist of an individual name, a preposition with or without an article, and a kennel name. Most if not all German breeds require litter registration, all puppies carrying the breeder's registered kennel name, while it is usual for all of a single litter to have individual names beginning with the same letter. Kennels' names often refer to the town, village or local area in which the breeder lives. Sometimes they are related to the name of the breed or the breeder, and puns are not uncommon. Thus Herr Berger, breeder of German Shepherds, used the kennel name *Bergerslust,* meaning "Shepherd's Delight" or "Berger's Delight" as one prefers. The impressive-sounding "Fiffi v. Rhein-Herne-Kanal" is only Fiffi of the Rhine Canal at Herne, where her breeder lived. Wilhelm Schwaneberg took the kennel name "v.d. Schwanburg," meaning "of or from the Swan Castle." The owners of "Neckarlust," "Neckarstadt" and "Neckartal" all live along the Neckar

57

River. "Zwergschnauzerheim" is nothing but "Home of Miniature Schnauzers."

Because so many common words are frequently abbreviated, both in pedigrees and show reports, a list of abbreviations is given in addition to the regular vocabulary. The meanings of the words for which the abbreviations stand may be found in the vocabulary itself.

Up to 1934 many of the larger German specialty clubs published their own studbooks. Included among these were the Verein für Deutsche Schaferhunde, devoted to German Shepherd Dogs, and the Pinscher-Schnauzer-Klub, which registered six breeds: Giant, Standard and Miniature Schnauzers, Smooth-haired Pinschers (not Dobermans), Miniature Pinschers, and Affenpinschers. The Deutsches Kartell für Hundewesen (DKH) was the all breed club recognized by the AKC, and the papers of imported dogs had to be endorsed by them before they were accepted for AKC registration. In 1934 the Nazi government reorganized the dog fancy, like so many other things. The national organization became the Reichsverband für das Deutsche Hundewesen (RDH) and the specialty clubs were absorbed as Fachschafte or sections of the RDH, though they continued to publish their stud books and breed papers as before, at least up to 1938. What has happened during the war remains to be seen. On July 1, 1937, the RDH was reorganized as the Reichsverband Deutscher Kleintierzüchter (RDK). The old styles of *Sieger,* or *Jahressieger* were changed to Reichssieger, while the Klubsieger title became Fachschaftsieger. Bitch titles were similarly changed to Reichsiegerin and Fachschaftsiegerin.

German training commands are given in quotation marks (e.g. "Fuss"). The English translation is followed by an exclamation mark (e.g. Heel!).

A number of abbreviations are used for more than one word. In such cases the various German words are given and the translator may choose the one which best fits the sense. Initials are frequently used for the names of specialty or other clubs, as we speak of the AKC. These initials are included among the abbreviations so far as possible.

German Vocabulary

"Ablegen" .... Lie down and lie still!

Abstammung .... Origin, descent, ancestry

Abzeichen .... Markings

Abzugeben .... Available, offered (e.g. for sale or at stud)

"Achtung" .... Look out! Watch! On guard!

Ahn, Ahnen .... Ancestor, ancestors

Ahnentafel .... Pedigree

Allgemeiner Deutscher
Rottweilerklub e.V. .... German Rottweiler Club

Allgemeiner Eindruck .... General impression

Alter .... Age

Altersklasse .... Open class

Amme .... Foster mother

Angekört .... Inspected and certified suitable for
breeding

Ankörung .... Official inspection for breeding suitability

Anwartschaft .... Prospective championship; accumulated
wins toward a championship

"Apport" .... Fetch!

Apportierbock .... Dumbbell (for training to carry and
retrieve)

"Auf" .... Up! (when the dog has been sitting or
lying)

Aufbeisser .... Dog with undershot mouth

Augen .... Eyes

"Aus" .... Out! Let go!

Ausbildung .... Improvement or advancement of a breed

Ausbildungskennzeichen .... Standard

Ausstellung, Austellungen........... Show, shows

Band, Bände .... Volume, volumes (of stud book or
magazine)

Befehl .... Command, order (in training)

Befriedigend .... Satisfactory (used in rating on show
points)

Begleithunde .... Companion or house dogs

Begrenzte Klasse .... Limit class

Behaarung .... Coat, hair

Beisskorb .... Muzzle (worn by dogs)

Belassen .... Left (with dam after birth); kept

Belegt .... Bred (of bitches)

Besitzer, Besitzerin .... Owner

Besitzwechsel .... Change of ownership

Bewertung .... Qualification; value; rating (e.g.
"excellent," "very good," "poor")

Bild, Bilder .... Picture, pictures

Blau ....Blue; slate-grey
"Bleibsitzen" ....Stay! Keep sitting!
Blindenführer Hund ....Guide dog (for the blind)
Blindenführerhundprüfung ....Guide dog trial or examination
Boxer-Klub e. V.............................Boxer Club (incorporated)
Braun ....Brown
Braungestichelt (Elchfarbig)......Elk colored; mixed brown not solid color
"Bring" ....Fetch!
Bringbock ....Dumbbell (for carrying)
Bringen ....To fetch
Bruder, Brüder ....Brother, brothers
Brustfleck ....Spot on chest
Brustgeschirr ....Dog harness

"Daun" ....Down! Drop! (when dog off leash is to
                                                         be halted at a distance from trainer)
Decken ....To breed, to cover by a stud
Decken frei, zum ....At public stud (for the usual fee)
Decktag ....Breeding date
Der, dem, den ....The (declined like an adjective or
                                                         pronoun and agreeing in gender with
                                                         its noun)
Deutsche Dogge ....Great Dane
Deutsche Pointer u. Setter-
    Verein ....German Setter and Pointer Association
Deutsche Schäferhund ....German Shepherd Dog
Deutsche Teckelklub e.V. ....German Dachshund Club (inc.)
Deutsche Vorstehende,
    Kurzhaarig ....Shorthaired German Pointers
Deutsche Vorstehende,
    Langhaarig ....Longhaired German Pointers
Deutsche Vorstehende,
    Stichelhaarig ....Roughhaired German Pointers
Deutscher Doggenclub e. V. i.
    Kartell ....Great Dane Club (inc.)
Deutscher Reichsverband für
    Polizei und Schutzhunde
    e. V. ....German Reich Association for police and
                                                         guard dogs (inc.)
Deutscher Schaeferhund
    Verband ....German Shepherd Dog Association (com-
                                                         paratively little known compared to
                                                         the S.V.)
Deutsches Hundestammbuch ......The official all-breed German stud book
Deutsches Kartells für
    Hundewesen ....Pre-Hitler all-breed German club corre-
                                                         sponding to the AKC.

Diensthund	Service dog; trained dog in actual service
Dienstsuchhund	A tracker on active police duty
Dienstsuchhundprüfung	A trial or contest for trained trackers
Dobermannpinscherverein	Dobermann Pinscher Association (commonly called D.V.)
Dogge	Bulldog (see also *Deutsche Dogge*)
Drahthaarigen	Wire-haired
Dressierung, Dressur	Training
Dressurprüfung	Training test, now called Zuchtprüfung
Dritter	Third
Dunkel	Dark
Dunkelrot	Dark red
Ehrenpreis	Trophy
Eigentümer	Owner
Eingetragener Verein	Registered association (i.e. incorporated)
Eintragung	Entry (at a show or in a stud book)
Eintragungsbestätigung	Certificate of entry; registration
Elchfarbig	Elk colored; a brownish mixture, not solid tan or chocolate
Ellenbogen	Elbows
Eltern	Parents
Enkel, Enkelin	Grandson, granddaughter
Entwartung	Cancellation
Ersatzpreis	A prize given in special recognition of the runner-up to the prizewinners at a show
Erster	First
Fachschaftssieger	Formerly Klubsieger
Fachschaft	Department; division; branch
Fachschaft für Schweizer Sennenhunde im R.D.H.	Swiss Sennenhund Division of the R.D.H.
Farbe, farbig	Color, colored
"Fass"	Take it!
Fédération Cynologique Internationale	International Dog Federation which awards World championship titles
Fehler	Faults
Fehlerhaft	Faulty
Führer	Handler
"Fuss"	Heel!
Gau	District
Gebrauchshund	Working dog
Gedeckt	Bred, covered

Gefleckt .... Spotted
Gelb .... Yellow
Genannt .... Called, alias, known as
Geschlecht .... Sex (also species, family, kind)
Geschutzter .... Protected
Geschutzter Zuchtname .... Registered kennel name
Gesellschaft für
    Hundeforschung .... Association for dog research
Gestreift .... Brindled, striped
Gestrommt .... Brindle
Getötet .... Killed, destroyed (when a litter is too
                                                            large to raise advantageously)
Gewinkelt .... Angulated
Gewolkt .... Clouded
Geworfen .... Whelped
"Gib laut" .... Speak!
Glanz .... Lustrous
Glatthaarig .... Smooth coated
"Gradaus" .... Straight ahead! Forward! (for *gerade*
                                                            aus)
Grau .... Grey
Gross .... Big, large
Grösse .... Size
Grosseltern .... Grandparents
Grossmutter .... Granddam
Grossvater .... Grandshire
Gut .... Good

Haar .... Coat, hair
Hals .... Neck, throat
Halsband .... Collar
Hasenfarbig .... Hare colored, mixed brownish grey
Hauptgeschäftstelle .... Main office, headquarters
Hauptprüfung .... Championship contest or trial
Hauptpreishüten .... Herding championship trial
Heisst .... Called, known as
Hell .... Bright, light colored
Herdengebrauchshund
    (HGH) .... Trained herding dog
"Hier" .... Here! Come here!
Hinterhand .... Hindquarters
Hinterläufe .... Hind legs
Hirschrot .... Reddish fawn
Hitze .... Heat, season (in bitches)
"Hoch" .... Up! Over! (command for jumping)
"Hopp" .... Away! Over! (command for jumping)
Höchstlobende Erwähnung .... Very highly commended

Höhe	Height
Holländische	Dutch
Hund, Hunde	Dog, dogs (male or in general)
Hundefreunde	Dog lovers, fanciers
Hündin, Hündinnen	Bitch, bitches
Inzucht	Inbreeding
Jahressieger, Jahressiegerin	Dog and bitch winner of the annual specialty championship show, thereby becoming champions of the year. After Hitler called Reichssieger and Reichssiegerin
Jahrgang	Annual volumes, year's issue of stud book or magazine
Jugendklasse	Youth class (12-18 months for German Shepherds)
Jung	Young
Junger, Junge	Puppy, puppies, youngsters
Junghundklasse	Junior class (18-24 months for German Shepherds)
Jungtier	Young animal, youngster, puppy
Kampioen	Champion (Dutch)
Katalog	Catalog
Kind, Kinder	Get (of a sire or dam)
Klein	Small
Kleintierzüchter	Small animal breeder
Klubsieger, Klubsiegerin	Club champion dog or bitch. (Winner of First Open with rating of Excellent under three different judges.)
Knochen	Bone
"Komm"	Come!
Komondor-Klub im Kartell	Komondor Club, affiliated with the D.K.H.
Konkurrenz	Competition
Kopf	Head
Koppel-Klasse	Brace class
Körbuch des Vereins für Deutsche Schäferhunde	Book of breeding suitability inspection of the S.V.
Körzeichen	Certified as suitable for breeding
Kräftig	Strong
"Kriech"	Crawl! Creep!
Kriegshund	War dog
Kruppe	Croup
Kurz	Short

63

Langhaarig .... Long-haired
"Lass" .... Let go! Out!
Läufe .... Running gear, legs
"Leg dich" .... Lie down!
"Legen" .... Lie down!
Leine .... Leash
Leistung .... Field training
Leistungsbuch .... Field trial registration book
Leistungsprüfung .... Field trial
Leistungssieger
   Leistungssiegerin .... Field trial champion dog and bitch
Leistungswanderpreis
   des S.V. .... Field trial trophy of the S.V.
Liebhaber .... Fancier
Links .... Left, lefthand
Lobende Erwähnung .... Highly recommended

Mangelhaft .... Passable, mediocre
Maske .... Mask, face
Melde Hund .... Army messenger dog
Meldehundprüfung .... Messenger dog trial
Meldeschein .... Registration certificate
Meldung .... Entry, registration
Mit .... With
Mit Amme aufgezogen................... Raised with a foster mother
Mitglied, Mitglieder .... Member, members
Monatshefte .... Unbound monthly issue of a publication
Monatsschrift .... Monthly magazine

Nachgewiesen .... Indicated
Nase .... Muzzle, nose
Nederland Hundestammbuch...... Netherlands stud book (all breeds)
Neulings-Klasse .... Novice class
Nicht nachgewiesen .... Not indicated; not shown on the record
"Nimm" .... Take it!
Nummer .... Number

O .... Zero; failed
Offeneklasse .... Open Class
Offeneleistungsklasse .... Open Class for dogs with training degrees. The winner of this class in each sex, if qualified Excellent (V) wins the Reichssieger title at the annual Reichssieger show, provided he or she has attained the minimum age for the breed, even though defeated in another class by a dog not eligible or not entered in OLK.

Ohne Amme	Without a foster mother
Ohren	Ears
Osterreichischer Verein für deutsche Schäferhunde	Austrian Association for the German Shepherd Dog
Osterreichisches Hundestammbuch	Austrian stud book (all breed)
Ortsgruppe	Local group; local club
Paar	Pair, brace
"Pass auf"	Watch out! Alert!
Pfeffer und Salz	Pepper and salt
Pfote, Pfoten	Paw, foot
"Pfui"	Shame! No!
Pinscherklub	Pinscher Club (Köln) founded 1895
Pinscher-Schnauzer-Klub (P.S.K.)	Pinscher and Schnauzer Club
Pinscherzuchtbuch (PZ)	Pinscher Club stud book
Pinscher-Schnauzer-Zuchtbuch (P.S.Z.)	Pinscher and Schnauzer Studbook
Platz	Place (in competition)
"Platz"	Down!
Prämierung	Award
Polizei Dienst Hund	Trained dog in actual police service
Polizei Dienst Hund Prüfung	Test or field trial for working police dogs
Polizeihund	Police-trained dog (of any breed)
Preis, Preise	Prize, prizes
Preishüten	Herding trial
Preishüten Sieger	Herding champion
Preishüten Siegerin	Herding champion bitch
Prüfung	Test, trial, examination
Prüfungsverband der Zuchtvereine für Diensthundrassen in Kartell	Training competition organization of specialty clubs for service dog breeds affiliated with the Kartell
Rechts	Breed
Reichsfachgruppe Deutsches	Breed standard, breed characteristics
Rasse	Right (righthand)
Rassekennzeichen	
Hundewesen e.V.	Post-Hitler name for D.K.H.
Reichsobmann	Chief of a nationwide organization under Hitler
Reichsverband Deutscher Kleintierzüchter e.V.	German Small Animal Breeders' Organization (inc.) Established under Hitler regime

Reichsverband für das
   Deutscher Hundewesen ....Hitler equivalent of D.K.H.
Reichssieger, Reichssiegerin ....Hitler equivalent of Jahressieger and
                                      Jahressiegerin
Rein ....Pure, entire, solid (of color)
Reinzucht ....Pure bred
Richter ....Judge
Richterbericht ....Judge's report
Riesenschnauzer ....Giant Schnauzer
Rot ....Red
Rücke ....Back
Rude ....Stud dog, male
Rute ....Tail, stern

Salz und Pfeffer............................Salt and pepper color
Sanitätshund (SH) ....Red Cross dog
Sattel ....Saddle
Schäferhund ....Shepherd Dog
Schäferhund Verein (S.V.)........German Shepherd Dog Club
Schau ....Show
Schecken ....Parti-colored
Schnauzer Klub e. V....................Schnauzer Club, Munich, founded 1907
Schnauzer mittelschlag ....Standard Schnauzer
Schnauzer Zuchtbuch ....Stud book of Schnauzer Club, Munich
Schönheit ....Beauty, bench
Schönheitsieger ....Bench champion
Schokolade ....Chocolate
Schriftleiter ....Editor
Schulhalsband ....Spiked training collar
Schulter ....Shoulder
Schulterhöhe ....Shoulder height
Schutzhundprüfung I ....Formerly Zuchthundprüfung
Schutzhundprüfung II ....Formerly Schutzhundprüfung — Guard
                                    dog trial
Schutzhundprüfung III ....Formerly Polizeihundprüfung or Deinst-
                                    hundprüfung
Schutzhundhauptprüfung ....Protection dog championship contest
Schutzhundvorprüfung ....Preliminary trial for protection dogs
Schutzhundprüfung ....Trial for protection dogs
Schwarz ....Black
Schwarz mit braunen
   Abzeichen ....Black with brown markings; black and
                                    tan
Schwarz mit grauer
   Stichelung ....Black with grey markings; grizzled
Schwarz mit kleinem
   weissen Brustfleck ....Black with small white breast spot

Schwartz mit hellem Brustfleck..Black with light spot on breast
Schwarz mit rostbraun...............Black with rust brown
Schwarzbraun .... Dark brown; black with brown markings
Schwarzbraun mit weissen
   Brustfleck ....Dark brown with white chest spot
Schwarzgelb ....Tawny; dark yellow
Schwarzgrau ....—Black with grey markings
Schwarzrot ....Dark red
Schweitzer Hundestammbuch......Swiss studbook
Schweitzer Sennenhund-
   Verein für Deutschland............Swiss Sennenhund Club of Germany
Schwester ....Sister
Sehr gut ....Very good (rating next below
                            "excellent")
"Setzen" ....Sit!
Sieger, Siegerin ....Champion dog or bitch
Siegerausstellung ....Championship show
Siegeranwärter,
   Siegeranwärterin ....Certificate winner; prospective champion
                            dog or bitch with wins toward the
                            Fachschaftsieger or Klubsieger title
Siegeranwartschaft ....Prospect of a championship
Siegerprüfung ....Championship contest
Silbergrau ....Silver grey
Stattspreis für Zucht oder   Government prize for obedience or work
   Gebrauchsleistung .... training
Sonderausstellung ....Specialty show
Sonderverein ....Specialty club
Sprungwand ....Hurdle; jump used for training to scale
                            fences, etc.
"Such" ....Seek! Trail!
"Such, verloren" ....Seek a lost object!
Suchhund der Polizei
   (SuchH) ....Police tracker
Suchhundprüfung ....Trailing test

Teckel ....Dachshund
Teil...Part, section, volume
Tiefschwarz ....Solid black
Tier ....Animal
Töten ....To destroy (as unwanted puppies in a
                            litter)
Totgeboren.. Stillborn

Übung ....Training exercise
Unbekannt ....Unknown
Und ....And

Unterschrift	Signature
Urgrosseltern	Great-grandparents
Ungrossenkel, Urgrossenkelin	Great-great-grandson or granddaughter
Urgrossmutter	Great-granddam
Urgrossvater	Great-grandsire
Ururgrosseltern	Great-great-grandparents
Vater	Sire
Verbindung	Mating
Verein	Club, association
Verein für deutsche Schäferhunde e.V. (S.V.)	German Shepherd Dog Association (inc.)
Verein für deutsche Schäferhunde in der Tschecho-Slowakei	Czecho-Slovakian German Shepherd Dog Association
Verein für deutsche Spitze	German Spitz Association
Vergebung	Award, bestowal
Vierter	Fourth
Vorderbrust	Forechest
Vorderhand	Forequarters
Vorderpfote	Forepaw
Vorprüfung	Preliminary trial
Vorsitzender	President, chairman
"Vorwärts"	Go ahead!
Vorzüglich (V)	Excellent (highest rating)
Wanderpreis	Challenge trophy (best of breed)
Wanderzuchtpreis	Breeder's challenge trophy
Wasserhundprüfung	Water dog trial
Weiss	White
Weitsprung	Broad jump
Welp, Welpen	Young puppy, young puppies
Weltsieger, Weltsiegerin	World champion dog or bitch
Werfen	To produce, to whelp
Wesen	Character, temperament, disposition
Winkelung	Angulation
Wurf	Litter
Wurfdatum	Whelping date
Wurfmeldung	Litter entry, litter registration
Wurfstärke	Size of litter
Zimmerrein	House-broken
Zotthaarig	Shaggy coated
Zucht	Breeding, rearing, breed, race
Zuchtbuch	Studbook

Zuchtbuchamt	Studbook office
Züchter, Züchterin	Breeder (masculine and feminine)
Zuchtgruppe	Team
Zuchthündin	Brood bitch
Zuchtpreis	Bred by exhibitor prize
Zuchtprüfung (Schutzhundprüfung)	Obedience test. (Not exactly corresponding to those given in this country, but required of dogs not having a more advanced training degree in order to be eligible for a championship.)
Zuchtverein	Specialty club
Zulassung	Allowed, permitted point or characteristic
"Zur Spur"	Trail!
"Zur Wache!"	Watch! On guard!
Zur Zucht nicht zugelassen	Not to be used for breeding
Zur Zucht nur mit Genehmigung des Zuchtbuchamtes zugelassen	Can be used for breeding only with approval of the Stud Book office
Zweiter	Second
Zwergpinscher	Miniature Pinscher
Zwergschnauzer	Miniature Schnauzer
Zwinger	Kennel
Zwingerklasse	Team class
Zwingername	Kennel name

Nightwatchman, 1608. A forerunner of the Police Dog

German Terms and Abbreviations

A. .... Amme
A.D.R.K. .... Allgemeiner Deutscher Rottweilerklub
          e.V.
Abz. .... Abzeichen
AK .... Altersklasse

B. .... Band. Befriedigend.
B.F.H. .... Blindenführer Hund
BK .... Begrenzte Klasse
Bel. .... Belassen
Bes. .... Besitzer, Besitzerin
Bl. .... Blau
BlHPr .... Blindenführerhundprüfung
Blbr. .... Blau mit braun
Br. .... Braun
Brgest .... Braungestichelt (elchfarbig)

CAC .... FCI award at smaller shows or to dogs
          not judged good enough for CACIB
CACIB .... International bench championship award-
          ed by FCI for three firsts with excel-
          lent under different judges

D. .... Der, dem, den. Dunkel.
D.H.S. .... Deutsches Hundestammbuch
D.K.H. .... Deutsches Kartells für Hundewesen
D.V. .... Dobermannpinscher-Verein
DSuchH .... Dienstsuchhund
DSuchHPr .... Dienstsuchhundprüfung
Dr. .... Dunkelrot
DrPr .... Dressurprüfung
D.S.V. .... Deutscher Schäferhund Verband

E. .... Eigentümer
E.V. .... Eingetragener Verein
Ep. .... Ehrenpreis

F. .... Fehlerhaft. Führer.
FCI .... Fédération Cynologique Internationale
FS (FSg) .... Fachschaftssieger

G. .... Gut
Gb. .... Gelb
GfH .... Gesellschaft für Hundeforschung

Gen.	Gennant
Gestr.	Gestromt
Gew.	Geworfen. Gewolkt
H.	Hündin
HPrHt	Hauptpreishüten
H.G.H.	Herden Gebrauchs Hund
H.L.E.	Höchstlobende Erwähnung
Hr.	Hirschrot
JK	Jugend-Klasse
JS	Jahressieger
JSn	Jahressiegerin
JunghK	Junghundklasse
K.	Kampioen
KB	Körbuch des Vereins für deutsche Schäferhunde e. V.
KS	Klubsieger
KSn	Klubsiegerin
KoK	Komondor-Klub im Kartell
LE	Lobende Erwähnung
LS or LSg	Leistungssieger
LWP	Leistungswanderpreis des S.V.
M.	Maske. Mutter. Mangelhaft.
MA	Mit Amme aufgezogen
MH	Melde Hund
MHPr	Meldehundprüfung
NHSB	Nederland Hundestammbuch
N. nachgew.	Nicht nachgewiesen
Nr.	Nummer
O.	Zero (Failed; no good). Ohne.
O. A.	Ohne Amme
OK	Offeneklasse
OLK	Offeneleistungsklasse
OSV	Osterreichischer Verein für deutsche Schäferhunde
P.D.H.	Polizei Dienst Hund
P.D.H.Pr	Polizeidiensthundprüfung
P.D.Z.	Prüfungsverband der Zuchtvereine für Diensthundrassen im Kartell

P.H.	Polizeihund
P.K.	Pinscherklub (Köln)
P.S.K.	Pinscher-Schnauzer Klub
P.S.Z.	Pinscher-Schnauzer-Zuchtbuch
P.Z.	Pinscherzuchtbuch
Pfslz.	Pfeffer und Salz
P. u. S.	Pfeffer und Salz
R.	Rot. Rüde.
R.D.H.	Reichsverband für das Deutsche Hundewesen
R.D. Kl.	Reichsverband Deutscher Kleintierzüchter
S.	Sieger. Sattel.
Sbgr.	Silbergrau
SH	Sanitätshund
SHSB	Schweitzer Hundestammbuch
SPr	Siegerprüfung
SSZB/AS	Schweitzer Sennenhund Zuchtbuch, Appenzeller Sennenhund
SSZB/BS	Schweitzer Sennenhund Zuchtbuch, Berner Sennenhund
SV	Verein für deutsche Schäferhunde
SV-TS	Verein für deutsche Schäferhunde in der Tschecho-Slowakei
SZ	Zuchtbuch für deutsche Schäferhunde
SchH I	Schutzhundprüfung I (formerly Zuchthundprüfung)
SchH II	Schutzhundprüfung (now Schutzhundprüfung II)
SchH III	Schutzhundprüfung III (formerly Polizeihundprüfung and Diensthundprüfung)
SchHHPr	Schutzhundhauptprüfung
SchHVPr	Schutzhundvorprüfung
SchZ	Schnauzer Zuchtbuch (München)
Schwz.	Schwarz
Schwz-B	Schwarz mit hellem Brustfleck
Schwz. m. rostbr.	Schwarz mit rostbraun
Schwzbr.	Schwarzbraun
Schwbrws.	Schwarz mit weissem Brustfleck
Schwzgb.	Schwarzgelb
Schwzgr.	Schwarz mit grauer Stichelung; Schwarzgrau
Sg.	Sehr gut
StP	Stattspreis für Zucht oder Gebrauchsleistung

73

SuchHPr.	Suchhundprüfung
SuchHHPr.	Suchhundhauptprüfung
Sn.	Siegerin
T.	Teil
U.	Und
V.	Vorzüglich. Vater. Verein.
W.	Weiss. Wurfstärke
WPr	Wasserhundprüfung
WS	Weltsieger
WT	Wurftag
WZPH	Wanderzuchtspreis des SV für Hündinnen
WZPR	Wanderzuchtspreis des SV für Rüden
Z	Zuchter, Züchterin
ZDS	Zuchtbuch für Deutsche Spitze
ZK	Zuchtklasse
ZP	Zuchtpreis
ZPr	Zuchtprüfung (now Schutzhundprüfung I)
ZPr	Zuchtprüfung
ZPrH	Zuchtprüfunghund
Zh.	Zotthaarig
ZwK	Zwingerklasse
*	Körzeichen (heisst angekört)
(!)	Zur Zucht nicht zugelassen
(?)	Zur Zucht nur mit Genehmigung des Zuchtbuchamtes zugelassen

This snapshot of Father Flanagan was taken shortly before his death. It symbolizes so well his life, his work and his interest in boyhood.—*Father Wegner*

HEAD STUDY OF CH. WARLORD OF MAZELAINE
BEST OF BREED 69 Times
Best In Working Group 48 Times
First Boxer to win Best in Show at Westminster (1947)

CHAPTER VII

The Boxer in America

WHEN and by whom the Boxer was first brought to America is sheer guesswork. In the 18th century, when the bullenbeisser still held his place at court, among the nobility there were wealthy and aristocratic Germans who obtained extensive grants of land and brought their families and retainers to settle here. Their favorite dogs could easily have been included along with other possessions. It is less likely that the middle class and peasant immigrants of the late 18th and early 19th centuries could have brought dogs with them, for they were often herded like cattle on the ships, hundreds died, and it became the practice to make all of a ship's company responsible for the passage money of those who died on the way. Those who could not pay became bound servants who had to work without wages for a term of years for whoever bought their time. Apparently this was more profitable to the captains of the immigrant vessels than receiving their legitimate passage money for every effort seems to have been made to run the wretched passengers into debt on one pretext or another.

Later on, when the Boxer had lost caste, the wealthier immigrants are unlikely to have been interested in taking him with them on the long voyage. However, there well may have been importations in the later 19th century which have left no recorded trace, for the earliest definite statement I have found on the subject is that the late Charles G. Hopton remembers seeing two Boxers at the Westminster Show in New York in

1898. However, a search of the early Westminster catalogs reveals no entry before the turn of the century which can be identified as a Boxer.

The first Boxers in America of which I have found definite record came over about 1903. One of them was a dog called Peter owned by the late Chief Judge Irving Lehman of the Court of Appeals of New York, whose home was in Rye. Peter was never registered with the A.K.C. and no definite records about him are available. His breeding, age and German kennel name, and even the exact date of his importation could not be recalled by Ex-Governor Lehman, his owner's brother. Most of Governor Lehman's early importations came from Switzerland, so perhaps Peter was Swiss likewise.

Owing to the loss of his kennel records, Ex-Governor Herbert H. Lehman of New York was unable to supply as many details as could be wished about his own early importations. His first importation was Flock v. Salvadore who was not registered in this country. Although not a very good show specimen he was intensely loyal and a wonderful guardian for his master's children. Flock was already established as a household pet of long standing and jealous of his privileges when the Lehmans imported Sieger Dampf v. Dom in 1914. The brindle Dampf, the only son of the great Ch. Rolf v. Vogelsberg who is known to have reached America, became the first American Boxer champion. He was whelped September 28, 1912, out of Bella v.d. München Ort. Flock v. Salvadore, known to the family as Flops, refused to accept the newly arrived Dampf and never made friends with him. As they had to be constantly kept apart Dampf, whose disposition was as fine as his looks, was loaned to a friend for the summer. On his return, in his enthusiasm he jumped out of the car and was immediately rushed by Flops. The two dogs fell over a steep embankment into heavy bushes and before they could be separated the fight was pretty well over. It was Flops, and not the prize-winning Dampf, who won the battle.

The first Boxer registered by the A.K.C. was in 1904, and surprisingly enough he was an American-bred. Arnulf Grandenz, No. 78043 was owned by James E. Welch of Harvey, Illinois, and bred by Max H. Schachner of Downers Grove in

FLOCK v. SALVADORE
First Boxer imported by ex-Gov. Herbert H. Lehman
This Boxer's pet name was "Flops"

FLORA v. NEAPEL
Owned by The Hon. Herbert H. Lehman of New York

the same state. He is described as a brindle, black and dark gray and was whelped April 2, 1903. In breeding he was close to recorded beginnings of the modern breed, for his sire was Prinz Mark v. Graudenz, a son of Wotan and Meta v.d. Passage. Since there is no indication that Prinz Mark ever left Germany it is probable that Arnulf's dam came over in whelp. She was Rose v. Graudenz, by Bosco Immergrun out of Flora Fuhr, a daughter of Flock St. Salvator and Molly (or Walby) St. Salvator. (Perhaps the latter should be Wally St. Salvator, since a nearly white bitch of that name is shown in a group benched at an early German show before 1900.) Arnulf's sire was thus a full brother to Ch. Gigerl and his dam a half-sister to Mucki v. Vogelsberg, the parents of Frigga v Vogelsberg, whose daughters Venus and Dora v. Vogelsberg were, respectively, the dams of Ch. Rolf v. Vogelsberg and Ch. Rolf v. Walhall.

Rose v. Graudenz is the first Boxer in this country known to us by name. She was shown at Chicago (March 25-28, 1903) only a few days before Arnulf was whelped and placed second in the Miscellaneous Class. The following year the Chicago Kennel Club offered Boxer classes and seven of the breed were exhibited. The judge was apparently Mr. J. Mortimer, who was scheduled to do "all other breeds". None of the entries except Arnulf were registered, but all carried the Graudenz name and one can assume that they were Rose's puppies. Huldah and Flora, owned by Schachner, were in the Puppy Class. Arnulf, owned by Welch, was first Novice, with Count Arnim of Graudenz, owned by J. H. Eckels, second, and Schachner's Ralph of Graudenz third. Schachner's Davo of Graudenz won the Open, defeating Arnulf and his dam, Rose, who was third. Arnulf again defeated Rose at Chicago the following year, but by this time she had changed hands and was owned by H. W. Carpenter of Harvey, Illinois. On September 2, 1905 she had a second litter, sired by her son Arnulf, for one of them was registered in 1906 as Kolbs von Graudenz 97079, owned by W. A. Rider of Milwaukee. Kolbs was a brindle, like his sire. Perhaps an exhaustive search of show awards in the AKC Gazette would reveal other appearances of some of these Boxers but they do not seem to have

HEAD STUDY OF SIEGER
DAMPF v. DOM
First American Champion

GRIEFF v. RIMBAL
Owned by the Hon.
Herbert H. Lehman

SIEGER DAMPF v. DOM
First American Boxer Champion (1915)
Sire: Ch. Rolf v. Vogelsberg
Owner: The Hon. Herbert H. Lehman, Albany, N. Y.

left any recorded offspring for there are no further registrations until 1914.

The first Westminster appearance of the breed which I have been able to find was in 1906. In that year C. Balme won VHC and fifth place in the miscellaneous class, seven competing, with the only Boxer entry, Tom II, by Sernhos II out of Flora. Tom II, whelped August 7, 1904, was bred by F. Valery, and from this fact and his sire's name it is possible that he was French or French Swiss. Forty-one years later another Boxer, Ch. Warlord of Mazelaine, made breed history by going Best in Show, all breeds.

In 1907 the Chicago show seems to have brought out only a single entry. "Boxer", owned by Miss B. Whiting, placed first in Open. Then comes a gap of some six years. In 1914 Westminster brought out an entry of eleven and offered regular Boxer classes: Puppy, Dogs and Bitches; Open Dogs; Open Bitches; Brace and Team. The exhibitors were Herbert H. Lehman, Jesse I. Straus and Nathan Straus, Jr. Entries included Flops (breeding unknown), Merry (whelped in 1911 by Ajax v. Siegthal out of Miela) and puppies from this pair. Although Mr. Lehman does not recall that Flock v. Salvator was ever used for breeding he was probably the "Flops" in question. In 1915 the Westminster entry dropped to eight but included three new owners, Mr. and Mrs. S. Lang Newman and Henry Esberg. Winners went to Mr. Lehman's imported bitch, Cilly v. Neapel, and Reserve Winners to her son, Rolf v. Neapel, whelped January 11, 1913, by Roland v. Lansitz. Rolf was owned by Nathan Straus, Jr. Dampf v. Dom, the first German Sieger imported to this country so far as is known, placed only fourth, but he finished his championship in the course of the year 1915 and for eleven years was the sole Boxer to hold an American title. He might have left his impress on the breed if there had been more bitches available or World War I had not broken out. As it was, although Dampf was registered in 1914 along with Cilly v. Neapel and her daughter Flora v. Neapel (both brindles like Dampf) there are no puppies by him recorded.

The Lehmans made a real effort to promote the Boxer in the East, but met with little success. Dampf sired two litters, which were nearly all lost with distemper, and none of whom was ever registered. Two other importations during the early 1920's, Grieff v. Renstal, a brindle, and Artus v. Hornfeld, met untimely ends, one killed by a car and the other shot by an unfriendly neighbor. Although Artus left one or two registered litters they have not appeared in any champion pedigrees, to date at least. About 1914, when the breed was still officially known as "German Boxer", there were attempts to have separate classification provided, outside of the Miscellaneous class, but they do not appear to have succeeded except at Westminster. Very likely the growing pressure of World War I had its effects in preventing a boom and after the Armistice the German Shepherd Dog brought home by many returning soldiers, rapidly became the breed of the moment. Discouraged by lack of competition and a disastrous epidemic of distemper which decimated their kennels, the Lehmans ceased breeding though they continued to import an occasional Boxer well into the '20s, and are still enthusiastic devotees of the breed.

In 1948 the only Boxer owned by the Lehmans was the ten-year-old fawn Mahderf's Leading Lady, AKC 247849, a daughter of imported Ch. Ferbo v. Königstor and Ch. Kitti v.d. Uhlandshohe, whelped January 8, 1938. A birthday present to the Governor from his wife, Leading Lady arrived at a time when Mr. Lehman was struggling with a large accumulated deficit in State finances. She was promptly rechristened "Budget", and two of the puppies from her second litter became "Surplus" and "Deficit." A newspaper article of 1942 describes Budget as a privileged character who sat in on practically all the state chief executive's private conferences, listened to the dictation of important letters but was never known to divulge any of the interesting things she heard. The newspaper men at that time derived considerable entertainment from watching development of both the state budget and the canine Budget's puppies. Eventually surplus won out on both counts.

Boxer entries at Westminster disappeared from 1915 until 1922, but there was still some slight activity in the Middle West. L. Reifess won second and third Open (Miscellaneous)

"SURPLUS" and "DEFICIT"
Out of Mahderf's Leading Lady whose pet name was "Budget"
mentioned in the text.
Owner: The Hon. Herbert H. Lehman, former Governor of New York

at St. Louis in 1916 with "Monday" and "Boxer". E. Seidel took first at Detroit with "Sepp", and J. C. Haviland's "Dude" was first in Limit and Open at Galesburg, Illinois, in 1917. Then war was declared and Boxers apparently went into the discard along with other German breeds, nor did they share the post-Armistice boom of the German Shepherd. Hufas v. Schladebach owned by W. Ulrich, was shown twice in June, 1922 and twice more the following year including Westminster, but he was never registered. In February, 1924, the tide began to turn, but even then it was a slow process. After the ten year gap from 1914 there were five registrations during 1924, but it was another decade before they reached the thirty mark. In 1934 there were 64 registrations. During 1947 there were more than ten thousand!

The first of these Boxers registered during the 1920's were Dina v. Thuringen, owned by J. G. Greef, and Max v.d. Elbe, owned by Sudie G. Huff. Both left descendants, though whether any of them are still in use for breeding today is uncertain. In April, 1924, two imported Boxers from a single litter were registered, Afra v.d. Alten Eiche by Edward Gollash and Anti v.d. Alten Eiche by Reinhold Henze. Nothing further is known of them, but in August Mr. Greef registered Ali v. Haldenberg.

The records on some of these early dogs are confusing. Ali v. Haldenberg and Dina v. Thuringen were both transferred to Ralph L. Raynor in October, 1926, but meanwhile they had produced a litter whelped October 18, 1924. A dog from this litter, Otto v. Haldenberg, was registered in March, 1926, by Clarence E. Hall, with J. G. Greef as breeder, but the previous January a sister, Helena v. Thuringen, is recorded as bred and owned by Mrs. Harvey K. Lines. Dina v. Thuringen's picture appeared in the 1926 edition of Dr. J. L. Leonard's "The Care and Handling of Dogs", where it must have helped to acquaint many readers with the fact that such a breed as Boxers existed. Dina whelped a litter in 1926 sired by Artus v. Hornfeld, a late importation of Governor Lehman's.

Some three weeks before the Ali-Dina litter, on September 27, 1924, arrived another which did leave its mark upon the breed in America. The dam, however, was not registered until March, 1925. Asta v.d. Adelegg must have been very light in

85

color for she is described as silver with white markings. She was by Arko v. Schoenbuch, a son of the undefeated fawn show winner, Milo v. Eigelstein (whose dam was a granddaughter of the light-colored Schani v.d. Passage) out of a daughter of the very prepotent brindle Ch. Rolf Walhall. Asta came over in whelp to Blitz v. Moosburg, whose sire was a Milo grandson and whose dam was by Rolf Walhall. Stockman speaks of Siegerin Asta v. Moosburg, sister or half-sister to Blitz, as Sieger Pascha v. Neunberg's best daughter. Three puppies were registered from the Blitz v. Moosburg—Asta v.d. Adelegg litter, Alex and Blackadarco in June, 1926, when they were a year and a half old, and a bitch, Alice, in July. All three seem to have been golden brindles. Once again there is some confusion as to ownership. Asta was registered by the Rev. Paul L. Phillipp and was transferred in July, 1926, to Harry W. Leonard, who is given as the owner of all three of the puppies. However, although the date of birth is the same, Mr. Philipp is recorded as the breeder of Alice, and Gotthilf Jeuther as breeder of the other two.

On May 28, 1925, Asta had another litter bred by Mr. Philipp. It included three bitches, Bessie, Daisy, and Nellie, two dogs, Moritz and Dewey, and probably another dog, Pax, as the latter's date of birth, May 28, 1926, could well be a misprint. All except Pax were owned by H. W. Leonard, to whom Asta was transferred in July and the sire in June, 1926.

The sire of Asta's second litter was Bluecher v. Rosengarten, whelped July 25, 1923, a fawn with a black mask who completed his championship late in 1926 and was the second Boxer and first fawn to do so. Bluecher was a somewhat old-fashioned type with no white and a rather weak muzzle.

The September, 1926, Dog News carried a half-page ad for the Jeuther Boxer Kennels, Woodlawn, Pa., offering Bluecher and Blackadarco at stud. Both had points toward their titles at that time but Blackadarco does not seem to have finished nor to have left any registered get. Bluecher's stud fee was $50 and puppies were advertised at $100. The ad was in the name of Mr. Leonard, which suggests that the dogs were owned by him but handled by Mr. Jeuther. Asta and four of the puppies were transferred to the latter in 1928. We hear no more of Ch. Bluecher but Mr. Jeuther continued to breed and is reported still active. The dog Alex from the litter by Blitz was mated to his half-sisters, Bessie and Daisy, and many of their descendants appear in the stud books down the years. They often bear the designation "of Adelegg". One such double granddaughter of Asta, Draga of Nipantuck owned by Rexob Kennels, was the dam of Rexob's Butch, sired by Ch. Egon v.d. Falkenburg. Butch placed second in a class of 15 under Herr Philip Stockmann at Westminster in 1938, with first and third going to future champions.

At least two present day champions are descended from this Jeuther strain. Ch. Airminded Miss of Airealm, who finished in 1946, traces back in the sixth generation to Asta v.d. Adelegg three times. In direct female line she goes through Bessie, while her dam is a granddaughter of Little Miss Muffet whose sire, Toby v.d. Adelegg, is by Alex out of Daisy. If the first American champion has left no known descendants, at least it is interesting to note that the second, Bluecher v. Rosengarten can still be traced at the back of today's winners. An even more recent champion, Puckety's Vorquelle, who finished in 1947, likewise traces in female line to Asta v.d. Adelegg, Bluecher and Blitz. The line comes down from the mating of Alex and Bessie through Lady Adelegg, Mary-Lu of Adelegg, and Dora of Adelegg to Vorquelle's dam, Larissa of Berwildun.

Although the vast majority of Boxer importations have come from Germany, other countries have also been represented, even in the early days of the breed. The first such recorded were an Austrian pair, Heissporn Falsaf and Ortelmabath Satan, whelped in July and April, 1923. They were received as a gift from a friend who was abroad by Dr. and Mrs. Edgar R. McGuire of Buffalo, probably during 1924. They were not registered until October, 1925 (when the bitch was recorded as Ortelmabeth Satien). Although both parents were registered as "golden yellow" their son, Valdar v. Segurt, whelped April 20, 1925, was registered as a brindle with white markings. Valdar was purchased as a six weeks old puppy by Emille M. Frost, now Mrs. John F. Pitass. At that time there were said to be nine Boxers in the United States, a

VALDAR v. SEGURT "Fritz" and John Pitass
When this picture was taken, Fritz was 8 years old
Sire: Heissporn Falsaf.   Dam: Ortelmabeth Satien
Breeder: E. R. McGuire, Buffalo, N .Y.
Owner: Emille M. Frost (later Mrs. John Pitass)
This was the only Boxer registered in May, 1926.

number which agrees precisely with the registrations for 1924 and 1925. Mrs. Pitass states that Valdar, despite his registered description, was a fawn with white markings—a perfect Boston blaze with a white collar. He lived to the age of fourteen and sired at least four litters out of Afra v. Rollbach, a bitch imported by Mrs. Pitass through Victor Moench. Registered in March, 1927, Afra was shown at Westminster the following February and took Best of Winners, but was not campaigned to her championship. At that time Boxers were still virtually unknown and Mrs. Pitass had great difficulty in disposing of her puppies. She gave away most of them to close friends or relatives and eventually ceased breeding. She recalls selling only four. One of Afra's daughters by Valdar, Gretchen v. Rollbach, was bred to Ch. Argus v. Königsee of Mazelaine, and an eight months old bitch from this litter won the puppy class at Morris and Essex in 1937. Afra, who lived to the age of ten, was a devoted guardian for the Pitass children and would never leave the baby's carriage while on watch. Once Mrs. Pitass left her baby with her mother while she went shopping but when the baby woke and cried Afra refused to let the grandmother come near the bassinet.

No recent registrations of descendants of Mrs. Pitass' stock have come to light and she herself believes that there are none, though at least five puppies were registered besides those she kept for herself. It is therefore unlikely that this early Austrian infusion had any permanent effect on the breed although Austrian stock did play an important part later and a number of champions came from the same kennels as Valdar v. Segurt's dam, Ortelma. The single Boxer registered during 1929 was a Valdar puppy, Samuel Slote's Bella Dona.

The first Swiss importation seems to have been Betty v. Limmatal, registered by Ex-Governor Lehman in March, 1927, the same month as Afra v. Rollbach. In February Alexander A. Nitt had registered two German importations, Berna v. Muehlen and Lenz v. Dom. This pair was mated and four "v. Lenz" puppies were registered in December, 1928, and four others during 1930. In 1935 a male of this breeding, J. v. Lenz, and a bitch Sylvia v. Arno, also bred by the Nitts, were registered by Jesse L. Livermore, Jr. of Santa Barbara,

AFRA von ROLLBACH
IMPORTED
BEST OF BREED at Westminster Show, 1928
Owned by Dr. John F. Pitass, Eggertsville, N. Y.

California. This pair seems to have produced the second Boxer litter west of the Rockies and may have living descendants today. However, Mrs. Nitt reports that she has no Lenz-Berna descendants in her kennels at the present time. Although the Nitt kennel name is now registered as "Esto Alpha" instead of v. Lenz, Mrs. Nitt has rounded out twenty years of Boxer breeding. While Mr. Lehman is probably the dean of Boxer fanciers in this country—having owned the breed continuously since before 1912, the oldest active breeders appear to be Mr. Gotthilf Jeuther of Valencia, Pa. and Mrs. Alexander Nitt, who both date back to the 1920's.

Discounting the registrations before World War I, Boxer registrations through 1929 totalled only 44, including both importations and American-breds; five in 1924, four in 1925 (all imported), 19 in 1926 with only one importation, seven in 1927, eight in 1928, one in 1929. In 1930 there were nine, and then the real upswing began—16 in 1931, 28 in 1932, 24 in 1933 and no less than 64 in 1934, by which date the breed had become established and was already making its mark in the variety groups. From that time Boxers have gained steadily, until in 1946 they ranked fifth of all breeds registered by the A.K.C. and during 1947 a total of 10,061 were recorded in the A.K.C. stud book. Championships too, increased rapidly. Following an interval of eleven years between Dampf v. Dom and Bluecher v. Rosengarten and a six year interval from Bluecher to Check v. Hunenstein, came three more in 1933, five in 1934, eleven more in 1935 and no less than nineteen in 1936. After a drop due to war restrictions, the record number of 69 new champions was recorded for 1946. (Figures as to the number of champions in various years often differ slightly according to whether the count is made on the basis of the actual wins or the date of official publication. Some figures give 79 champions for 1946.)

A careful examination of the pedigrees of all American champion Boxers published by the A.K.C. through December, 1947 has been made by the writer. In every case the line has been traced back to the original importations, so it is possible to say accurately just which foreign dogs and bitches have played a part in forming the title holders. Owing to the

91

AFRA v. KOLLPACH

Sire: Ch. Argus v. Konigsee of Mazelaine   Dam: Gretchen v. Rollbach
Owner: Mrs. Emille M. Pitass, Hamburg, New York
Date of picture, July, 1939

many thousands of Boxers which have now been registered however, it is impossible to say that there may not actually be descendants of other early importations which are still being bred from and which may eventually produce champions although they have as yet failed to do so. One need only point out that the two champions which are descended from Asta v.d. Adelegg and Ch. Bluecher v. Rosengarten of the mid-1920's did not finish until 1946 and 1947 to prove the truth of this statement. Unquestionably there are many other descendants of Asta and Bluecher still living. There may easily be descendants of Lenz and Berna or of other early sires and dams as well. It is also true that in some cases more than one generation was imported. So it sometimes happens that an imported dog or bitch carried on through an imported son or daughter, or even grandchild, although none of his American-bred get proved of value as producers.

There were so few Boxers available in the early days that many a sire has left registered progeny out of only one or two bitches, often his kennel mates and sometimes his own daughters. Regardless of how good an individual or producer a dog might be, his opportunities at stud were so limited that if he did not happen to be suited for the one or two bitches at his disposal that was likely to be the end of him so far as future generations were concerned. Thus there appear to be no descendants of the bitch Alma Mayer, imported in 1926 and bred to Max v.d. Elbe, nor of Artus v. Hornfeld, imported by Ex-Governor Lehman and registered in April 1927. Neither do the two importations of 1928, Rigo v. Lindengarten and Citta v.d. Drei Gleichen, owned by Benjamin N. Namm seem to have carried on, although two puppies from this pair were registered the same year.

Even before the depression started, 1929 was a poor year for Boxers, with only one registration, a puppy by Valdar v. Segurt out of Afra v. Rollbach. Although three of the nine puppies entered in 1930 were granddaughters of Asta v.d. Adelegg, none of these has carried on to date.

It was in 1931 that events of real importance began to take place affecting the breed's future. There were nine importations among the year's sixteen registrations and several of them are worth noting. In January B. L. Tuellmann of Baltimore registered the dog Querry Struthio, whose litter sister, Quinta Struthio of Mazelaine, was imported later. Quinta made her championship in 1935 and became the dam of two producers, Hekate and Ottilie of Mazelaine. Mr. Tuellmann did considerable breeding and showing and became one of the first Boxer judges.

Lillian C. Weaver of Tarrytown, N. Y., owner of Andrebrook Kennels imported Britta v.d. Magdalenenquelle, Schiele's Lily, and Hektor v. Alteneiche, registered in July. There are said to be descendants of these dogs still being bred, although I have not found their names among the ancestors of champions to date.

Hexe v.d. Magdalenenquelle, a sister to Britta, was imported by Mr. Tuellmann and registered along with Querry Struthio. Although she did not complete her title until 1935, Hexe eventually became a champion and seems to have been the next Boxer imported after Bluecher v. Rosengarten to do so, although intervening arrivals finished before she did. In September Kastor v. Vierenberg was registered by G. Albany Perryman and in December a Kastor daughter out of Fricka v. Lenz. Kastor, too, may possibly still have descendants.

The truly outstanding event of the year 1931 was the importation by Dr. Benjamin J. Birk of Milwaukee of two bitches and a dog. Prinz and Olly v.d. Magdalenenquelle have carried on through their daughter Lilo Lisalotta from Birkbaum. Bred to Sigurd v. Dom she produced Santel of Kenoosa (the dam of one champion and granddam of another) and Sigurd's Honig of Bluemound, dam of a champion and two producers. Dr. Birk's other bitch was Ella v. Werdenfels, by Egon v. Biederstein, the sire of Prinz, out of Fricka, a daughter of Egon v. Gumbertusbrunnen P. H. Ella was a yellow or fawn bitch with a black mask, whelped August 22, 1930. She had at least three litters by different sires, but only the first is important. It is probable that Ella v. Werdenfels is the ancestor of more American-bred champions than any other Boxer bitch ever imported, for just before her second birthday on August 14, 1932, she whelped the future Ch. Landa of Mazelaine.

94

Astor v. Thalreit, the sire of Landa of Mazelaine, was a brindle with a black mask who was imported at the age of four years and seems to have been the first Austrian Boxer to have a lasting effect upon the breed. Astor was by Moritz v. Tannich, a son of Astor v. Hiltensberg who was a Milo v. Eigelstein grandson.

The year 1932, when Astor was imported, was perhaps the most vital in the history of the Boxer in America. It saw the birth of Landa of Mazelaine and the arrival of Check v. Hunenstein.

Check v. Hunenstein, owned by Marcia and Joseph Fennessey of Cirrol Kennels, was a great show dog as well as an important sire, and really put the breed on the map. He was the first Boxer to win a Best in Show in America, under Alva Rosenberg at Mount Kisco, N. Y. in the summer of 1932. Although five years old, the brindle Check held his own in the hottest competition and by his marvelous personality, coupled with the fact that he was shown everywhere, he won hosts of friends for the breed. Boxers ceased to be virtually unknown and within fifteen years became one of the most popular breeds in the country.

Check's value to the breed through his phenomenal show career is incalculable. He finished his championship promptly in 1932 and was immediately in demand as a sire. However, he was handicapped by the scarcity of good bitches in this country at that time and left comparatively few litters behind him in Germany. Some of his German descendants were imported later. Ch. Astrid v. Lew who finished her title in 1938, was by a Check son, Gomo se Sumbula, out of Adeline of Pacific, a Check granddaughter. Dromeo of Cirrol, another Check son, is at the back of the pedigree of the 1946 champion Airminded Miss of Airealm. Aleda of Barmere, whelped in 1933 out of Ch. Dodi v.d. Stoeckersburg, carried down through Diane of Barmere and Karla of Barmere to Southdown's Vous and Ch. Southdown's Dinky and their sons Ch. Southdown's Fury and Ch. Southdown's Rector. A brother to Rector, Southdown Rabat, was officially proclaimed in 1948. Finally, out of Landa of Mazelaine Check sired two bitches, Alpha and Anitra of Mazelaine, who were outstandingly important producers. Alpha was the dam of one champion and two producers, Anitra of six champions and two producers.

However, if Check had never sired a puppy either here or abroad, his influence on the breed would still have been profound for he put Boxers on the map and set a high standard of quality for breeders. Moreover, though he did not sire a single American-bred champion and his producers numbered only two dogs and four bitches from a total of five matings, Check's place in American winning pedigrees is much greater than this would indicate. Through his American-bred get he left eight champion grandchildren and others in later generations. A more notable contribution however, came through his German get for Check was the grandsire of Ch. Dorian v. Marienhof, Ch. Brokas v. Germanenstolz and several other importations out of the litter sisters, Saxonias Andl and Saxonias Aska. A post-war importation, the 1943 Austrian Winner Hasso v. Landl owned by Bladan Kennels, is a descendant of Saxonias Assan, a brother to Andl and Aska. Check also sired the German Siegerin Yva v. Marienhof.

1932 saw other important happenings. The Stoeckersburg Kennels of Neptune, N. J. registered Ulotte v.d. Lowenburg, who finished her title in 1934 and two of her puppies whelped the previous November, Delma and Dolf v.d. Stoeckersburg. Ulotte, a fawn daughter of Ajax v. Durrenberg and Nanny v.d. Lowenburg (the latter a granddaughter of Max II v. Hohenzollernplatz, bred by Kaiser Wilhelm II) came over in whelp to Armin v.d. Mundsburg. Under the rules of those days her litter, whelped in the U. S. A., counted as American-bred. Ch. Dodi v.d. Stoeckersburg, registered by Ralph T. Miller in October 1932, was therefore the first American-bred Boxer as well as the first bitch to complete the title. She finished in 1933 and her transfer to Mrs. Young (now Mrs. Breed of Barmere) recorded in June of that year marks the beginning of Barmere Kennels. Ch. Arno v. Vogelsang also finished in 1933 but left almost no impression as a sire, despite several litters.

Besides Ch. Dodi, Ulotte's first litter contained three other bitches, Delma, Dora and Dutches v.d. Stoeckersburg, who appear in the pedigrees of later champions. She was also the dam of Ch. Lord v.d. Stoeckersburg, whelped November, 1933, by the imported stud Armin v. Hanseatenhof Stoeckersburg. Lord was the first American-bred male Boxer to complete his championship and the first champion who would rank as an American-bred under present day rules—being from a mating which took place in this country. He was a brindle with a black mask, as was Dodi. In 1934 Lord's registration was cancelled by the A.K.C.

Stoeckersburg blood played a prominent part in the foundation of the High Spot Kennels of Paul Ladin, which moved to California about 1936 where Mrs. Ladin is still breeding. Ch. High Spot Billy the Kid, who finished in 1947, comes down from Dora, but Delma was the dam of three champions in addition to Frazier's Liesel, granddam of Ch. Tanz of Danboro, who finished in 1944 and Ch. Wuttke's Bombardier in 1945. Another Delma daughter, High Spot Hilda, a sister to Frazier's Liesel, and also a Dutches son and daughter, appear in the pedigree of Baroness of Burmont. Baroness is the dam of 1947 Ch. Pendel Pepper's dam, Uhle of Berolina, and also the dam of Zita of Berolina, dam of Ch. Adair of Three Birches and his sister Aloha of Three Birches. Aloha is the granddam of 1947 Ch. Baron of Brightwood, and Adair sired Ch. Eldra of Yartrap, Ch. Brunhilda v. Waldes Ruhe, and is the grandsire of 1947 Ch. Forever Amber. Baroness of Burmont, incidentally, is about as intensively bred as a bitch can be and her pedigree is of interest from another angle also. While all but 2% of American-bred Boxer champions have at least one champion ancestor within two generations, Baroness not only fails to follow this pattern herself but her sire does likewise and her dam, Gretchen v.d. Stoeckersburg, has only one champion in the first two generations, her granddam Ulotte. Only 8% of American-bred Boxer champions have no more than one champion in the first two generations. Baroness has only one in the first three. Besides being a double granddaughter of Armin v. Hanseatenhof herself, Baroness's paternal granddam, Empress v.d. Stoeckersburg, is also his double granddaughter. Empress is also a granddaughter of the little sisters Delma and Dutches v.d. Stoeckersburg, while Gretchen is a Dutches daughter. This gives four crosses to

97

Armin in four generations and three to the D. Stoeckersburg litter. And as if all this were not enough, Armin v. Hanseatenhof is himself a grandson of Armin v. Mundsburg, who sired Delma and Dutches, and Armin v. Mundsburg was mated to his own dam, Cuny v. Flossachtal, to produce the daughter Carla v. Mundsburg who was Armin v. Hanseatenhof's dam. Several of the High Spot champions finished between 1937 and 1942 showed considerable inbreeding along similar lines, though less intensive. Ch. Banner of Barmere, a Sigurd v. Dom son of Ch. Dodi v.d. Stoeckersburg, was used successfully in some of these, combining with other members of the D litter.

Armin v. Hanseatenhof (the Stoeckersburg suffix was added upon his importation) is a dog who has received little or no mention among recent writers on the breed. His pedigree does not contain well-known names, though Cuny v. Flossachtal's sire, Benkur v. Israstrand, was a brother to Belfine v. Isarstrand, the dam of Sieger Edler v. Isarstrand. Consider, however, that Armin sired five champions and seven others who appear in champion pedigrees. And remember that his sons include Ch. Lord v.d. Stoeckersburg, the first American-bred male to win the title, and Ch. Baldur of Fostoria, the first American-bred to win the Group. Baldur is also the maternal grandsire of the 1947 Ch. Lady Belle of Little Nook. Armin, a brindle whelped February 22, 1931 and imported in 1933, sired a litter as late as 1937 which may or may not have been his last. No other dog imported up to that time did as well. Armin's second champion, High Spot Dotti, finished in July, 1937, the same year in which Ch. Sigurd v. Dom finished his second American-bred, Eitel of Barmere, but Dotti was first by four months. When Baldur of Fostoria finished in 1939, making Armin's fifth champion, only Dorian v. Marienhof and Sigurd v. Dom had more American-breds to his credit. Except Ch. Baldur of Fostoria, Armin's champions were all out of Ch. Ulotte v.d. Lowenburg or her descendants, Ch. High Spot Boots and High Spot Major both being out of Empress v.d. Stoeckersberg, a double granddaughter of Armin himself and double great-granddaughter of Ulotte.

During the 1930's there were forty-three Boxer champions

CH. DU BARRY OF KERNIA
Sire: Ch. Dorian v. Marienhof of Mazelaine
Dam: Lorna of Kernia
Breeder: Kernia Kennels, Philadelphia, Pa.
Owner: Keith Merrill, Herndon, Virginia

whelped in the United States, four of them from matings made abroad. Out of these, Ch. Dorian v. Marienhof sired 16, Ch. Sigurd v. Dom sired 7, Armin v. Hanseatenhof Stoeckersburg 5, Sieger Fachinger v. Neu Drosedow 3, and Ch. Argus v. Königsee 2. The other seven were divided among as many different sires. Three of the last group were American-breds, namely Gomo se Sumbula, sire of Ch. Astrid v. Lew (whose dam, Adeline of Pacific, was also American-bred) ; Ch. Banner of Barmere, sire of High Spot Miss Ritz (out of High Spot Letti, an Armin-Delma daughter) ; and High Spot Major (an Armin-Empress son who was full brother to Baroness of Burmont's sire). And so two of the first three American-bred champions by American-bred sires were Armin grandchildren. The third, Ch. Astrid v. Lew, was by a Check son out of a Check granddaughter, Cita of Cirrol. Astrid's dam, Adeline of Pacific, whelped October 9, 1935 and bred by Paul M. Streib of Los Angeles, was from the third California-bred litter appearing in the stud book. The first, bred by Dr. and Mrs. Clark James Burnham, Jr., of Berkeley, Calif., was by Bimbo I v. Preussenadler out of Elmi v.d. Hohen Schrott. Whelped March 29, 1935, it contained the bitch Carla v. Wachau, granddam of a champion, Baron v. Wachau Toepferhof, who was mated to a descendant of Bluecher v. Rosengarten (second Boxer to become an American champion), and produced the dam of 1946 Ch. Airminded Miss of Airealm.

Early California Boxers were well spread over the state, for the Burnhams were in Berkeley, Jessie L. Livermore, Jr., breeder of the second litter, was in Santa Barbara, and Paul M. Streib in Los Angeles. About 1936 Paul Ladin moved his High Spot Kennels from New Jersey to Hollywood and California became an active centre for the breed. Ch. Banner of Barmere, one of the first high quality American-bred champions, was purchased from the East and actively shown by Victor Young of Hollywood. With relatively limited opportunities at stud, Banner sired three champions and two producers, and his name appears in numerous modern pedigrees. Dr. and Mrs. Blake Watson of Hollywood were also keenly interested in the breed during the 1930's and imported or purchased from the East many great dogs, including Ch. Jod v.

Neu Drosedow and Ch. Ingo v. Heger se Sumbula. Ingo, a son of Sieger Fachinger v. Neu Drosedow and a double Sigurd grandson, died in 1945 at under ten years of age, leaving seven champions and two additional producers. Ingo's greatest success was in matings with Cynthia v. Tal, whose dam was a Fachinger daughter. The famous Barmere Kennels are now located at El Monte, California, and three regional specialty clubs, the California Boxer Club, the Pacific Coast Boxer Club, and the Boxer Club of Southern California, flourish in the state. The breed has been popular in the film colony, and in addition to Victor Young the many breeders and exhibitors include Bing Crosby, Robert Taylor, Clark Gable, Gary Cooper, Eddie Prinz and many others.

Boxers early gained an active foothold in Michigan, where Dr. Dan Gordon's Bladan Kennels was founded in 1936, and still earlier in the Chicago-Milwaukee area, where the breed had been exhibited as far back as 1904. John P. Wagner founded Mazelaine Kennels in 1933 in Milwaukee, where they are still located, with the purchase of Ch. Landa of Mazelaine from Dr. Birkbaum, who had had Boxers in Milwaukee since 1931. Between this area and California there was virtually no activity but as early as June 18, 1935, Mrs. Gerald W. Bennet of Colorado Springs bred a litter by Ch. Flott v.d. Blutenau out of Cita v.d. Solalinde. Early kennels in the South included Douglas Hunt's Birbama, still active in Alabama, Alfred B. Booth of Tennessee, whose Ch. Peter v. Dorian of Dunroaming was the first Ch. Dorian v. Marienhof son to finish, and Ben Matthews of New Orleans, who took Ch. Argus v. Königsee to that area.

Back in 1932 the New York section, stimulated by the show career of Ch. Check v. Hunenstein, was coming to recognize the Boxer. Mrs. Andrew T. Pierce imported Franzi v.d. Wurm who made her championship the following year. Franzi was good enough to place in the Group at four straight shows on the Southern circuit in April, 1935, and was the cornerstone of Frator Kennels, though she appears to have no champion descendants to date. Dr. R. G. Tunison of Orland, Maine, imported three Karlshohe Boxers in 1932 which were

101

the first registered in the state. There is now an active All-Maine Boxer Club.

The first imported Boxer bitch to become an American champion was the Siegerin Barbel v.d. Eibe, imported for Cirrol Kennels along with Check, who finished in July, 1933. She was also, probably, the first Siegerin imported. Although she had left at least one litter in Germany she proved unable to raise puppies over here and produced only a single American-bred litter, by Check. From it, the bitch Cita of Cirrol has carried on to a limited extent.

1931 marked the beginning of several kennels which are still breeding today. Max Ketzel and Valentine Martin had both raised Boxers in Germany, the latter from the early 1900's. Ketzel registered Bella v. Lowenstrutz in January, 1933, and she appears in the fifth generation of 1947 Ch. Lustig v. Baron Ingber (a bitch in spite of her name.) After his kennel name "v. Atlantic" was disallowed by the A.K.C. the name of "Edelstamm" was chosen, and this is still in use. Valentine Martin has bred several notable dogs. Gretl v. Berggeist produced two champions, Erick and Eda v.d. Stuttgarter, by Dorian, and a litter sister, Emmie v.d. Stuttgarter, is the granddam of Ch. Lady Belle of Little Nook. Erick sired two champions. More notable is Ch. Piccolo v.d. Stuttgarter, sire of six champions and an additional producer. He is the grandsire of three champions including Baron Trevor of Tredegar, and is the great grandsire of Ch. Alwin. Piccolo's dam, Glenda v.d. Stuttgarter, was out of Knirps v. Menchendal, an excellent Sigurd granddaughter and one of the few parti-colored Boxers imported. Glenda's sire, Alba v. Wasserschloss, was by Iwein v. Dom, the sire of Sigurd. As Piccolo himself is by Utz v. Dom, a double Sigurd grandson, he is strongly bred to Sigurd and his prepotency is not surprising.

As previously mentioned, Mazelaine Kennels began with the purchase of Landa of Mazelaine from Birkbaum in 1933 and Barmere with the purchase of Dodi v.d. Stoeckersburg in the same year. These two famous kennels, which are among the oldest and certainly the best known and most out-standingly successful of the breed have run a curiously paral-

CH. MARJACK'S GOLDEN WINDJAMMER
(with handler Phil Marsh)

Sire: Ch. Captain Lookout of Thorhall
Dam: Ch. Marjack's Golden Twist

Breeder: Mary Jackson
Owners: Mr. and Mrs. John P. Wagner

lel course. Started in the same year, within a few months at most, each by the purchase of an American-bred bitch, the said bitches became the first two American-bred champions of their sex. Both Landa and Dodi were bred to Check v. Hunenstein, the latter whelping in October, 1933, and the former in November. Bitches from each litter, though not themselves champions, left descendants which attained the title and are winning heavily today. Later each of these kennels achieved top distinction in the show ring and notable breeding success. And within a short period of their founding each kennel was headed by an imported Sieger who proved one of the great show dogs of the breed and one of the four record-breaking sires.

Barmere's Ch. Dodi v.d. Stoeckersburg left a son, Ch. Banner of Barmere, who has already been discussed, and three producing daughters. Aleda of Barmere, the only bitch in her first litter, was the dam of Diane of Barmere, a Sigurd daughter who died young, within a point or two of her title, leaving only one litter, by Ch. Kniff v.d. Blutenau. Karla of Barmere from this litter is the dam of the sisters Southdown Vous and Ch. Southdown Dinky, the former the dam of one champion and the latter of two. A litter sister to Ch. Banner, Barbara of Barmere, produced two champions by Bastel v. Elbufer in Ch. Rido of Dorick and Ch. Dorn of Dorick. Dorn sired the 1947 Ch. Lady Belle of Little Nook and is still advertised at stud in 1948. How close the Boxer still is to his beginnings in America is indicated by the fact that Dorn is an own grandson of Ch. Dodi, and that her accomplishment of the first American-bred championship occurred only fifteen years ago. In another litter by Sigurd, Dodi produced Frieda of Barmere, who became the dam of Ch. Helga by Dux v. Marienhof, a litter brother to Dorian. Helga's litter sister, Tyra, bred to Lustig v. Dom, was the dam of a champion, Christl of Kernia, who has made her mark in Obedience training and obtained the U.D. in addition to her bench title.

Ch. Landa of Mazelaine's litter by Check has already been mentioned. From it came Alpha of Mazelaine, who to Ch. Argus v. Königsee produced Mazelaine Frederika, the dam of Ch. Calmar v. Billyssa, and to Sigurd v. Dom had Ch. Glory of Mazelaine and Ginger of Mazelaine. Ginger was the dam of three champions in one litter sired by Lustig v. Dom and among them the outstanding American-bred sire, Ch. Dauber of Tulgey Wood. Anitra of Mazelaine, a brindle like her sister, was probably on a par with Check's German-bred daughter, Saxonias Andl. Bred to Dorian v. Marienhof, Check's grandson, Anitra produced six champions and a producer, not all, however, in one litter. Among them were the famous K quartet, Chs. Kavanagh, Keturah, Kobold and Kohath of Mazelaine. In her litter by Ch. Argus v. Königsee Anitra had Ch. Dagmar of Mazelaine. Dagmar was a lovely brindle whose matings to Dorian produced four champions, the dams of four more champions and the great-grandsire of two others. Three of the four Dagmar champions were also the dams of title winners. Ch. Nemesis of Mazelaine was the dam of four, Sir Galahad, Sir Royal, Blue Heaven and Blue Smoke of Bladan, and of three more non-champion producers. Ch. Nocturne of Mazelaine, one of the great bitches of the breed, produced six champions in her litter by Utz, Vassal, Vigilante, Vivace, Volante, Vorspiel and Vox Pop of Mazelaine, all but one of them parents of champions. Nocturne and Lustig v. Dom produced Ch. Kavalier of Mazelaine, an outstanding sire, and the bitch Kantratrix of Mazelaine, dam of three champions from one litter. Finally by Sigurd Nocturne produced Mazelaine Xenobia, the granddam of two champions, and Mazelaine Xidi whose Utz litter included the dam of Ch. Merry Monarch and the granddam of three champions by El Chico—Baron Trevor of Tredegar, Majestic of Crystal and War Major of Crystal. This does not exhaust the list of Nocturne's or Anitra's winning descendants, but gives some indication of the vital part which this line from Check and Landa has played in creating the modern Boxer.

The importance of Landa does not even end here, however. The only champion she produced herself was Xanderl of Mazelaine (by Dorian) who sired the dams of two champions. Xanderl's sister Xanti has carried on but is of minor importance. Like her daughter Anitra, however, Landa appeared to combine excellently with Argus v. Königsee, Dagmar's sire. Ar-

105

gus, an imported son of Udo v. Friedensengel II and Dina v. Königsee (dam of Ch. Baldur v. Königsee), was imported by Mazelaine and made his championship in 1935. He was sold to New Orleans not long after the advent of Dorian, I believe, and this doubtless limited his stud opportunities after that date. Argus nevertheless sired two champions and eight producers. Out of the police-trained Ch. Dirndl v. Stolzenhof came Ch. Fire of Mazelaine and three bitches including Fray, the dam of Ch. Brace of Briarnole, and Flame, the granddam of Ch. Overture of Mazelaine. From Landa herself Argus produced Etfa of Mazelaine. Etfa was bred to Ch. Just v. Dom of Barmere, a full brother to the sires of Lustig and Utz. Their daughter, Mazelaine Quagga, was bred to Ch. Dauber of Tulgey Wood, a son of Lustig out of a daughter of Sigurd (the grandsire of Just and Lustig) and Alpha of Mazelaine. This mating gave the champions Heigh Ho Carry On and Heigh Ho As You Were, both C. D. winners in Obedience. By Dorian, Quagga had a non-champion bitch more famous than either of the title holders. She was no other than Heigh Ho Bramble, who holds the breed record as a producer of champions. Bramble has produced nine champions in three litters, probably a record in itself, and seven of the nine were from a single litter which finished 100%. Bramble was first mated to Utz, who sired Ch. Suzette, and then to Ch. Konzert of Mazelaine, (son of Utz and Lorelei), who sired Ch. Clinaude's Majorette. When Bramble was finally mated to Lustig, the elder brother of Utz, he was more than nine years old and she was slightly over three and a half. Except in the matter of age this mating conformed to the general pattern which produces 88% of American-bred Boxer champions, namely the mating of a champion sire to a bitch who is either a champion or the daughter of a champion. · The Dorian-Lustig combination in the first two generations has also been markedly successful, but has not uniformly achieved such outstanding results. Bramble's famous litter contained three bitches, Chs. Better Still, Blossom Time, and Bright Maiden of Lilac Hedge and four dogs, Chs. Bright Feather, Bubbling Over, But Good and By Request of Lilac Hedge. Better Still finished in 1944 when under two years old, Bright Feather the following year, and

106

CH. PICCOLO v.d. STUTTGARTER
Sire: Ch. Utz v. dom of Mazelaine
Dam: Glenda v.d. Stuttgarter

Blossom Time and the three other dogs in 1946, with Bright Maiden completing her title in 1947. Bright Feather and But Good have already sired a champion apiece, and Bubbling Over has sired two.

Before the great pillars of the Boxer in America are discussed a few more early dogs and kennels deserve mention. In April, 1934, Mrs. Ida Gaertner founded Sumbula Kennels in Connecticut with the registration of Dromio ben Satan and Tirah bath Satan, while later in the year her daughter, Mrs. Harold Palmedo, brought over Gerik v. Schutzgeist. All three became champions during 1935, and both Tirzah and Gerik left their mark as producers. These and several other Sumbula importations were Austrian bred. Among notable names on the long roll of Sumbula-owned champions were Biene v. Elbe-Bogen se Sumbula, the first Boxer bitch to go Best in Show, Ch. Hermes v. Uracher Wasserfall se Sumbula, Ch. Ingo v. Heger se Sumbula, etc. For years this kennel ranked with Barmere and Mazelaine among the heaviest importers, breeders and exhibitors. Their home-breds included Ch. Sumbula's Gunnard, Ch. Magnet se Sumbula and Ch. Sumbula's Hot Stuff, all successful sires.

Walter Lippert founded another kennel which is still in existence with the registration of Berbel v.d. Falkenburg in October, 1934. Although she herself failed to carry on, her kennel mates, Chick v.d. Falkenburg, Dina v.d. Falkenburg and Ch. Egon v.d. Falkenburg, put the Hinshenfelde name on several champion pedigrees.

Besides the German and Austrian Boxers which largely made up the foundation stock of the breed in America there were two Swedish dogs who deserve consideration. Gotaholms Baron Fritz and Gotaholms Skal both completed their titles in 1936. Baron Fritz sired the dams of two champions and the grandsire of two more. Skal left a daughter, Deliah of Rexob, who was the granddam of two champions and the great-granddam of a third.

In April, 1935, the American Boxer Club applied for A.K.C. membership. Before this date there was no recognized standard, no regular breed organization and no Boxer columns in the dog press. (The casual mention of Boxers seen at the German Sieger Show in 1930, in the course of an article on Schnauzers by Anne Fitzgerald in *Popular Dogs* is perhaps the earliest mention of the breed.) The first Boxer delegate to the A.K.C. was Dr. Clinton R. Barker. The A.B.C.'s first slate of officers included Harold B. Palmedo, President; Mrs. Rudolph Gaertner, Secretary; Alexander A. Nitt, Treasurer. Mrs. Arthur M. Lewis (who wrote the Boxer column in the A.K.C. *Gazette,* beginning with the June, 1935, issue), Miss Marcia Fennessy, Mrs. L. W. Whittemore, Mrs. H. B. Palmedo, F. Greenhagen, A. V. Barber and Dr. C. R. Barker made up the first Board. That same July, 1935, issue of the *Gazette* saw Sigurd v. Dom's picture on the cover —the first Boxer to appear there. Show entries were on the increase, too, and Morris & Essex had a class entry of 26, with several specials for Bernard Tuellmann to judge. This was an amazing entry at the time, although today that number might be found in a single class, and total entries at the larger shows have nearly reached the 200 mark.

Another important event of 1935 was the transfer of Boxers from the Non-sporting to the Working group. Although dire predictions were made at the time, the shift has certainly not affected adversely the breed's record in group wins.

Several important bitches were imported during 1935. Mazelaine acquired Quinta Struthio, a daughter of Sieger Granti Struthio, and Lola v.d. Drei Gleichen, both of whom finished before the end of the year. Quinta left two good producers, Ottilie and Hekate of Mazelaine (the latter dam of Ch. Schottische of Mazelaine, the granddam of Ch. Schoolmaster among others.) Lola produced Lorelei of Mazelaine, dam of Chs. Kris and Konzert and granddam of Nylon and El Wendie, to name only a few of her descendants. Lola was out of Cilly v. Hohenneuffen. Ch. Paddy v. Hohenneuffen of Barmere, registered at the same time, was out of Cilly's daughter, Ida v. Hohenneuffen. Paddy, a beautiful fawn who made several Group wins, came over in whelp to Sieger Fachinger v. Neu Drosedow and this litter contained Chs. Candida and Commander of Barmere and Ch. Cynthia of Mazelaine. Bred to Sigurd v. Dom she produced two more champions, Etfa and Eitel of Barmere.

Cilly v. Hohenneuffen was also the dam of Siegerin Gretel v. Hohenneuffen by Hansl v. Biederstein. Gretel, like Cilly, remained in Germany, yet she holds the breed record for American-bred champions. More than a dozen of her progeny were imported and nearly all of them scored as producers, in the show ring, or both. She was the dam of eleven American champions in addition to Siegerin Dina v. Uracher Wasserfall who remained in Germany. Ch. Alex v. Uracher Wasserfall was by Sigurd v. Dom and so was Ch. Busa v. Uracher Wasserfall (imported in whelp to Droll v. Königstor). Busa was the dam of Ch. Alice of Barmere and Hetta v. Schoenegelbe, the double granddam of Ch. Adventure of Mossmont. Busa left in Germany another daughter, Gunda v. Hohenneuffen, who was the dam of Ch. Max v. Hohenneuffen and therefore the granddam of Chs. V-E Admiral and V-E Wave of Renrew. Chs. Cilly and Corso v. Uracher Wasserfall were also by Sigurd. (Corso sired three champions and seven producers.) Chs. Dora, Dorle and Draga v.d. Uracher Wasserfall were by Zorn v. Dom and all three were producers. Ch. Edler v. Uracher Wasserfall was by Dorian v. Marienhof. Chs. Hansl, Hermes and Heidi were also by Zorn. Hermes sired three champions besides the outstanding brood bitch Cynthia v. Tal and Hansl sired a champion and three producers. In addition to her eleven champions Gretel also produced Asta and Holda v. Uracher Wasserfall, each of whom was the dam of a producer. She was an example of a Siegerin who produced a Siegerin, and her influence on the breed in America has been very great.

The Four Horsemen of American Boxerdom have all been mentioned in the course of the foregoing discussion. Chs. Sigurd v. Dom of Barmere, Dorian v. Marienhof of Mazelaine, Lustig v. Dom of Tulgey Wood and Utz v. Dom of Mazelaine have records as yet unapproached and have gone far toward making the breed what it is today.

Sigurd was as important in Germany as in America and his descendants have dominated the Sieger titles and German breeding program. In 1938, before the beginning of the war, just over half the German litters registered carried the blood of Sigurd or his sire Iwein v. Dom. Yet both Sieger and Siegerin in 1938, and all but 7 out of an entry of 83 at the

110

CH. SALGRAY'S BATTLE CHIEF
(with handler Jane Kamp Forsyth)

Sire: Ch. Barrage of Quality Hill
Dam: Ch. Slipper of Grayarlin

Breeder-Owners: Mr. and Mrs. Daniel M. Hamilburg

111

1938 Sieger Show were of v. Dom blood. Sigurd's enormous influence in America is consequently due even more to the importations of his descendants—children, grandchildren and more remote generations—than to his actual get in this country, important as some of them were.

Sigurd belonged to the line of great dogs tracing back in male line to Box St. Salvator of which the highlights were Hugo v. Pfalzgau, Ch. Rolf v. Vogelsberg, Ch. Rolf v. Walhall and Ch. Cäsar v. Deutenkofen. Like these others, Sigurd was a great individual with extraordinary prepotency. Both of his parents carried Sieger Cäsar v. Deutenkofen (the sire of Check v. Hunenstein) as parental grandsires, and Sigurd was strongly linebred to Sieger Rolf v. Vogelsberg, appearing four times through his son S. Rolf v. Walhall, four times through Schelm v. Angertor and once through Siegerin Rassel v. Dom. Sigurd was a fawn, but sired both fawns and brindles. He was whelped July 14, 1929 and did not leave Germany until five years old, when he was already an established sire. He was imported by Charles Ludwig and immediately sold to Barmere. Mr. Ludwig became a Boxer fancier and breeder (like John P. Wagner of Mazelaine he had been earlier interested in Great Danes) and his daughter, Mrs. Lena Ludwig, is still breeding Boxers.

Behind him in Germany Sigurd left Sieger Fachinger v. Neu Drosedow, Sieger Zero v. Dom, International Ch. Xerxes v. Dom (owned in Switzerland), Just v. Dom who later became an American champion, the great sire Zorn v. Dom, Siegerin Zeila v. Dom and Siegerin Yva v. Marienhof. Eventually ten of his sons and daughters were imported and became American champions, while two more left champion descendants. Chs. Corso v. Uracher Wasserfall, Just v. Dom and Hatto v.d. Karlshohe were the most successful as sires. Starting in 1936 with Banner of Barmere, Sigurd also produced 16 American-bred champions and no less than 27 producers. Altogether 55 of Sigurd's get made their American titles or left champion progeny. He lived to be nearly thirteen, passing away March 3, 1942. Imported in May, 1934, not long before his fifth birthday, the fawn Sigurd won Best in Show that same year at San Mateo, California and in 1935 was

Best of Breed at Westminster, where he defeated the brindle Check v. Hungenstein. Sigurd, like Check, was an important factor in making the general public aware of the Boxer. Widely shown from coast to coast he piled up an impressive record of breed, group and best in show wins.

Imported only two years after Check, Sigurd undoubtedly suffered to a somewhat less degree from the same scarcity of suitable bitches which limited Check's activities as a sire. In the interval, however, some good Check daughters had matured and good bitches were being regularly imported. Nevertheless, only seven out of his sixteen American-bred champions finished their titles by 1939, while one, Ch. Clarice of Balancing Rock, was not whelped until May of 1941, only a couple of months before his twelfth birthday. Had Sigurd remained in Germany it is probable that he would have surpassed all records as a sire of Siegers. Even leaving when he did, he ranks with Rigo v. Angertor and the two Rolfs, in addition to his American get.

The importance of Sigurd to the American Boxer does not become fully apparent, however, until it is pointed out that all three of the other members of the Big Four were his grandsons! Hence, all of their great achievements must be credited in some degree to Sigurd also. Lustig and Utz were full brothers with three years difference in age. Sired by Zorn v. Dom, a great sire who never became a Sieger, out of Esta v.d. Wurm, they were double Sigurd grandsons. Esta was out of the Sieger Edler v. Isarstrand daughter, Uni v.d. Wurm, and Zorn out of Dudel v. Pfarrhaus, a daughter of Sieger Cäsar v. Deutenkofen and half-sister to Check v. Hunenstein.

The only brindle among the Big Four was Int. Ch. Dorian v. Marienhof. Sired by Int. Ch. Xerxes v. Dom, a full brother to Zorn, Dorian was out of the Check v. Hunenstein daughter, Saxonias Andl, and so combined the blood of Check and Sigurd. He was whelped April 15, 1933 and died March 24, 1941. Never defeated in his breed in Europe or America, he was 22 times Best in Show. Dorian was a contemporary of Lustig v. Dom in Germany, being only some eight months older than his fawn rival. He was imported before his third birthday and so, like Check, left few German get. Several

113

of these, however, were eventually imported and two made American championships. Ch. Biene v. Elbe Bogen se Sumbula, who finished in 1937, was one of the outstanding bitches of her day. Dorian's record of 37 American-bred champions stands unbeaten. In addition, he sired the Canadian Ch. Allison Adonis (sire of Ch. Major Bruce), two imported champions, and 23 American-bred producers.

Dorian leaped immediately into the front rank as a sire. Although he was imported only in 1936, four of his get made their championships before the end of 1937. At Westminster that year he won the Group—the first Boxer to do so—and showing superbly, was the apparent runner-up for Best in Show. The highest award at Westminster was not to fall to a Boxer for another ten years, but when it did come the successful contender was a Dorian grandson, Ch. Warlord of Mazelaine. Warlord's dam, Ch. Symphony of Mazelaine, was one of eight by Dorian out of the imported Ch. Crona v. Zwergeck, seven of whom became champions while six have a total of fifteen champion grandchildren. The eight were not from a single litter, however. Crona was an imported Lustig daughter out of Britta v. Königsee, the latter a litter sister to Ch. Baldur v. Königsee and half-sister to Ch. Argus v. Königsee. Dorian and Argus more than once proved an excellent combination. Besides Symphony, Crona and Dorian produced Ch. Serenade of Mazelaine, a great winner with nearly a hundred best of breeds, some 84 groups and three best in shows to her credit at five years old and the dam of Chs. First Fiddle and Fandango of Dorick. Ch. Symphony was the dam of four champions, and Ch. Duke Cronian the sire of five.

From Anitra of Mazelaine, a Check daughter, Dorian sired five champions and two producers, and from Anitra's daughter, Ch. Dagmar he sired four champions and four producers. Out of Dagmar came two great bitches Chs. Nocturne and Nemesis of Mazelaine, the latter granddam of 16 champions and the former of 17 and one Canadian champion. Nemesis is the dam of Ch. Sir Galahad of Bladan, Nocturne of Ch. Vorspiel and Kavalier of Mazelaine.

Dorian sons who are proving prepotent sires include several of the most outstanding American-breds. Sir Galahad of

CH. BAROQUE OF QUALITY HILL

Sire: Ch. Bang Away of Sirrah Crest
Dam: Valley Groves Applause

Breeders: Mr. and Mrs. M. E. Greiner
Owners: Mr. and Mrs. John P. Wagner

Bladen, a grandson, out of Nemesis, died in 1946 at the age of ten with 11 champions and three producers to his credit, and was still siring puppies within a few months of his death. His get included Ch. Heigh Ho Painted Chief, Ch. Bladan's U-Chetnik and Ch. Lady Jill of Marmac. Ch. Archduke of Valcar, a son of Dorian and Valwa v. Dom (by Lustig out of Blanka v. Fohlnhof) is credited with ten champions in the space of three years starting in 1945. They include Ch. Nylon of Mazelaine, one of the outstanding bitches of her day. Ch. Mahderf's El Chico, out of double Lustig granddaughter, has sired 10 champions and a producer, including Ch. Merry Monarch, Baron Trevor of Tredegar, War Major of Crystal and Baron of Brightwood. Ch. Endymion of Mazelaine is the sire of seven champions and a producer, including Ch. Schoolmaster of Mazelaine, already the sire of seven and Nightcap of Sirrah Crest the sire of three champions. The Dorian grandson Warlord is also the sire of seven champions, with plenty of time to add to the list.

Int. Ch. Lustig v. Dom was whelped during the same year as Dorian, 1933, but was several months the younger and was not imported until 1937. After a magnificent show career abroad he was acquired by the late Erwin O. Freund of Tulgey Wood. Lustig was extensively used at stud in Germany and resembles his grandsire, Sigurd v. Dom, in the fact that his influence upon the breed has been to an important extent through his important get and grandget. In contrast, Dorian and Utz are important almost entirely through their American-bred progeny.

Lustig sired 24 American-bred champions and 17 imported dogs who gained their titles in this country, a total of 41 which exceeds by 2 Dorian's total of 39. In addition, Lustig sired at least one Canadian champion, 23 American-bred producers of champions and two imported producers, making a grand total of 67 against Dorian's 63. However, both Dorian with 37 and Utz with 35 American-bred champions exceed him in this respect.

Whelped December 28, 1933, Lustig died on June 14, 1945, at the age of eleven and one-half years. He therefore outlived his younger brother Utz by some two months and ranks next

116

to Sigurd among the Big Four in respect to age at the time of his death. Lustig was a fawn, like both Utz and Sigurd, although his sire, Zorn v. Dom, was a brindle. Oddly enough the Int. Ch. Xerxes v. Dom (Zorn's brother) who sired the brindle Dorian was himself a fawn. Lustig combined power and tremendous substance with elegance and grace, and his splendid personality and true Boxer temperament were among the outstanding qualities which he handed on to his progeny. He left behind him in Germany such outstanding males as Sieger Danilo v. Königsee, Sieger Ajax v. Holderburg, Ernstlustig v. Zollernhof and Stolz v. Friedenheim, top quality Boxers who were active at the beginning of the war.

Of Lustig's imported get, Ch. Crona v. Zwergeck has already been mentioned as the dam of seven champions by Dorian. Ch. Kniff v.d. Blutenau, his brother Ch. Kurass v.d. Blutenau, and sister Ch. Lisl v.d. Blutenau, all out of Cora v.d. Blutenau, were the parents of ten champions and grandparents of some thirteen others. Kurass, in particular, sired Mahderf's Miss Eva, the dam of Ch. Mahderf's El Chico. Another imported Lustig daughter, Ch. Herta v. Pfarrkirchen, was likewise bred to Dorian and produced Mazelaine Leocadia, dam of two champions, Gavotte and Groomsman of Mazelaine, and the non-champion Whirlaway of Mazelaine, who left four champions including Apollo of San Joaquin at his early death when only six years old. Ch. Valwa v. Dom, the dam of Chs. Archduke and Ardeth of Valcar, was another Lustig daughter who produced notably to Dorian.

Lustig's stud record includes the famous B-litter of Lilac Hedge Kennels from the Dorian daughter Heigh Ho Bramble. All seven of this litter made their championships and three of the four males have already sired title winners.

Lustig's most successful imported son was Ch. Brokas v. Germanenstolz, whose dam, Saxonias Aska, was a Check v. Hunenstein daughter and a litter sister to Dorian's dam, Saxonias Andl. Brokas sired four champions and three producers, of whom the most outstanding was the late Sir Galahad of Bladan, discussed under his grandsire, Dorian. Ch. Brace of Briarnole, who finished his title back in 1939, must have been one of Lustig's earliest American-bred get. He was out of Fray of Mazelaine, a daughter of Ch. **Argus v.** Königsee and Ch. Dirndl v. Stolzenhof (the police-trained bitch Mr. Bigler described as "a tough old lady who slept with a night-stick in her mouth). Brace was the first American-bred **Boxer** to win a Best in Show all breeds and in addition he sired six champions and eight producers. His best known son is Ch. Adair of Three Birches.

Among American-bred sires Ch. Dauber of Tulgey Wood, whelped July 20, 1937, by Lustig v. Dom out of Ginger of Mazelaine, still ranks first at the time of writing and at past ten years of age was still siring puppies. He has to his credit no less than thirteen champions and one additional producer. His dam was the Sigurd daughter, Ginger of Mazelaine, out of the Check-Landa daughter, Alpha of Mazelaine. As a Lustig son, Dauber consequently carries three lines to Sigurd, while the female line on his dam's side is one of the most prepotent in the country. Apparently he got off to a slow start for none of Dauber's get made their titles until 1941. In that year, however, four of his sons finished—Adonis v. Volk, Royal of Tulgey Wood, Yeoman of Tulgey Wood and Yopo of Tulgey Wood. A son and daughter, Ch. Heigh Ho As You Were and Ch. Heigh Ho Carry On, finished in 1945 and are both Obedience Class winners with the C.D. title. Ch. Dauber's Debutante finished in 1947 at more than four years of age.

A Lustig son with an interesting record, probably unique, is Ch. Kavalier of Mazelaine, out of Ch. Nocturne of Mazelaine. Kavalier, whelped in 1939, has to his credit only one champion, the Canadian champion son, Kavaliero of Briarnole. However, he has sired two non-champion sons and eight non-champion daughters who have proven their worth as producers and he bids fair to have an important influence upon the future of the breed. Kavalier's outstanding producing son, Whirlaway of Mazelaine, C.D., a litter brother to Wiegenlied, is out of the Dorian daughter, Mazelaine Leocadia, whose dam was the imported Ch. Herta v. Pfarrkirchen of Mazelaine. Whirlaway, Obedience trained, was whelped in 1941 and died prematurely when only five or six years old, leaving four champions from three different matings. Ch. Apollo of San Joa-

118

CH. TRECEDER'S PAINTED LADY
(with handler Joe Gregory)

Sire: Ch. Treceder's Selection
Dam: Treceder's Discovery

Breeders: Don and Rita Montier
Owners: Mr. and Mrs. Donald Smith

quin, who finished in 1946, has made an excellent show record on the West Coast and finished his title before he was two. Another dog, Udandie of Sirrah Crest (out of Ch. Oracle of Sirrah Crest), and two bitches, Calada and Camarada Del Ray (out of Alice v. Jansu, dam also of Ch. Blason Del Ray) finished in 1947, all of them between two and two and a half years of age.

Kavalier's producing daughters include Psyche of Mazelaine, the dam of Ch. Schoolmaster (out of the Dorian daughter, Ch. Schottische of Mazelaine) and five sisters out of Ouida of Mazelaine (an Utz v. Dom daughter), namely Ovation of Sirrah Crest, dam of Ch. Questa of Sirrah Crest; Ozanna of Sirrah Crest, dam of Sirrah Crest Manx; Ornadoon of Sirrah Crest, dam of Ch. Bianca of Canyonair and granddam of Ch. Clinaude's O'Flap Jack; Onyx of Sirrah Crest, granddam of three champions; and Ouinkle of Sirrah Crest, dam of Nightcap of Sirrah Crest, who sired three champions out of Madcap of Sirrah Crest, the daughter of his dam's sister Onyx. Few non-champion sires have left as many good producers as Kavalier.

Among Lustig's imported get were three champions out of Cora v.d. Blutenau, all of whom have carried on successfully. Ch. Kniff v.d. Blutenau, sired six champions, Bravenhartz Ensign Easy, Bravenhartz Nova Norma, Meritaire's Bravenhartz Wish (a litter sister of the Seeing Eye Dog, Bravenhartz the Wizard), Kim of Solway, Augusta of Brielynn and Allgau of Brielynn. In addition he sired six producers, including Karla of Barmere, dam of one and granddam of three champions. Ch. Kurass v.d. Blutenau, Kniff's litter brother, sired three champions and two producers. His daughter, Ch. Mahderf's Miss Eva, a double Lustig granddaughter, was the dam (by Dorian) of Ch. Mahderf's El Chico. Ch. Lisl v.d. Blutenau, a younger full sister to Kniff and Kurass, produced Ch. Xylan of Tulgey Wood by Ch. Dauber (making him a double Lustig grandson), Quinella, the dam of Ch. Dondera of Tulgey Wood, by her own sire, Lustig, and two non-champion producers by Dorian. These were Elda of Tulgey Wood, the dam of Ch. Yactor of Tulgey Wood, and Eagle of Tulgey Wood, sire of Ch. Carter of Roanne and Ch. Bonita of Cross Acres. Bonita, bred to Ch. Schoolmaster, who also combines Dorian and Lustig, is fast acquiring fame as the dam of a remarkable litter which finished three champions during 1947, Neff, Nemesis and Nonita of Cross Acres, with very probably more to come. This N-Cross Acres litter shows a most interesting pedigree, with five crosses to Dorian in five generations, three to Lustig and four to Sigurd. Since Dorian is a Sigurd grandson and Lustig a double grandson there are at least nine more crosses to Sigurd beyond the fifth generation. There are also seven crosses to Check v. Hunenstein, five of them through Dorian, but only two within five generations. Ch. Bonita of Cross Acres belongs to the 2% of Boxer champions with neither parent a champion. Nevertheless, she has three champion grandparents, for in addition to Dorian and Lisl on her sire's side her dam, Bravenhartz Ionic Irene, is by Ch. Haris v.d. Uetliburg, an imported brindle dog of excellent quality. Irene's dam was by Lustig out of a Dorian daughter. Cora v.d. Blutenau, the dam of Kniff, Kurass and Lisl (and of a non-producing champion, Flott v.d. Blutenau, by Sigurd) was a daughter of Sieger Edler v. Isarstrand out of a daughter of Sieger Alex v.d. Magdalenenquelle.

Another imported Lustig son who has been carrying on successfully is Ch. Eros v. Luisenblick. From the Sigurd daughter, Paulette of Barmere, Eros sired Ch. Adolf of Balancing Rock (grandsire of Ch. Trinka of Gor-Wen), Adroit Lady of Balancing Rock (dam of Ch. Clarice of Balancing Rock) and Ch. Axel of Balancing Rock. Axel, who died of leptospirosis at the early age of six years, has been called one of the finest American-bred males. For some obscure reason, despite a really impressive show career, Axel seems to have been greatly underrated and was comparatively little used at stud. However, he left a number of sons and daughters who may still perpetuate his name. Eros v. Luisenblick also sired Lore of Kernia, dam of Ch. Du Barry of Kernia and of Kantata of Wolf Trap, dam of Ch. Halgeo's Spike v. Berube.

The fourth of the great quartette of Boxer sires, Ch. Utz v. Dom of Mazelaine, was a full brother to Lustig but nearly two and a half years younger. Whelped April 18, 1936, Utz died April 9, 1945, some two months before his famous

121

brother. Thus after Dorian, Utz was the shortest-lived of the Big Four. Like Lustig and Sigurd, Utz was a fawn. (Dorian was the only brindle of the four.) He was imported by Mazelaine in 1939, just before the War, and for that reason his get which have influenced the breed in this country have all been American-bred. Up to the end of 1947 Utz had sired 35 champions and 16 non-champion producers. Although the total of 51 is less than for any of the other three, his American-bred total is second only to Dorian's 60, and Dorian, who was imported several years earlier, died early in 1941.

For five successive years, beginning with 1942, Utz was the leading sire. In that year he had nine champions to his credit, out of six different bitches. They included Ch. Suzette, the brothers Konzert and Kris of Mazelaine, and three from the Nocturne litter (Volante, Vorspiel and Vox Pop of Mazelaine). No other sire has had nine American-bred champions finished in a single year. Sigurd had nine in 1936, but all except one were imported. Dorian had eight in 1938 and led again in 1940 with seven. (In 1941 he tied for first place with Lustig, both having five champions finished, and in 1942 was second to Utz, with six.) Lustig had eight champions in 1939, but two were imported. Despite his great record, that is the only year in which Lustig was squarely in the lead. He tied for first with Dorian in 1941, was second to him in 1940, 1938 and 1937. Sigurd was first only in 1936, second in 1939, and tied for second in 1940. Utz' record of five straight firsts is therefore unique. Besides nine champions in 1942 he had six in 1944 and seven in 1946. Both Utz and Lustig had a single champion in 1947, giving Lustig a record of from one to eight champions per year for eleven years without a break.

Utz was fortunate in his timing. When he appeared upon the scene the condition of the breed in America was very different from what it had been upon the arrival of Sigurd, Dorian or even Lustig. Utz found an array of excellent bitches awaiting him, including Dorian, Sigurd and Utz daughters and granddaughters. Owing to the outbreak of the War importations were suspended for several years, so that Utz had to compete with only his older rivals in addition

CH. DORN OF DORICK
Sire: Int. Ch. Bastel v. Elbufer of Barmere
Dam: Barbara of Barmere

to the growing list of good American-breds. Moreover, his get, excellent as many of them were, did not face the competition of successive importations of European title winners. Up to 1936 only one Boxer champion in eight was an American-bred—five out of the first forty champions, and two of the five were from bitches imported in whelp. Ten years later, in 1946, the only imported dog to finish was Karlo v.d. Wolfschlucht, whelped in March, 1939, and still good enough to become a champion when seven years old.

Utz was a great show dog as well as sire. He was the second Boxer to win the Working Group at Westminster (Dorian was the first) and sired the only Boxer to win it more than once. Utz's greatest claim to fame is undoubtedly his son, the great Ch. Warlord of Mazelaine. Whelped in October, 1942, Warlord is a magnificent fawn with a long record of Best in Shows. He won the Group at Westminster for three years running, in 1945, 1946 and 1947, a feat no other Boxer has equalled; was the first of the breed to go Best American-bred at Westminster, and retired after topping his record by placing Best in Show at Westminster in 1947. In addition, he has a record of seven champion get at five years old. Warlord's dam is Ch. Symphony of Mazelaine, a Dorian daughter out of Ch. Crona v. Zwergeck. Crona was by Lustig and produced seven champions to Dorian, though not all in one litter. Her get includes Ch. Duke Cronian, sire of five champions and a producer, and Ch. Serenade of Mazelaine, dam of two champions and herself a show bitch par excellence, with an unequalled record of Best of Breed and Group wins. At the age of five Serenade had been thrice Best in Show and won the Group 84 times. Symphony, the dam of Warlord, has four champions to her credit, as well as the dams of two others. Warlord is certainly one of the young American-bred sires who can be expected to strongly influence the breed in the future. His show record is bound to produce a continuing demand for his services, and both his pedigree and past success at stud indicate that he will live up to his promise.

Utz can claim some of the credit, likewise, for another great performer, the fawn bitch, Ch. El Wendie of Rockland. Wendie, like Warlord, is a great showman. In 1944 all-round and group judges voting on a ballot prepared by the Gaines Dog Research Center pronounced her the best dog or bitch of the year, regardless of breed, and she won most Best in Shows of any dog in 1944. Wendie's sire, Ch. Konzert of Mazelaine, is a son of Utz out of the Dorian daughter, Lorelei of Mazelaine, whose dam was by Sigurd. Konzert was a litter brother to Ch. Kris of Mazelaine, a successful sire, and a full sister, Swagger of Mazelaine, is the dam of Ch. Nylon of Mazelaine, one of the most notable show bitches of the present day. El Wendie's dam, Tilda of Rockland, is a Sigurd daughter out of Hulda of Rexob, whose sire is a Sigurd grandson. El Wendie herself has already made a name as a producer, with four champions from three litters. Bred back to her grandsire, Utz, she produced Ch. Gentleman Jim of Rye Top and El Dandie of Rye Top, each of whom has already sired two champions, plus a bitch, Ch. Miss Spitfire of Rye Top. She also produced Ch. Victory Song of Rye Top by Ch. Beacon Out of Bounds (a Sigurd grandson), and Ch. Model Lady of Rye Top by Revelation of Barmere, another Sigurd grandson. Few bitches of El Wendie's quality have been so successful as brood bitches.

As the sire of Warlord and grandsire of El Wendie and Nylon, Utz has earned a secure place in Boxer history, but there are others as well. Ch. Yller of Mazelaine is another Utz bitch combining show and breeding qualities. From Ch. Nocturne of Mazelaine, Utz sired a litter of six, all becoming champions and five of whom are producers. Nocturne, a Dorian daughter, was the only American-bred among the top placings when Herr Philip Stockmann judged the breed at Westminster in 1938. From the Utz-Nocturne litter came Ch. Vorspiel of Mazelaine, sire of six champions, Ch. Vox Pop, sire of two, Ch. Vassel, sire of one, and the bitches Vivace and Volante with four more. All told, Utz has eleven champion grandchildren from this one litter. Vorspiel, with his Utz-Dorian breeding and his record of six champions from six different bitches, is another of the coming sires who will bear watching.

In judging the value of a sire to the breed, perspective is necessary. Time does strange things to reputations. The dog

125

CH. RANCHO CHIQUITO YANNA

Sire: Ch. Jered's Spellbinder
Dam: Rancho Chiquito's Dancer

Owner: Miss Joan Johnson

who is a sensation in his day as a show winner is likely to receive many of the outstanding bitches available, as well as others of lesser quality whose owners hope to improve their stock by his use. With many matings and a large crop of puppies being shown, such a dog has every opportunity to prove himself, and if he is genetically a really prepotent sire, with the ability to pass on desirable characteristics to a high degree, he will sire not only winners but producers who will carry on his blood for generations. If, however, he is not really prepotent and able to transmit his qualities down the generations, his line will gradually disappear. Such a dog may produce a considerable number of excellent get, probably in large part because of the high quality of bitches mated to him, but he will fail to carry on beyond the first or second generation. Other dogs may have the qualities requisite for a great sire, but for various reasons may lack opportunity to show what they can do. A dog of this latter type may be sold, perhaps as a puppy, to an owner who is not interested in showing or breeding. Though the equal or superior of the first type, he may never have the chance to make a championship. If bred to at all, it is likely to be by his breeder, or by owners of one bitch located in the vicinity who may well lack superior quality. Probably many a possible Sigurd or Dorian leaves nothing behind him from lack of opportunity. Even if he is freely shown a dog may for some reason fail to go to the top and never complete his title. For this reason or another he may have little chance to show what he can do. Sometimes a top show dog is not as prepotent as a brother who is less successful in the ring. And sometimes there seems to be no reason except fashion or prejudice to explain why one dog is sought after and another is not. Herr Stockmann, for many years the owner of Ch. Rolf v. Vogelsberg, the great brindle sire who proved to be the foundation of today's Boxer breed, writes that Rolf was at stud in Munich for seven years. During all that time only two bitches outside the von Dom kennels were bred to him! Local breeders were prejudiced against him (or may it have been against his owner?) and what a golden opportunity they missed!

A dog of the type described, whose opportunities at stud

have been curtailed for extraneous reasons, or who perhaps died young through accident or disease, sometimes leaves a few outstanding get. If these have better opportunities than their sire, particularly if there are several sons or grandsons of quality, it becomes apparent in due course that their sire or grandsire was a great producer, his stock is sought after and his reputation grows accordingly. A dog whose producing get are largely daughters, however, is likely to have much of his worth credited to the studs to whom his daughters are mated. And of course, other things being equal, a dog can produce as many litters in a year as the average bitch can whelp in a lifetime. This not only increases the mathematical likelihood of a male leaving individuals who will carry on successfully but means that his name occurs more frequently in the stud books.

It sometimes happens that even a dog with ample opportunities at stud sires daughters who are superior to his sons and carries on principally through them. Such was the case of the great German Ch. Rigo v. Angertor, whose granddaughter, Liesel v. Deutenkofen, through her son, Ch. Cäsar v. Deutenkofen, was the ancestress of all the Big Four.

Some fifteen or twenty years are generally required before the breeding value of a dog can be properly adjudged in long range terms, though it may be fairly evident by ten or twelve. There is certainly no doubt that Utz v. Dom, whelped in 1936, has had and will continue to have a tremendous influence on the breed, for instance, but twelve years is not enough to predict with certainty his relative standing as compared with his brother, Lustig.

Utz's best producing son to date is unquestionably Warlord, whose seven champions include several sons. It is too soon, however, to judge whether they will carry on the male line, or whether Warlord stands a chance of approaching his sire's record. Only five years old as yet, he should have many years at stud ahead of him and comparatively few of his get can have attained the age of the average Boxer champion, for 71% of the breed's title winners finish between the ages of 1½ and 3½ years. Warlord himself was not whelped until Utz was six and a half. Ch. Vorspiel of Mazelaine, with six champions to his credit, has only one son among them, though he may yet have others. Chs. Kris and Konzert of Mazelaine are both dead at a comparatively early age, and so are two of their three champion sons. Ch. Piccolo v.d. Stuttgarter has three sons among his six champions and there are others who will have plenty of time to do as well. On the record to date, however, Warlord leads strongly.

While Sigurd far excels all others in the number of male lines descended from him, since the rest of the big three are his grandsons, his best American-bred son is Ch. Edel of Barmere, with four champions and four additional producers. Out of the seven Edel sons several have already sired champions. Ch. Quixote of Mazelaine (by Sigurd out of Ophelia v. Marienhof, by a Sigurd son out of Dorian's dam) left three sons, Ch. Beacon Out of Bounds whose first three champions finished within a year, Ch. Drum Major of Rockholl, and Alladin of Echo Lane. Sigurd's notable American-bred daughters include the dams of Ch. El Wendie of Rockland and Ch. Dauber of Tulgey Wood.

The greatest number of important American-bred sires thus far trace in male line to Dorian and Lustig. Ch. Dauber of Tulgey Wood, by Lustig, was still siring puppies in 1947 and ten of his 13 champions were sons. None of them has yet come near his sire's record. Ch. Sir Galahad of Bladan, who died in 1946 at the age of ten, also sired litters only a few months before his death. His 11 champions are more evenly divided between the sexes than in the case of Dauber. This list may well receive additions, for the success of his get made him in demand again toward the end of his life and a daughter finished in 1947. Another Lustig son, Ch. Brace of Briarnole, has three sons among his six champions, including Adair of Three Birches, most likely to carry on according to present indications. The four Lustig sons in the Lilac Hedge litter out of Heigh Ho Bramble were not whelped until 1943, when Lustig was nine and a half. Given the quality of this litter and the fact that four 1947 champions, three of them males, were sired by its members, there is every promise that the line will carry on.

Ch. Kavalier of Mazelaine has been mentioned elsewhere as

the sire of ten producing daughters and a Canadian champion son. There seems, however, a good chance that he may carry on in male line through Whirlaway of Mazelaine. Although Whirlaway died comparatively young without completing his title (a litter brother, Wiegenlied of Mazelaine lacks only a few points to finish) he is credited with four champions, two of them sons. One of the latter, Mr. J. Howard Davis' Ch. Apollo of San Joaquin, was Best Boxer at the 1948 specialty show of the American Boxer Club, with an entry of 235. This is the largest Boxer show ever held in this country. Not yet three years old, the fawn Apollo should have a big future ahead of him. He was bred in California, and the specialty show was his first appearance in the East. Unfortunately, his entry was received too late for Westminster 1948. He has already sired a number of litters and after such an important win should receive every opportunity to prove what he can do. Besides tracing in male line to Lustig, through Whirlaway and Kavalier, Apollo's pedigree shows Lustig twice more in the fourth generation and Ch. Hermes v. Uracher Wasserfall, a half-brother to Lustig, once also. On his sire's side Apollo has two lines to Dorian and on his dam's side at least four to Sigurd (two of them through Fachinger v. Neu Drosedow).

It may be that some of Lustig's other imported sons will also carry on his male line. However, to date the most promising is that of Ch. Brokas v. Germanenstolz, the sire of Sir Galahad of Bladan.

When it comes to a consideration of Dorian's male lines, one of his leading sons is Ch. Mahderf's El Chico, whose ten champions include several proven sires. Among them Ch. Chriss of Treceder, Ch. Baron Trevor of Tredegar, Ch. Merry Monarch, Ch. War Major of Crystal are already earning laurels. Ch. Archduke of Valcar by Dorian had likewise ten champions to his credit at the end of 1947 (an eleventh was published in the first month of 1948) and his get includes the outstanding bitch, Ch. Nylon of Mazelaine. However, since only one of the lot finished before 1946, the Warlord daughter Ch. Aftermath of Woodcrest is as yet his only champion granddaughter. A highly promising Dorian line comes through Ch. Endymion of Mazelaine, whose seven champions include Ch. Schoolmaster of Mazelaine (also with seven). Nightcap of Sirrah Crest, with 12 points himself, has sired three champions.

Six of Schoolmaster's get finished in 1947, and this makes him the leading sire of that year. It is the first time since 1942 that Utz has not headed the list and Schoolmaster is the first American-bred who has ever done so. Archduke with four came second and Nightcap with three tied for third with Vorspiel of Mazelaine, the only Utz son among the first four. Schoolmaster's sire, Endymion, was one of thirteen sires with two each. Ch. Duke Cronian, a Dorian son who finished his championship back in 1942, brought his list of winners up to five champions and two producers by finishing two sons in 1947, Krackerjack and Yobang of Sirrah Crest. Krackerjack, out of a Lustig daughter, is a full brother to Ch. Kobang of Sirrah Crest and the latter's sister, Kokokreme. Krackerjack already has three champions to his credit and Yobang added two to the role of Duke Cronian grandchildren in 1947. Yobang is out of an Utz daughter, Madeira of Sirrah Crest, who is herself a Duke Cronian granddaughter. Ch. Yobang is therefore inbred to Duke. He also carries a third line to Dorian v. Marienhof in the fifth generation, two lines to Utz on his dam's side, and two to Lustig through Duke Cronian's dam. Yobang of Sirrah Crest, bred by the R. C. Harrises of California and owned by Mrs. Henry W. Lark of Meritaire, was Best Boxer and winner of the Working Group at Westminster in 1948. Thus he follows in the footsteps of his grandsire, Dorian, the first Boxer to win the Group at Westminster.

The Dorian male line is responsible for six more of the 1947 champions, one by El Chico and five by the latter's four champion sons, Baron Trevor of Tredegar, Chriss of Treceder, War Major of Crystal and Merry Monarch. More than a third of the year's new champions thus trace in male line to Dorian.

Three of the 1947 champions, for the first time in years, were imported. They were the litter brothers Zack and Zick v. Dom, and Check v.d. Bavaria-Quelle. The two former are by

131

Heiner v. Zwergeck, a son of Arno v. Grafensprung. Arno's sire, Sieger Danilo v. Königsee, was probably the most outstanding Lustig son who remained in Germany. Petra v. Dom, the dam of Zack and Zick, also carries two crosses to Lustig. She is out of a Lustig daughter and is sired by Ch. Milo v. Pfarrkirchen se Sumbula, imported some years since and by the Lustig son, Zunftig v. Dom.

Ch. Check v.d. Bavaria-Quelle is the only imported champion, so far as I am aware, who traces to Utz v. Dom. His sire, Bajazzo v.d. Bavaria-Quelle is a son of Axel v. Puckheim, a son of Utz and Hedy v. Zenith. Actually, however, Check probably carries much stronger breeding to Lustig, for he comes from the dam and son mating of Bajazzo and his dam, Petra v. Friedenheim. Petra is a double granddaughter of Stolz v. Friedenheim, who was a litter brother to American Ch. Stern v. Friedenheim, a winner of note in his day, and a Lustig son.

Another of the few imported Boxers to finish since the War is Ch. Karlo v.d. Wolfschlucht, who completed his title in 1946. He is by Arno v.d. Holderburg (a litter brother to Sieger Ajax v.d. Holderburg), out of Alma v. Grund, a Hermes v.d. Uhlandshohe daughter. Hermes never came to America, but several of his get have played a prominent part here. Among the most important have been Ch. Blanka v. Bopserwald, dam of two producing champions, Quality and Qui Sais of Barmere; Ch. Viktor v. Kraichgau, a successful sire; and Ch. Betti v.d. Schlusselberg of Marenore. Betti was the dam of Karlo v.d. Wolfschlucht's sire (which makes Karlo inbred to Hermes v.d. Uhlandshohe). In addition to Arno and Sieger Ajax v.d. Holderburg, she sired two imported American champions, Kitty and Klaus v.d. Uhlandshohe (all these four by Lustig) and was bred in this country to Dorian v. Marienhof by whom she had Cilla v.d. Marenore, the dam of Ch. Yller of Mazelaine. Betti's imported daughter, Ch. Kitti v.d. Uhlandshohe, is the dam of Ch. Mahderf's Miss Eva, through whom she is the granddam of the great American-bred sire, Ch. Mahderf's El Chico.

None of these four post-war imported champions can be said to introduce a really new strain, but they do provide the

CH. BLADAN'S U-CHETNIK
Sire: Sir Galahad of Bladan
Dam: Blue Glow of Bladan
Breeder and Owner: Dr. Dan M. Gordon, Bladan Kennels

different line of descent from a common source which can prove very valuable to breeders.

In studying the sires and bloodlines which have proved most successful since 1940 it quickly becomes apparent that the male lines from Sigurd v. Dom have virtually ousted all others. Out of 321 champions published in the American Kennel Gazette from 1940 through 1947 inclusive all but eight have been tail male descendants of Sigurd through either imported or American-bred sons. Of the remaining eight, three go to Ch. Cäsar v. Deutenkofen, Sigurd's own great grandsire in tail male (and these three finished during the first three years of the period, 1940, 1941 and 1942). The remaining five are all descendants of Golf v. Frankonia, son of Ch. Egon v. Gumbertusbrunnen, by Ch. Rolf Walhall (Cäsar's grandsire). Hence they, too, go back to a common source. Golf sired Benno v.d. Helenenquelle, the sire of Alex v. Königstor, who is represented by two lines. One comes through Droll v. Königstor to Ch. Max v. Hohenneuffen and his son Ch. V-E Admiral of Renrew (whose litter sister, V-E Wave, is also a champion. The other comes through Castor v. Hohenneuffen and his imported son Buko v. Kerspetal (whose litter sister, imported Barbel v. Kerspetal, is also a champion) to Ch. Aurelius of Kesthal. Admiral, whelped in May, 1945, and finished in 1946, is still a young dog with every promise of carrying on the line, and his sire, Ch. Max, at nearly eleven years of age is still alive and active.

Going back to the 313 champions from 1940 on who trace in male line to Sigurd it will be found that 101 trace through Lustig and his sons, 85 through Dorian and his sons (plus two more through Dux v. Marienhof, Dorian's litter brother), 67 through Utz and his sons, and 57 are by Sigurd himself (whose daughter, Ch. Rexob's Indian Penny, finished as late as 1943), or are descended from other Sigurd sons. This does not mean 57 other male lines from Sigurd, for a considerable number of the champions among these 57 were of course bitches, and not all of the dogs have left producing sons. Indeed the Sigurd male lines aside from Dorian, Lustig and Utz which show substantial promise of continuing

134

at the present time (though five, ten, or twenty years from now the picture may be quite different) are only three in number: Fachinger v. Neu Drosedow through Ch. Ingo v. Heger; Ch. Edel of Barmere; and Ch. Quixote of Mazelaine. Another which is interesting on paper, though I have seen neither the dog himself nor a critique, is the 1947 Ch. Ritter v. Oberehnhof. His sire, Adalric v. Oberehnhof, is by the Sigurd son, Ch. Corso v. Uracher Wasserfall (a successful sire, whose sons seems to have produced champion daughters) out of Clare v. Dom, who is by a Lustig son from Ursel v. Germanenstolz, a half sister to Ch. Brokas v. Germanenstolz (their dam, Saxonias Aska, was a litter sister to Dorian's dam). Ursel was sired by Udo II v. Friedensengel, whose son Ch. Argus v. Königsee left his mark indelibly on the breed as the sire of Ch. Dagmar of Mazelaine and Etfa of Mazelaine (granddam of Heigh Ho Bramble). I cannot recall any other Udo importations, though perhaps there have been some. Ch. Ritter's dam, Britta v. Oberehnhof, is by Ch. Konzert of Mazelaine who combines Utz, Dorian and Sigurd, out of Jill of Barmere, a double Sigurd granddaughter.

Of course descent in male line tells only part of the story. Some notable sires have carried on chiefly through their daughters, or a line may appear only once in a pedigree yet happen to be in tail male, while another may occur several times in other places on the pedigree, resulting in strong inbreeding to a dog which does not occur in tail male at all. Nevertheless, as has been stated elsewhere, there is a strong tendency for certain male lines to absorb all others, not only in Boxers but in other breeds of dogs and other kinds of animals, such as horses and cattle. The fact that less than twenty years after his birth in 1929 the Sigurd male line has almost completely ousted all others is an excellent example of this. If the principle holds good in the future as it has in the past it may be that one of the leading Sigurd representatives, Dorian, Lustig or Utz, will gradually push out the other two, leaving them represented only by lines which eventually end in bitches. This is sheer speculation, however, and even if it were to happen at some future date it is too soon to hazard even a guess as to which line might ultimately predominate.

The fluctuations of the past few years are interesting and are included for what they are worth, but it was not a normal period in any sense. Wartime restrictions on gasoline and show fixtures seriously limited the number of dogs shown and the number of champions completed. Some dogs, due to the accident of their geographical location, were virtually debarred from the ring. Others were severely restricted or withdrawn for the duration. Hence, in judging the performance of the various sires of this period it must be remembered that an unknown number of champion-calibre get lost their chance at the title for good. Dogs who were unshown during the War may have died before they had a chance to prove their worth in the ring, or they may have passed their prime and thus unable to compete against the younger specimens who have matured in the meantime. Much the same thing has probably happened to some potential sires and dams of quality stock, since breeding operations were frequently curtailed during the war, also. However, this may have had some advantages, since breeders cutting down their operations would tend to eliminate first the stock of poorer quality and retain or breed only the best.

BOXER CHAMPION MALE LINES

	Sigurd	Dorian	Lustig	Utz	Misc.	Total
1940	18	7	12	2	3	42
1941	9	9	16	3	1	38
1942	5	6	9	7	1	28
1943	4	3	2	5	1	15
1944	6	6	13	10	0	35
1945	3	7	5	8	0	23
1946	4	18	26	20	1	69
1947	10	29	19	12	1	71
Total	59	85	102	67	8	321

Before 1940 there were 129 American Boxer champions. The earliest Sigurd descendant is not found until 1935. Lustig and Dorian appear in 1937, and Utz for the first time in

136

CH. FLINTWOOD'S RABBLE ROUSER

Sire: Ch. Brayshaw's Masquerader
Dam: Flintwood's Banned in Boston

Breeder: Dr. Lloyd Flint
Owner: Mrs. Cheever Porter

1940. The figures for the five years from 1935 to 1939 are given in the following table for Sigurd, Dorian and Lustig only, to complete the records of these dogs.

	Sigurd	Dorian	Lustig	Utz	Misc.	Total
1935	1					1
1936	12					12
1937	9	6	4			19
1938	13	8	6			27
1939	9	3	9			21
Total	44	17	19	0	0	80
Gr. Total	103	102	121	67	8	401

It must be remembered that Sigurd's 103 is in addition to all the rest and that actually 393 champions out of 401 are descended from him in tail male.

The remaining champions before 1940 can nearly all be traced to the same sources a few generations farther back. Two go through Sigurd's sire, Iwein v. Dom, and fourteen more through Iwein's grandsire, Ch. Cäsar v. Deutenkofen (plus three more from the period beginning with 1940, giving Cäsar 19 in all exclusive of Sigurd). Cäsar's sire, Ch. Moritz v. Goldrain, was responsible for eight more (four through Sieger Alex v.d. Magdalenenquelle, three through Ch. Gerik v. Schutzgeist who was himself the eighth). Moritz's half-brother, Ch. Egon v. Gumbertusbrunnen (already mentioned as the ancestor of five champions who finished from 1940 on) is responsible for 14 more, making a total of 19 tracing to Egon up to 1947. Egon was not in direct male line back from Sigurd, but was sired by Ch. Rolf Walhall (sire of Moritz and grandsire of Cäsar). One other Rolf Walhall son besides Egon and Moritz must be credited with a champion descendant—Basso v. Annburg—making 28 in all for Rolf besides the lines through Cäsar. Ch. Rolf v. Vogelsberg, the sire of Rolf Walhall, was himself the sire of Ch. Dampf v. Dom, the first American champion. The second American champion, Bluecher v. Rosengarten, is the single title holder who comes in tail male from the great show dog, Ch. Milo v. Eigelstein.

138

Both Milo's sire, Ch. Remus v. Pfalzgau, and Rolf v. Vogelsberg's sire, Ch. Curt v. Pfalzgau, were by Hugo v. Pfalzgau.

Only two out of the entire list of AKC champions cannot be traced to Rolf v. Vogelsberg in male line. One of them is the Swedish Gotaholms Skal, whose line ends with Holmgards Box II in the fourth generation. The other is Ulotte v.d. Lowenburg, dam of the first two American-bred champions, Dodi and Lord v.d. Stoeckersburg. Ulotte was by Ajax v. Durrenberg, a half-brother on the dam's side of Zitta v. Durrenberg, granddam of Check v. Hunenstein. Ajax was by Sieger Lump v. Volkerschlachtsdenkmal (a mouthfilling kennel-name which means Monument of the Massacred Populace). Lump was a contemporary of Sieger Pascha v. Neunberg, whelped about 1919, and appears to have been considerably used at stud during the early 1920's. He was by Sekt aus der Haitha out of Rita v.d. Spreeau, but as the stud book volume containing Sekt is not available it is impossible to state whether or not he is a Rolf descendant.

In compiling the foregoing figures on male lines all the American champions have been included. However, since close to half of them are bitches and some sires left no sons which were either champions or sires of champions, not all of these lines are represented by studs who are producing winners today. Indeed, I know of no lines not coming from one of the Big Four which are represented at the present time with the exception of Ch. Max v. Hohenneuffen and his son Ch. V-E Admiral of Renrew. A champion son of Admiral, Oracle of Renrew, was published in the Gazette while this chapter was being written.

Alma of Skole Gate, one of the four Boxers with the U.D. in Obedience work, with a perfect score in the Utility class and 249½ in Open B, a record for all breeds in this country, is a brindle daughter of Xari of Barmere and Rexob's Brightness. Xari, by Ch. Bastel v. Elbufer, although not a champion himself is a Lustig grandson of a strain of big show winners. Rexob's Brightness is by Ch. Egon v.d. Falkenburg out of Draga of Nipantuck. Draga was bred by Mr. J. G. Jeuther, the oldest continuous breeder in the United States. Draga's parents were Alex and Daisy, the former from the first American-bred Boxer litter known to have left descendants still being bred; the latter by the earliest American champion with registered get, Blücher v. Rosengarten. Alma, along with Ch. Puckety's Vorquelle and Ch. Airminded Miss of Airealm, make a trio of descendants of Blücher and Asta v.d. Adelegg who achieved fame during 1947 and are definitely putting this old strain on the map.

The age at which Boxers have finished their championships is most commonly from a year and a half to three and a half. Only about one in five finishes earlier and only some eight percent later. Seven out of more than four hundred Boxers were past five years old when they finished their titles. The youngest seems to have been a Sigurd v. Dom daughter, Betta v. Sigurd-Nike. Early in 1939 her owner, Mr. Morgan Milner, started out to three southern shows with half a dozen puppy bitches. At that time and place six bitches made a five point show. Mr. Milner encountered no outside competition and all three judges put Betta to the top, so he returned home with a seven months old champion! A feat which is not likely to be duplicated today!

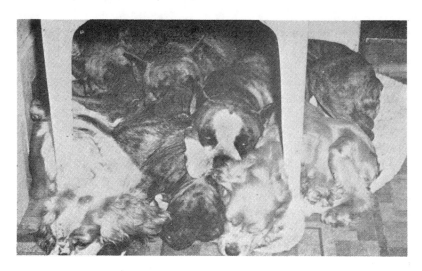

"PEACE ON EARTH"

This picture was taken on Christmas Eve by Paul Streib of Los Angeles, California

CH. FRAZER'S PARADE MEISTER
(with handler Joe Gregory)

Sire: Mazelaine's Kapellmeister
Dam: Frazer's Miss Boots

Bred and owned by Mr. and Mrs. Eugene Frazer

AIVI BOXER KENNELS IN HABANA, CUBA
Belonging to Mr. Crispulo D. Goizueta

CHAPTER VIII

The Boxer Around the World

The Boxer in Italy

ANOTHER country in which postwar conditions have not been able to stifle interest in dogs and breeding is Italy. An illustrated booklet on The Boxer, by Mario Confalonieri, was published in 1947.

Boxers were shown at Milan, Italy, under the Swiss judge, Fritz Leimgruber, in 1928, but they were of very poor quality, according to his report. After 1930, however, the situation improved and there were some notable importations. Esta v.d. Blutenau was purchased at Munich by Piero Scanziani and was a brindle bitch who placed first at the show with the qualification Excellent. The first Italian champion was Nathan v. Edelwante, back in 1925, after which there was a gap of nine years. Then came Drill v. Bauremberg and Resi v.d. Ickstatt in 1934, imported by Cav. Lucio Ausiello. Rassel v.d. Wurm followed in 1937, and the next year Raoul di Ponente, as his name suggests, the first Italian bred. The Ponente Kennels are owned by Conte E. Scotti Douglas of Savona. In 1939 there were three more champions, Vera v. Grünen Inn (probably Austrian), Bayard v.d. Wurm, and Hector v. Seeburg. Then the War intervened, but in 1946 Harry di Dargo and Coo di Virmar finished their titles. Only three out of the ten were bitches—Resi, Rassel and Vera, but they were all important.

One of the outstanding sires in Italy has been Alf v. Christofsbad, imported from Germany in 1943 with the rating "Excellent" and a son of Buten v. Elbufer out of Sonia v.

Christofsbad. Buten, a well-known winner, was a litter brother to Ch. Bastel v. Elbufer of Barmere and so was a son of Ch. Lustig v. Dom out of Siegerin Tea v. Isebeck, who was by the sire of Sigurd v. Dom. The Virmar kennel, registered in 1941, produced one of the first postwar champions in Coo di Virmar, a son of Alf. The latter also sired the outstanding bitch Ch. Crea di Virmar. In 1943 the kennel also acquired from Germany the bitch Betty v.d. Uracher Alb, by Ernstlustig v. Zollernhof (another Lustig son) out of Kletta v. Uracher Wasserfall. Betty's son Artu di Virmar has also proved a successful sire. In 1944 came Alex v. Steinweg, unfortunately killed in an automobile accident, and the bitch Assi v. Stromberg, also from Germany. Assi was by Arno v.d. Holderburg, a son of American Ch. Betti v.d. Schlusselburg of Marenore, out of Amsel v.d. Konradsburg. Assi, whelped in 1943, was the dam of Ch. Crea di Virmar, by Alf v. Chrisofsbad. The Virmar Kennels also include Cilli, a daughter of Ch. Vera v. Grünen Inn (Ch. Yuwel v. Tiroleradler out of Cylli v. Königsee). Cilli is the dam of Clo di Virmar and Ch. Coo di Virmar. During 1946 and 1947 Virmar bred a number of times to the Swiss stud Arno v. Turnellen, a son of Kobold v.d. Schlossgrotte out of Fixi v. Limattal, thereby introducing a new strain, developed in Switzerland during forty years of breeding.

It is evident that Sigurd and Lustig blood is strong in the Italian Boxers. Ch. Rassel v.d. Wurm, owned by the Ponente Kennels, is by Zimmt v. Dom out of Uni v.d. Wurm and is consequently a full sister to American Ch. Pitt v.d. Wurm of Tulgey Wood. Other kennel names in the pedigrees have a familiar ring—Blutenau, Hohenneuffen, Königsee, etc. Aldisia Kennels' Swiss bitch, Rita, for instance, is by Fels v. Blutenau (in all probability a litter brother to Am. Ch. Flott v.d. Blutenau, by Sigurd) out of Nira v. Hohenneuffen, whose sister, Nilse v. Hohonneuffen, was the dam of Am. Ch. Ferbo v. Königstor and the granddam of Ch. Max v. Hohenneuffen.

The Boxer Club of Italy was formed after the War, on November 3, 1946, by a small group including Mario Confalonieri of Virmar, Piero Scanziani of Villanova, Comm. Virgilo Favara and Signora Théa Favara of Miramare, Edoardo Barbiellini Amidei, Giulio Bettoja and Capt. Louis Cerutti of the American Army. This nucleus grew rapidly and in a few weeks the Club included more than a hundred members from all over Italy and is still growing.

The objectives of the Boxer Club of Italy are threefold. First the institution of a Libro d'Oro (roll of honor) to record the names of dogs and bitches of high quality, with pertinent information for the reference of future breeders. This is intended as a means of informing breeders of the worth of individuals whose names are found in pedigrees although they did not win the title of champion. The second object is the examination of prospective stud dogs and brood bitches by qualified judges or breed wardens. If the dogs are approved, recommedations as to the choice of bitches to be mated to them will be made, in an effort to improve the quality of the breed. The third and last objective is the promotion of training for the Boxer. The Boxer Club is anxious that some sort of training qualification be required before a dog can become a champion.

Boxer kennels are located in Rome, Milan, Padua, Mantua, Savona, Ravenna and Brescia among other cities. The Italian Kennel Club, officially the Ente Nazionale Della Cinofilia Italiana (E.N.C.I.), registers purebred dogs in its stud book, Libro Origini Italiano (L.O.I.), which is under the scrutiny of the Ministry of Agriculture. Owing to the loss of records during the War the E.N.C.I. also keeps a second book, the Libro Italiano Riconosciuti (L.I.R.), in which it records dogs of unknown breeding which appear to be purebred. After three generations the descendants of dogs entered in the L.I.R. become eligible for the L.O.I. In France there is a similar Registre Initial d'Inscription (R.I.)

The general oversight of European dog affairs is carried on by the F.C.I. with headquarters in Brussels. Germany, Switzerland, Holland, etc., follow the system of awarding annual Sieger titles which are in practice the equivalent of an ordinary championship. In Italy, France, and Belgium, however, a championship is awarded to the winner of three C.A.C. awards under three different judges. This Certificato di Attitudine al Campionato is comparable to the Challenge Certificate in

England. A dog must be qualified "Excellent" to receive a C.A.C. and six months must elapse from the date of the first win. In Italy a dog with three C.A.C.'s is then examined by a special commission of three judges who award the final P.D.C. (Preposta definitiva di Campionato). To win an International Championship a dog must obtain three C.A.C.I.B.'s (Certificato di Attitudine al Campionato Internazoinale di Bellezza) under three different judges in three different countries. In 1935 and 1937 World Champion titles were also awarded. Separate Field championships and international championship are also awarded for the working breeds.

FIETJE V. KLABAUTERMANN, 52150
Won many first prizes at German Shows

"He too wants to become a Boxer Champion. . . ."
MAKRO V. KLABAUTERMANN, 38245
Germany

FIETJE V. KLABAUTERMANN, 52150
Head study, at the age of six months
Germany

GERMAN CHAMPION WISCHEL V. KLABAUTERMANN, 43467
German Champion, 1947

FRANZE V. KLABAUTERMANN, 35780
Boxer female
First class German type

The Boxer and the Boxer Club in Germany Since 1945

By Gerda Umlauff

RIENDS of the German Boxer may have been wondering what has happened to the Boxer fancy and to the Boxer Club in the native country of the breed after the dreadful war with its bombs, fires, death, flight, hunger, cold, and deprivation of every kind, and whether there were any good Boxers left in Germany after that country's defeat and capitulation in 1945. The German Boxer breeders and fanciers were forced to supply a large number of dogs to the German army during the war, and other valuable Boxers were killed and lost in the air raids. Nevertheless, the love of the breed persisted in the hearts of those persons familiar with its charm and virtues, and interest in the breeding and training of dogs was resumed immediately after the end of the war.

After the Nazi regime was overthrown, it was possible to restore the old name of the club—the "Boxer Klub e. V. Sitz München"—with a remaining membership of two thousand fanciers. At the beginning of this period, the activities of the club were thwarted in many ways. The use of the postwar mails was forbidden to Germans, and permission for meetings of the club was unobtainable.

After a short while, however, restrictions were somewhat relaxed, and the Boxer fanciers, particularly those enthusiasts in Hamburg, put forth their greatest efforts to build up the club and to restore to it its former prewar state and functions. As soon as it was possible to hold them, meetings

151

of the club were arranged for at Hamburg, Cologne, Munich, Berlin, and Schwetzingen. Mr. Wilhelm Niemann of Hamburg, who is now President of the Boxer Club, has kindly given us some details about Boxer happenings since the ending of the war.

The Military Government since 1945 has not requisitioned valuable breeding stocks of Boxers, but because of events that took place during 1945, famous aggregations of Boxers were lost to the fancy; these included the well-known Marienhof Kennels and the Drosedow Kennels, which before the war had included many of the greatest Boxers in the world. In spite of the many losses of fine breeding stock, however, it has not been found necessary to register Boxers without pedigrees in the stud book of the club, as had been feared. A large number of breeders established or re-established their kennels in the first three years after the termination of the war; but, particularly because of the introduction of a new currency in Germany in June of 1948, many of those persons whose interest in the breed is not profound are being forced to lessen or abandon their Boxer operations.

Shows have been held since the autumn of 1945, with larger and yet larger entries of Boxers. In May of 1946, we saw 67 Boxers at Hamburg; in September of the same year there were 76 Boxers; and at Munich in the autumn of 1948, there were 186 Boxers. Several Boxer trials have been held; for instance, at Leipzig, Hamburg, and Munich, at all of which the large number of entries was most encouraging.

The Boxer Club of Germany currently has 84 branches with a total enrollment of 3,500 members, with three full-time officials employed in the office of the club in Munich. Since October of 1948, the club has published monthly a little magazine devoted to the Boxer and its interests. Among the afore-mentioned 3,500 members of the Boxer clubs, there are no fewer than 700 breeders, and 4,000 Boxers are registered each year in the stud book of the club. The last stud book published appeared in the year 1942, and it is proposed to publish the next one in the spring of 1950.

The Boxers of the Russian Zone of Germany are recorded in the stud book of Munich. Registrations have grown more numerous because there are three times as many breeders

152

of Boxers as before the war. The chief centers of Boxer breeding in Germany at the present time are: in the North, Hamburg; in the West, Cologne; and in the South, Munich.

The Boxer club recommends Boxers as a breed for guide dogs for blind persons. Exceptionally good results have been attained for this purpose by experimentation with some two dozen Boxers, especially because Boxers are of quiet temperament and do not seek fights with other dogs.

, The new pedigree published by the club not only sets forth the names and stud book numbers of the dog's ancestors, but also states the colors of their coats and of their eyes. Beginning soon, it is proposed to tattoo Boxers on the inside of their thighs with their stud book numbers for purposes of identification.

At this time, defects of Boxer type are in some measure overlooked in dogs employed for breeding, but breeders are careful to avoid matings likely to produce light-eyed progeny or those with light and fading colors. There are in Germany many more yellow Boxers than brindles. In this breed, missing teeth are not a problem, as in some of the other breeds, but, on the contrary, Boxers very often possess more than their full compliment of forty-two teeth.

Only those dogs are acceptable for registry in the Boxer club stud book which are bred under certain rules laid down by the club. These rules include that either the sire or the dam of the dog for which registration is sought shall have qualified at a trial for guard dogs. For breeding, the male must be at least eighteen months of age, and the female not less than fourteen months. Before breeding is permitted under the club rules, the dogs to be mated must have competed at a so-called breeding show where they are examined by judges for their conformation and their qualities of character. In no cases are nervous dogs sanctioned for breeding. The judges rate the dogs sanctioned as "excellent," "very good," "good," or "deficient." The male dog with which the breeder chooses to mate his bitch must achieve at least the rating of "good" at such a show; otherwise the club will not authorize his use for breeding.

At another special inspection for suitability for breeding it is required that both proposed parents shall have passed

153

GERMAN CHAMPION HARRY V.D. STORCHENBURG, 44100
German Boxer, yellow male

the guard dog trials; and for the so-called field training breeds it is necessary that three generations of ancestors, without any exceptions, must have passed the guard dog trials. The breeder is not permitted to raise more than six young Boxers from any litter, and the use of another bitch as wet nurse or foster mother is forbidden.

There is now but one championship title per year for each color for all the three western zones of Germany. In the Russian zone, there is also a title called "Zonen-Champion."

The best dogs receive from the Club gold, silver, or bronze medals at the shows. In addition to these, exhibitors may compete for other major awards, such as:

The Philipp Stockmann Challenge Trophy, which must be won under three different judges during two years;

The Club Champion Title, which the dog must win under three different judges; and

The Annual Specialty Championship, the dog winning it becoming the champion for the year. This title is awarded only to a dog that has previously qualified in the trial for protection dogs.

Some of the champions for the last two years have been:

1948, Arno v. Isebeck, Hany v.d. Starkenburg (yellow), and Fera v.d. Starkenburg (yellow). United States zone of Germany, Yvonne v. Biederstein (brindle).

1949, Harry v.d. Storchenburg, 44100 (yellow), Calo v.d. Wupperstadt, 44973 (brindle). Bitches, Hoheit v. Dom, 43634 (yellow), and Monika v.d. Reiterstadt, 48555 (brindle), for the British and American zones. For the Russian zone, male, Droll v. Loberstrand.

The best Boxers in Germany today are perhaps the following: Champions Alex v. Grunwaldpark, Carlo v. Rasmus, Erlo v.d. Mumsel, and Arno v. Isebeck. The last named of these won the championship title for three consecutive years.

Among the top bitches may be mentioned: Burgel v. Grunwaldpark, Assi v. Niemannseck, and Zissy v.d. Lindenburg.

The high quality of present-day German Boxers has created interest and brought inquiries from Switzerland, Great Britain, Austria, the Netherlands, Belgium, the United States of America, and various parts of Africa, Italy, and Canada.

BOY von TRUNELLEN 12832/46, e. Billo v d Brunegg SHSB 80442 u Anita v Turnellen SHSB 93308, 1:a pris skl, certifikat, HP, CACIB SKK Göteborg 1948, 1:a pris skl, certifikat, HP SBK Linköping 1948, 1:a pris skl, certifikat, HP SBK Stockholm 1949, äg. fru Inez Engström, Herrekiperingen, Folkungagatan 110, Stockholm, tel. 47 71 91. (Foto: B. Rosengren)

The Boxer in Sweden

By C. Andreason

Stockholm, Sweden

WEDEN has, through its geographical position, always kept up very close relations with Germany regarding canine matters and it is not surprising that the first Boxers came to Sweden as early as 1909. This year three Boxers, two males and one female, were shown at the Swedish Kennel Club Show in Stockholm. The males both won a first prize and the female a second prize in the open class. The following data about these dogs are available in the Swedish Kennel Club Stud Book, SKK, for the year 1910: Males: **1) King (Pascha) DBSB** vol. 2, fawn, whelped in 1905 by Lord DBSB 177 ex Mayers Flora, breeder Herr Lorenz Mayer, Muenchen. **2) Lord v. Angerthor,** fawn with white markings, whelped in 1906, by Ch Rigo v. Angerthor DBSB 299 ex Mirzl v. Angerthor DBSB 498. Bitches: Alla v. Angerthor, fawn with black markings (brindle) whelped in 1907. Breeder of Lord and Alla was Herr Jacob Dauer, Muenchen.

The above dogs started the Boxer activities in Sweden and during the following years many good dogs were imported. In 1914 **Dora Walhall,** a red bitch with a black mask, came to Sweden. She was whelped in 1911, sired by Ch Remus v. Pfalzgau DBSB 719 ex Dora v. Vogelsberg DBSB 939.

Here for the first time we encounter the kennel-suffix von Vogelsberg, which later was destined to go down in Boxer history through the great Ch Rolf v. Vogelsberg.

Another bitch importation followed in 1915, namely, **Isolde v Stolzenfels DBSB 2821,** whelped in 1913. She was by Ch.

157

Maiers Blitz DBSB 1285 ex Siegerin Graefin Rita v Stolzenfels. In the Swedish Stud Book for the year 1915 are registered nine dogs and five bitches. The year of 1916 was a very active one regarding Boxer importations. First came **Milo v Blankenburg,** whelped in 1914 by Rex v d. Kynast-Burg Blankenburg ex Ella Freigericht v Blankenburg, then the bitch **Austrian Ch. Frohgunde v Marienhof,** she by Ch. Maiers Blitz DBSB 1285 ex Helianthe v Marienhof DBSB 1289. The event of the year, however, was the arrival of two males from Germany's most outstanding kennels, known the world over as "von Dom." The dogs were Wotan v Dom DBSB 2176, a grey and brown brindle by Ch. Rolf v Vogelsberg ex Trudel v Sternhausen, and **Othello v Dom DBSB 3967,** a red fawn with white markings whelped in 1915 by Flott v Dom DBSB 3201, a grandson of Ch. Rolf v Vogelsberg, ex Derby v Dom DBSB 2473, a daughter of Ch. Rolf. In the fourth generation of Othello's pedigree, Ch Rigo v Angerthor appears three times.

In 1917 followed two new importations, the male **Harro v Marienhof,** a red fawn with white markings by Edel v Marienhof DBSB 2140 ex Hortense v Marienhof DBSB 1290, and the brindle bitch **Eris v Dom DBSB 2734,** whelped in 1912 by Ch. Rolf v Vogelsberg ex Reichles Julchen DBSB 2255. This year Isolde v Stolzenfels became the first Swedish boxer champion of record, closely followed by Ch Othello v Dom and the other male, Ch. Wotan v Dom.

The following year nothing of importance happened, but in 1919 a German Sieger, **Rino II v d Elbe,** began his Swedish career. He was a red fawn whelped in 1911 by Ch. Rigo Angerthor DBSB 299 ex Ella v Osterland DBSB 1899. He completed his Swedish title the following year.

For quite a long period of years no more dogs were imported from Germany, but the Swedish breeders got along quite well with their stock and the Boxer became more and more popular. The sire that influenced the breed most was, without any doubt, Ch. Othello v Dom, and his most famous son, **Holmgards Box II SKK 7 U.** Box II in his turn became the sire of Ch. Sir Bull av Lillbo SKK 429 DD, which was bred by Herr Carl Borg, one of the pioneers for the breed in Sweden, and owned by Herr A. Fogelberg, Kennel Rolands, who later came to

CHAMPION NICOTIN SKK 5049/47
Nicotin is a son of Ch. Axons Fock SKK 730TT
and a Swedish top winner in 1949.

dominate the Swedish breeding program up to the present period.

In 1930 another German-bred dog appeared at the shows. His name was **Rietz-Fritz v Gerhardsbrunnen SKK 189 EE, a** brindle whelped in 1929 by Flock v Zenith BZB 19730 ex Asta v Gerhardsbrunnen BZB 16985. He became quite popular as a stud, but did not influence the breed to any great extent.

In The Stud Book for 1931 we find a Danish-owned male, **Ch. Schach v Dom SKK 1290 FF** which was shown once in Sweden and topped the winners class. Schach was a full brother of the great Sigurd, whose descendants were destined to great wins in every country where the boxer is known.

The Sigurd blood became a fashion, and many of his descendants found their way to Sweden. However, before the Sigurd strain began to overshadow other lines in the breeding program, there were some other dogs imported from Germany. All had their share in the creating of the modern Swedish Boxer. The males, the brindle **Ch. Max v Isebeck SKK 868 JJ** and the fawn **Ch. Fels v d Teck SKK 1124 HH,** both won their titles in Sweden. Max was sired by Alex v Alsterblick BZB and Fels by Illo v Hohenneuffen BZB 22480, a son of Sieger Alex v d Magdalenenquelle. Fels and Max were both used much at stud and left many good dogs. Neither Fels nor Max have left behind any tail male line of note.

A brindle imported from Denmark also deserves to be mentioned. She was **Marmons Glori SKK 911 KK,** sired by Ch. Ajax v d Gralsburg BZB 19232 ex Edel v Schölerberg, she by Ch. Aspirin v Neu-Drosedow. Glori was destined to become the dam of **Danish Champion Rolands Kadett,** which became the best and most dominating stud Sweden has ever seen to the present time, comparable to what Sigurd meant to the breed in Germany.

The sire of Rolands Kadett SKK 743 MM was Bastel v. Elbufer SKK 823 LL, a son of the immortal Lustig v Dom BZB 28518 ex Weltsiegerin Tea v Isebeck BZB 27560, she a daughter of Iwein v Dom, the sire of Sigurd. Bastel was shown once in Sweden and topped the winners class, winning his first championship certificate. Quite soon after this event Bastel was sold to America.

160

Silwos Buster II.
A Swedish-bred, Silwos Buster II SKKS 36FX, whelped
in 1922, a current winner in 1924 and 1925.
A good type only two decades ago.

161

Two males of great importance to the breed in Sweden were **Wotan v. Isebeck SKK 793 LL,** a brindle sired by Athos v. Dom BZB 26668 PH ex Amer. Ch. Venus v Isebeck BZB 29666, both of them sired by Sigurd, and another brindle imported from Denmark, **Marmons Harro SKK 656 PP,** sired by Zorn v Dom BZB 26394 ex Andl v Dom BZB 26669, both Zorn and Andl also by Sigurd. Andl was a litter sister of Athos, the sire of Ch. Wotan v Isebeck.

It is rather amazing how the breed pattern is congruent in Germany, U.S.A. and Sweden. Here we have the intensified Sigurd breeding, and to the Swedish breeding program, Marmons Harro and Ch Wotan v Isebeck seem to play the same part as Lustig and Utz have done in America. Lustig is also strongly represented in Sweden and his line has come to dominate the breed here through his grandson, Ch. Rolands Kadett. Kadett's success as a sire must depend on the lucky combination of Bastel v Elbufer and the Ch. Ajax v d Gralsburg daughter, Marmons Glori, because Bastel, in spite of his excellent background, has not sired any dogs of great importance since his arrival in America, as far as can be ascertained by studying the records.

Kadett's litter brother, **Ch. Rolands Kyras SKK 47 NN,** has also contributed a great deal to strengthen the Lustig strain. However, he met an untimely death at only seven years of age and consequently did not have the same chance to stamp the breed as Kadett.

Probably Kadett's most promising son is the brindle Ch. Axons Fock SKK 730 TT, whose dam is a daughter of Marmons Harro.

Fock's best son seems to be Ch. Nicotin SKK 5049/47, whose dam is by Ch. Rolands Symftig, a Harro-son.

The latest Boxer import came to Sweden in 1946 from Switzerland. He is a brindle dog, and has won at our shows every time shown. His name is **Boy v Turnellen SKK 12832/46,** sired by Billo v d Brunegg SHSB 80442 ex Anita v Turnellen SHSB 93308. The future will show his worth as a stud dog.

What the Swedish Boxer fancy badly needs, in the opinion of the author of this article, is a good stud dog carrying an

Dansk Champion Rolands Kadett 743 MM

	⌈Amerikansk Ch	⌈Zorn v. Dom
Amerikansk Ch.	⎪Lustig v. Dom	⎬Esta v. d. Würm
Baste v. Elbufer	⎬Weltsiegerin	⌈Iwein v. Dom
	⌊Tea v. Isebeck	⎬Peppi v. Isebeck
	⌈Ch Ajax v. d.	⌈Sgr. Hansel v. Stolzenfels
Marmons Glori	⎪Gralsburg	⎬Anni v. d. Capadocia
	⎬Edel v. Schölerberg	⌈Ch Aspirin v. Neu-Drosedow
		⎬Adda v. Maschsee

A great show dog and the dominating stud dog in the breed in
Sweden, bred and owned by A. Fogelberg, Malmoe, Sweden.

163

intensified Dorian-strain. Dorian is not yet represented here, but we hope that a dog with that blood could do the same good to the Swedish Boxer as has been experienced in America.

The Boxer is very popular in Sweden because of his many good traits and the following table shows his popularity as compared to other breeds for the last five-year period (1944-1949).

	Number of Dogs registered in SKK	Utility (working) dogs registered	Boxers	Collies	Dobermann Pinschers	Rottweilers	Giant Schnauzers	German Shepherds
1944	5727	1267	200	145	30	110	105	677
1945	9842	2380	280	331	91	126	174	1378
1946	12925	3404	451	799	86	190	214	1664
1947	11060	3126	263	1016	100	118	142	1487
1948	12907	3738	346	1288	90	139	94	1781

Here in this country the Boxer is mainly used as a companion, though the breed is listed among the "brukshundar," which is best translated as "utility dogs," including the following breeds used for police and army work: Boxer, Dobermann Pinscher, Collie, German Shepherd, Giant Schnauzer and Rottweiler. A dog of any of these breeds must pass an obedience test comparable to your C.D.X. before he can obtain the champion title. The necessary show wins for the title are: three champion certificates, won under at least two different judges.

Because of his thin coat, the Boxer (and also the Dobermann) cannot stand the rough Swedish winter climate as well as the other breeds, and this is probably the reason why, with a few exceptions, he is not used in police and army work. During the second world war, however, the Boxer made himself very useful as a guard and sentry dog and proved himself a sturdy, hardy and fearless co-operator. The Boxer has not been used in Sweden as a Seeing-Eye dog. The one and only breed used for this purpose here seems to be the German Shepherd.

The breed is at present suffering under the ban of a prohibition against ear cropping, authorized by the Swedish Government on April 1st in 1947, and inspired by the Swedish Association for Prevention of Cruelty to Animals. This prohibition has proved to be a very unfortunate one, because it is isolating Sweden from the other Scandinavian countries and puts an end to Swedish dogs showing in inter-Scandinavian competition.

The hope of all sincere Swedish breeders is that the ear cropping prohibition shall not last for long, and that we shall soon be able to see the Boxer again in a shape that is congruent with the international standard.

Much could be said about the most important Swedish Boxer kennels. Those who are interested are advised to study the Swedish Kennel Club Stud Book for thorough information. One kennel, however, may, without unfairness to other breeders be mentioned, and that is Herr A. Fogelberg's "Rolands" Kennels.

The Rolands prefix has for a long period of years been the Milky Way on the Swedish Boxer sky.

The Boxer's future in Sweden is an interesting question. The fact is that we badly need new blood that can be successfully blended with the old strains. We hope that new and potent imports will come to our country and that the development of the breed will proceed in the right direction. The Boxer is a splendid breed, a utility dog, and the desire and goal for the Swedish breeders is to create still better Boxers.

Ch Fels v. d. Teck 1124 HH (t. h.) är inavlad pa Ch Rolf v. Vogelsberg (t. v.) och sonsonssonsonsso till denne, Fels kan tjäna som exempel pa hur en typ kan nedärvas sa gott som exakt i manga generationer.

Ch. Fels v.d. Teck S.K.K. 1124HH is inbred to Ch. Rolf v. Vogelsberg and a great-great-great-grandson to Rolf, shows a striking example of heredity true to type through many generations.

166

THE IRISH KENNEL CLUB

23 Eden Quay
Dublin, C.8

Milo G. Denlinger, Esq.,
Denlinger's,
117 Hamilton Avenue
Silver Spring, Maryland,
U. S. A.

Dear Sir:

The Boxer has never been a popular breed in Ireland but has been gaining steadily in recent years.

In 1946 the registrations in the breed were 33
In 1947 "   "   " "   "   " 67

The principal exhibitors of Boxers in Ireland are: Mrs. J. C. Sugars, Miss Patricia Victory, Mr. Alfred Davis, Jun., Major J. H. Craig-Wilson, Robert McCartney and Mrs. Knox Ingram.

We will be glad to correspond with any American breeders who care to write us.

Yours very truly,

(Signed)   Richard G. Quirk,
                    Secretary.

167

A "Federation Cynologique Internationale" (FCI) Altal Magyarorszag
Vezeto Szervezetenek Elismert

MAGYAR EBTENYESZTOK ORSZAGOS EGYESULETE

Membre de la "Federation Cynologique Internationale" a' Bruxelles

KENNEL CLUB	HUNGARIAN	UNGARISCHER
HONTROIS	KENNEL CLUB	KYNOLOGEN VEREIN

BUDAPEST
VIII. Rakoczi-Ut 29. SZ.

DENLINGER'S
Mr. Milo G. Denlinger
117 Hamilton Avenue
Silver Spring, Maryland, U.S.A.

Dear Sir:

We beg to inform you that since 1945, there have been
no registrations of Boxers. They, and their breeders, mostly officers,
never turned up since the war.

There are a few old specimens, mostly males, that may
still be seen on the streets but breeding is at a standstill. The Boxer
never has been a very popular dog in our country and was seldom used
as a working dog. He was chiefly used for guard work.

There has never been a book published in Hungary dealing exclusively with the Boxer.

Our Club is a member of the "Federation Cynologique
Internationale" but has lost many of its members and breeders from the
war. We are trying to build up our club again but have to cope with
many difficulties.

Very truly yours,

(Signed)   Lewis ILOSVAI-HOLLOSSY
Managing Director
Hungarian Kennel Club

SUOMEN BOKSERIYDISTYS - FINLANDS
BOXERFORENING r. y.

Helsingfors,
Doebelngatan 2 E 28

MR. MILO G. DENLINGER,
Silver Spring, Maryland

Dear Sir:

As far as we know, the first Boxer was imported to our country from Germany in 1920. His name was Asgard von Kellerhof. The next to come was Harno von Tetterode in 1922. Later on some bitches were imported but we do not know if they were used for breeding purposes.

Our Boxer breeding really begins with Wotan von Georgsheim which was registered with our Club in 1935 FKK 12288/XXI and Jutta von der Danziger Hansa FKK 13075/XXII, both imported from Germany. From those we got the dog Negus av Hansastam FKK 14719/XXIV who appears very often in the certificates of later Boxers.

The bitch, Cassandra av Hansastam FKK 14719/XXIV was sent in 1939 to the Swedish stud Ch. Katias Tobo SKKS 1026 JJ, and thus we obtained some new blood. Since 1944 we have sent some bitches to Sweden to be covered by Ch. Rolands Ukas SKKS 2943 PP and Ch. Rönnvikens Sintram SKKS 1250 PP. In the last few years we have imported some dogs from Holland and Denmark, among which the bitch, Bellahjs Senta Dsk.HSB 119405 seems to develop favorably.

It is difficult to tell exactly how many Boxers there were in this country in the beginning, perhaps only about ten or so. From 1939 on and especially after 1944, the number has increased and now there should be over 300 of them. Our records do not show so many of them because some owners have not registered their dogs. We can well say that the Boxer dog is gaining in popularity every day.

169

NAOKI AV NIGGERSTAM
SKL 15F91/XI
Whelped February, 1946
Owner: Mr. Kaarlo Helenius
Finland

CH. PONTUS NEGUSSON   CH. PEPITA PONTUSCLOTTER
SKL 5F1F/VII   VON DER AUE
Whelped June 30, 1942   SKL 10162/X
Whelped August 3, 1945
Owner: Miss H. G. Westerlund, Helsingfors, Finland

170

The most popular working dog in our country for years has been the German sheep-dog, the "Schäfer," because this dog is best fitted for our climate and is a bigger and stronger dog. The Boxer is second in order. Our association however, is working hard to make the Boxer the most popular one in the future. We got our first working champion this year, Ch. Topi av Gronskog FKK 21211/XXX, and three other Boxers will become working champions in a short time. Our Boxers have taken part in many working tests with very good results. In October, 1948, our team won a competition with our biggest "Rottweiler" club.

Our most noted Boxer breeders are:

Earlier breeders:
Mr. B. Schwindt (Kennel von der Aue)
Mrs. A. Vilonen (Aidan Kennel)
Mrs. X. Ekman (Prickens Kennel)
Mrs. E. Löyskä (Kennel av Hummeli)
Mrs. S. Ericsson (Kennel av Barberina)
Mrs. M. Nystedt (Kennel av Niggerstam)

New breeders:
Mrs. A Rinne (Kennel Borealii)
Mr. B-E. Ericsson (Kennel de Babette)
Miss H-G. Westerlund (Kennel Boxergarden)

You can get in touch with them through our association.

Finally we wish to tell you a little about our association. We started in 1944 and determined to give good advice to the owners of Boxers, arrange training courses for working dogs and make the Boxer breed known. We have in all about 170 members all over the country. We are working hard and we are glad to say that some results can be seen. Now we have nearly twice as many Boxers as in 1943 and have attained good results in competitions and exhibitions. We are trying to get in touch with as many foreign Boxer associations and Boxer breeders as possible and we have already many good connections abroad.

We arrange courses regularly and enclose a picture taken when 17 young Boxers joined a two-weeks working dog course. In the winter time we arrange occasions when our dogs pull children in small sledges, earning money for our expenses.

171

We enclose some pictures of our Boxers. We have selected good looking dogs which are good working dogs also, because we pay so much attention to that point.

We would be more than happy if you would mention our association as the contributor of this information and would be very glad to have a copy of your book. We are sorry to tell you that there has been no book published about Boxers in our country but our association intends to publish one as soon as funds are available.

With our best kennel-regards,

Yours very truly,

SUOMEN BOKSERIYHDISTYS-
FINLANDS BOXERFORENING r.y.

(Signed) G. EKMAN   K. EKELUND

Chairman   *Secretary*

BARRY AV BARBERINA
SKL 9F63/X
Whelped April 4, 1945
Helsingfors, Finland

172

NORSK KENNEL CLUB
Stiftet 24, Januar 1898

Oslo, Norway

MESSRS. DENLINGER,
Silver Spring, Maryland, U.S.A.

Gentlemen:

It is more than forty years ago that the first Boxers came to Norway from Germany. The Norwegian breed is grounded upon these German dogs and those that, in the following years, were sent to Norway chiefly from the famous German kennel, von Dom, but there were also important specimens from the kennels of von Marienhof, von Pfankirchen and others.

The first von Dom Boxer to come to Norway was Champion WOTAN. In Mr. J. P. Wagner's book on the Boxer, it is incorrectly stated that this famous dog was exported from Germany to Sweden.

During the late World War, 1940-1945, when Norway was occupied by the German forces, they requisitioned all the Boxers they could get hold of here in Norway. Many owners, however, preferred to destroy their dogs rather than to let them be of use to the enemy, consequently much damage was done to the stock of Boxers in Norway during these years.

The number of Boxers registered by the Norwegian Kennel Club was in 1946, 228; and in 1947, 121.

The Boxer is very popular in Norway and this popularity has continually increased. Barring the Alsatians (German Shepherd Dogs), the Boxer can show the largest number exhibited at Norwegian shows among the working dogs.

In later years some of the most successful breeders are:

Mr. Eyv. L. Dahl, Hafrsfjordgt. 39, Oslo,
Mr. Björn Stenström, Torggt. 8, Oslo,
Mr. Rolf Ostdahl, Nordbergvn. 14, V. Aker,
Mr. and Mrs. Vesla and Ole Skjeslien, Dunkersgt. 3, Oslo.

There is no book about the Boxer published in the Norwegian language. A number of special articles on the breed have, however, been published in the Norwegian Kennel Club Gazette.

Yours very truly,
NORSK KENNEL KLUB
(Signed)   RAGNAR HALLE   C. T. GJERSOE, JR.
Chairman   *Secretary*

173

RAAD VAN BEHEER OP KYNOLOGISCH GEBIED
IN NEDERLAND

Goedgeķeurd bij Koninklijk Besluit van 16 April 1925, No. 33
Gewijzigd bij Koninklijk Besluit van 5 Huni 1929, No. 20

Amsterdam Z.,
Emmalaan 16.

Mr. M. G. Denlinger,
117 Hamilton Avenue,
Silver Spring, Maryland (U.S.A.)

Dear Sir:

The Raad van Beheer op Kynologisch Gebied in Nederland wishes to inform you that in 1946 and 1947, 1010 Boxers were registered into the Nederlands Hondenstamboek (N.J.S.B.).

The Boxer is a popular dog in Holland but is not used as a working dog.

The address of the Nederlandse Boxer Vereniging is: Mr. L. P. Knapen, Vosmaerstraat 49 at Haarlem.

We are sorry to tell you that no book that deals exclusively with the Boxer has ever been published in our country.

Yours faithfully,

(Signed)   W. Thijsse
Manager

174

The Boxer in Spain

By Rosemary Douglas

Barcelona, Spain

T THE request of the Count of Zenete, President, Real Sociedad Central de Fomento de las Tazas Caninas en Espana, I am writing you regarding Boxers in Spain. Until a year or two ago, I bred pedigreed Boxers for sale and show purposes and have always been sincerely interested in the breed.

The development of the present day Boxer in Spain can be said to date from 1939, as during the Spanish Civil War very many dogs were destroyed or lost trace of, and the records of the Real Sociedad de Fomento de las Razas Caninas en España (Royal Society for the Development of the Breeds of Dogs in Spain) were not able to be kept up to date.

Prior to 1936, the only Boxers bred in Spain and registered in the Society's Stud Book (L.O.E.) were D. Pedro Bustingorri's Jai-Alai strain. His bitch, Frau Berta, was sired by D. Gonzalo Figueroa O'Neill's Ferrum v. Neu Drosedow, a son of Sigur v. Dom and grandson of Iwein v. Dom and Belinda Hassia. This dog also had Iwein v. Dom blood through his dam, a daughter of Ch. Aspirin v. Neu Drosedow. Ferrum won a 1st class medal and Premio Extraordinario (Special Prize) in Madrid in 1935. Frau Berta's dam was the Duque de las Torres' bitch Elida v. Neu Drosedow. Sr. Bustingorri crossed Frau Berta with Arras v. Bamberg, an imported dog belonging to D. Jose Antonio Olano, and produced some good puppies which were registered in the L.O.E. just prior to the outbreak of the Spanish War.

175

By the end of the war in 1939, there were very few Boxers in Spain, and no registered bitches. At the same time the popularity of the breed increased greatly, and this was unfortunately exploited commercially by some breeders who had no interest in showing or improving the breed and who kept no records of pedigrees, but produced a large number of puppies of unknown origin in order to take advantage of the high prices paid for Boxers at that time. Some of these dogs, however, were of good type, and the result is that there are now quite a number of good-looking Boxers in Spain of unknown origin and not registered in the L.O.E.

In 1939, Bynie Bella of Luckings, a bitch bred in England by Mr. F. W. Burman, was brought to Spain by the writer. Bynie, although not of perfect conformation herself, having rather too much of the bulldog type jaw (in common with many of the English Boxers), had good blood and proved an excellent brood bitch. Her sire was Fritz of Leith Hill, a dog imported by Mr. Burman from France, by Armin v.d. Haake and Philippa; her dam was Birka v. Emilienhorst by Tasso v. Isebeck out of Weltsiegerin 1935 Alice v. Emilienhorst. Tasso was a son of Iwein v. Dom out of Peppi v. Isebeck.

Bynie Bella of Luckings was first mated to Moucky, a dog belonging to D. Jose Antonio Olano. Moucky's sire was Herisson, a son of Flex of Sun Brand and Mirka. His dam was Addi v. Haus Germania, a daughter of Dingo v. Valtenberg and Armin Krekeltje. Both Bynie and Moucky's forebears had been registered in foreign Kennel Clubs, and they were registered in the L.O.E. in 1940 and the kennel name Bira was authorized by the Society.

This cross proved very successful and some good puppies were produced, but then there arose the difficulty of finding suitable dogs for crossing purposes and, as these were not available, and the importation of dogs was impossible owing to the European war situation, it was decided to resort to consanguineous crossing. D. Jose Antonio Olano kept a bitch from the first litter, Bira Miss Addi, and bred her to her sire, Moucky. Bira Kennels kept the best dog of the first litter, Bira Beowulph, and bred him to his dam, Bynie, and also to a sister, Bira Mitzi, both of which crosses produced some good puppies. As a result of this breeding policy, by the end of 1946, nineteen out of the twenty-two Boxers registered in the L.O.E. since 1939 were direct descendants of this Bynie-Moucky cross with no other admixture of blood. Though few outstanding dogs were bred, owing to the difficulty

176

BYNIE BELLA OF LUCKINGS
and a litter of pups
(Uncut ears owing to English law)
Sire: Fritz of Leith Hill
Dam: Birka von Emilienhorts
Breeder: Mr. F. W. Burman, England
Owner: Mrs. Rosemary Douglas, Barcelona, Spain

BIRA MAXIMILIAN
Sire: Bira Beowulph   Dam: Bira Mitzi
with Maria Paz, two-year-old daughter of
Mrs. Rosemary Douglas, Barcelona, Spain

177

of correcting defects with consanguineous crosses, the general standard was fairly good, and Bira Kennels took a Cup at the 1943 and 1946 Barcelona official Dog Shows for the best group of Boxers presented, as well as silver and bronze medals. In 1947 in Madrid, Bira Moritz took a First class medal and Premio Extraordinario. Various people who have bought Bira dogs and bitches and bred from them have decided to continue the consanguineous policy, owing to the difficulty of finding suitable fresh blood.

In 1947 the Bira kennels closed down owing to the number of dogs (which had hitherto been exceptionally healthy in spite of inbreeding) lost owing to infection with leishmaniasis or kala-azar which is very prevalent along the Mediterranean coast in Spain, and to which Boxers seem to be particularly prone as a breed. This disease, which is transmitted mainly by ticks, many of which are brought over from Africa by swallows after having been parasites on infected cattle, is caused by a spirochete which invades the whole organism and particularly the spleen, causing a great variety of symptoms and ultimately death. Until recently the only treatment available was an antimony product, Neostibiosan, which however failed to effect a permanent cure in a large percentage of cases. Lately better results have been obtained by using a French product, Lomidine, and the veterinary surgeons in Barcelona have hopes of checking the spread of this disease which has caused a high mortality among dogs.

Other breeders of Boxers whose dogs are registered in the L.O.E. are D. Federico Duran Falp of Barcelona, and Srta. Maria Fernandez de la Gomera, both of whom have used exclusively Bira blood. A recent enthusiastic addition to the Boxer world in Spain is Captain Allen, head of the Trans-world Airlines in Barcelona, with his American-bred Igor, for which dog he is hoping to import a Swiss-bred bitch shortly, and which should introduce some very badly needed new blood into Spanish Boxers.

From the above, some idea may be had of the difficulties facing breeders of Boxers in Spain. The Real Sociedad de Fomento de las Razas Caninas en España is of course faced with the same problem. After the Spanish War it was decided that any dog or bitch of unknown origin winning a First Prize in one of the official Dog Shows organized by this Society, should be admitted to the L.O.E. In other cases dogs and bitches of unknown origin can also be registered in the

L.O.E. after they have been examined by a committee of the Society and a representative of the Ministry of Agriculture. If this committee is satisfied by the dogs' appearance and conformation that they are pure-bred, they can be registered in the L.O.E. In spite of these facilities many breeders still do not care to register their dogs, and the dog-loving public rarely asks for a pedigree when buying a puppy.

In the Exhibitions or Dog Shows organized by the Society a First, Second and Third class medal are awarded in each class as an Ordinary Prize, and four Mentions: Special Reserved Honorary Mention (M.H.E.R.), Special Honorary Mention (M.H.E.), Honorary Mention (M.H.), and Mention (M.). There are also Premios de Honor (Prizes of Honour) presented by the authorities and which are given only to dogs or bitches winning a First Prize. These often correspond to a Best of Show award, being a single prize open to all breeds. The Premios Extraordinarios are given by other Societies or groups and are generally awarded in each breed, and are limited to dogs or bitches with a First, Second or Third class medal. There are also Premios Especiales given by private individuals for various things . . . sometimes the best pair or best group, or best Spanish-bred dog or bitch, etc., etc. No Championship certificates or titles have been given since 1936 owing to the small number of dogs shown, but in the 1949 exhibitions the Society is starting to award Championship certificates (C.A.C.) again. Three of these Certificates of Aptitude for Championship must be won, and at least one in Madrid, for the dog to become eligible for the title of Champion, and at least a year must have elapsed between the winning of the first and third of these.

Yours faithfully,

(Signed)   Rosemary M. Douglas

Tuvo lugar recientemente en el local de
la Sociedad Rural Argentina la 41ª ex-
posición internacional organizada por el
Kennel Club Argentino. En la foto-
grafía aparece Oberon of Berolma, de
la raza Boxer Alemán, campeón brasi-
leño, que fué expuesto por la señorita
Alzira B. Cabaleiro, delegada del Brasil
Kennel Club.

180

KENNEL CLUB de CHILE

El Registro Genealogico del Kennel Club de Chile es reconocido por la Sociedad Nacional de Agricultura como organo oficial para inscripcion de perros de pura raza dentro de la Republica de Chile

Vina del Mar

DENLINGER'S,
Silver Spring, Maryland

Gentlemen:

We have received your letter and hereby we answer your questions.

The Kennel Club registrations for the Boxer in 1946 were seven, nine in 1947 and twenty-four in 1948.

The Boxer is gaining in popularity.

The Boxer is not the most popular working dog in our country. The most popular is the German Shepherd.

There are only two breeders of the Boxer in our country. They are:

Gregorio Amunategui, Teatinos 20, Santiago
Hernand Cuevas, Fundo Monte Blanco, El Monte

Very cordially yours,

(Signed)   Victor Wiedmaier
Secretary

The Boxer in England

70 Warwick Road
New Southgate,
London, N. 11.

MILO DENLINGER, ESQ.,
117 Hamilton Street,
Silver Spring, Maryland

Dear Sir,

I am a comparative newcomer to dogs, having been interested in Boxers for the past two years. Incidentally, as a matter of interest, it was due to the fact that I was told that Boxers were so popular in America, that gave me such an interest in the breed.

I am enclosing a short history of the breed in England which I have compiled from various sources, records, etc., which may be of some use to you in your next edition, also a list of Champions which is correct up to the present date.

Sincerely yours,

(Signed)   A. Charles Evered

The first Boxer to be registered in England was a bitch owned by E. Goujons, Jondy, by Remos von Pfalogan out of Flora Frierla von Goppingen and whelped on 29th July, 1911, but it would appear that she was not used for breeding. Since the breed was previously unknown in this country it must have been quite a rarity and apparently no other Boxer came into the country until a bitch Cilly von Rothenburg was imported by Miss P. M. Rogers in 1932. This bitch was in whelp to Drill von Kurland and a litter of three dogs was born on 16th

182

June, 1932, one of whom, Riverhill Racketeer, was bred to his dam and on 21st December, 1934, a litter of two dogs and a bitch was born.

From 1935 onwards there was a slow but steady stream of importations until 1939 when importations from Germany were impossible. A few importations are listed below with the date of registration.

1935. Quitta von Biederstein by Hansl von Biederstein out of Judra von Biederstein.

Derb von Menchendahl sired by Sieger Edler von Isarstrand.

1936. Tell von der Magdalenenquelle by Egon von Biederstein.

Gretl von der Boxerstadt who was imported in whelp to Hansl von Biederstein. To Gretl fell the honour of being the dam of the first English Boxer Champion, Ch. Horsa of Leithhill.

1937. Burga vom Twiel a granddaughter of Sigurd's sire, Iwein von Dom. This bitch was imported by Allon Dawson and was in whelp to Lustig von Dom, the litter which was born on 13th January, 1937, resulting in three bitches. Of this litter Stainburndorf Wendy won two Certificates and Stainburndorf Vanda won one in 1939.

Rex von Durrenburg who was a grandson of Sieger Check von Hunnenstein.

Bessi von Trauntal, a Sigurd granddaughter.

1939. Stainburndorf Flori von Dom a son of Zorn von Dom and a grandson of Hermes von der Uhlandshohe.

Stainburndorf Flori von Dom whose pedigree is given below. Both of these dogs were bred by Frau Stockmann, who with her husband, the late Philip Stockmann owned the famous Dom kennels and bred so many fine dogs.

Stainburndorf Zunftig von Dom	Lustig von Dom	Zorn von Dom
		Esta von der Wurm
	Blanka von Fohlhof	Alf von Uracher-Wasserfall
		Eukutol von Neu-Drosedow

Zunftig was later exported to America, where he finally gained his American Championship.

At this point it should be mentioned that in England, Boxers who have cropped ears cannot be exhibited at shows except as "Not for Competition," i.e., for advertisement purposes only, and it is a recent edict of the ruling body of the English Dog Fancy, the Kennel Club, that no dog may be registered who is the progeny of a dog or bitch who had been cropped in this country. The National Veterinary Medical Association strongly deprecates the practice of cropping Boxers' ears and has advised all veterinary surgeons against carrying out this operation. This does not debar an imported, cropped dog from being registered or from being used for breeding purposes.

The newcomers to the breed in this country have been handicapped to a certain extent by the fact that up to the present, the only books on the breed are either American or Continental and consequently the illustrations are of cropped dogs. However, now that the breed has become popular and more Boxers are seen in the streets, the natural ear, strange as it may sound, seems natural.

It was not until 1939 that there were sufficient registrations of Boxers for them to be given Championship Status. In order to qualify for the title of Champion, a dog must win three Challenge Certificates under three different Judges (this does not apply to Gundogs), the Challenge Certificates being granted by the Kennel Club to certain Canine or Breed Societies for certain breeds at Championship Shows. The number of Certificates available to each breed is dependent, at present, on the number of registrations in that breed during the previous year.

In 1939 there were five shows at which Certificates were offered in Boxers, one Certificate to each sex, and Ch. Horsa of Leithhill was the first Boxer to gain his title in this country, winning his three Certificates under the following Judges: C. Houlker Esq., Tom Scott Esq., and F. N. Pickett Esq. Then came the war and breeding operations were suspended for the most part while operations of a more deadly nature were engaged in.

In 1946 however, dog shows recommenced in a small way and the British Boxer Club held its first Championship Show on the 10th October at Coventry, and was fortunate enough to engage the famous American breeder and judge, J. Phelps Wagner, to officiate. The Challenge Certificates were awarded to Monarchist of Maspound and Panfield Serenade, both of whom were to gain their titles at a later date, Monarchist in 1948 and Serenade in 1947. The Reserve Best of Sex Dog was awarded to a puppy, Holger von Germania, who had been imported from Germany, uncropped, and who won his title in 1948.

In 1947 twelve shows, eleven of them all-breed shows, offered Certificates in Boxers, and three bitches became Champions: Champions Panfield Serenade, Thornick Beta of Oidar and Cuckmere Krinetta. No dog completed his title in this year.

In 1948 twenty shows, nineteen of which were all-breed shows, offered Certificates in the breed, and five dogs and four bitches won the coveted title. Dogs: Champions Holger von Germania, Panfield Tango (who is half brother to Panfield Serenade through their dam, Alma von der Frankenwarte), Bucko of Gerdas Hofstee, Monarchist of Maspound and Holmehill Faust of Gerdas Hofstee (who is a litter brother to Bucko of Gerdas Hofstee and who won his third Certificate at Cruft's Dog Show which was revived after nine years' absence). Bitches: Champions Florri of Breakstones, Asphodel of Knowlecrest (who was the first champion in England with an English Champion parent), Cuckmere Bomza Ficsta, and Annelie von Eddys-Gluck (who was imported uncropped).

Only three of the Champion Boxers have won more than the requisite three Certificates, Ch. Panfield Serenade who won five Certificates under five different judges (English, American and Dutch), Ch. Bucko of Gerdas Hofstee who has also won five under five different judges and Ch. Asphodel of Knowlecrest who won her fourth Certificate recently at the Ayr Agricultural Show. Furthermore, to Bucko fell the honour of winning the British Boxer Club's Championship Trophy at the Championship Show in 1948 under three judges, Mrs. H. Gamble, Mr. J. Keet and Mr. P. Zimmerman. The runner-up for the Trophy was Ch. Panfield Serenade and seven Champions competed. The Trophy which is for competition annually, is confined to Champions. In February another milestone was passed in English Boxer history when Mrs. C. L. Hullock's bitch, Orburn Kekeri, after winning her first Certificate went on to win Best in Show all breeds at Birmingham. This was the first time a Boxer had won Best in Show at an all breed Championship Show in England. It is a coincidence that a few days later, Ch. Mazelaine's Zazarac Brandy went Best in Show at Westminster and then went on to win Best in Show at Hartford on the Saturday following.

Until quite recently there was little or no Dorian or Utz blood in English Boxers but since the end of the war there have been many importations, some being:

America	Finemeres Flip of Berolina
	Fostorias Chieftain
	Am. Ch. Applause of Emefar
Germany	Collo von Dom
	Gremlin Gernot von der Herreneichen
	Champus von der Fischerhutte
Switzerland	Arras von der Schusselburg
Holland	Breakstones Helios vom Haus Germania
	Breakstones Faust vom Haus Germania
Sweden	Carlshead Master Fra Sverige
	Strandborg Lustig af Barbel

The breed has rapidly become popular in this country mainly due to the fact that Englishmen serving in the Forces on the Continent were attracted by the Boxer's qualities which were so aptly described by Alfred Putnam in the first edition of "The Complete Boxer." The same thing happened after the 1914-18 war with the German Shepherd Dog (Alsatian as it is known in England) which became so popular that in 1948 they were the second breed in order of registration totals. From being an almost unknown breed in 1938 the Boxer climbed to twentieth in popularity in 1947 and to sixteenth in 1948, which is remarkable, as very little breeding was done during the war years owing to the difficulty of feeding.

Comparative Tables showing the rise of registration totals of Boxers in England (in 15 years)

Year	Total	
1933	2	
1934	1	
1935	14	
1936	11	
1937	48	
1938	83	
1939	74	
1940	33	
1941	23	
1942	79	Wartime period when breeders, under the circumstances, voluntarily did little breeding
1943	139	
1944	246	
1945	399	
1946	707	
1947	1412	
1948	1922	

At the present time there are four Boxer Clubs in England and Scotland:

The British Boxer Club.   (The first to be formed.)
The Northern Boxer Club.
The Midland Boxer Club.
The Scottish Boxer Club.

These Clubs do a great deal to assist the breed by holding breed shows, offering Special Prizes, guaranteeing classes at General (all breed) Shows, giving lectures, etc.

Up to the present, little has been done with regard to the working qualities of the Boxer, but a few enthusiasts are advocating competition in Obedience Tests, which are mainly held by the Alsatian Clubs but which are sometimes open to all breeds. The Associated Sheep, Police and Army Dog Society annually holds Police Dog and Tracking Trials and it is to be hoped that Boxer owners will train their dogs for these Trials, since it would be a great pity for such a readily trainable breed to lose the qualities for which it is renowned in America.

A. Charles Evered.

English Boxer Champions

DOGS

Name	Born	Made Champion	Sire	Dam
Ch. Horsa of Leithhill	1936	1939	Hansl von Biederstein	Gretl von der Boxerstadt
Ch. Holger von Germania	1947	1948	Rex von Hohenneuffen	Favoriet vom Haus Germania
Ch. Panfield Tango	1946	1948	Panfield Flak	Alma von der Frankenwarte
Ch. Bucko of Gerdas Hofstee	1947	1948	Faust vom Haus Germania	Britta van Gerdas Hoeve
Ch. Monarchist of Maspound	1945	1948	Mutineer of Maspound	Marienlyst of Maspound
Ch. Holmehill Faust of Gerdas Hofstee	1947	1948	Faust vom Haus Germania	Britta van Gerdas Hoeve
Ch. Golf von Kunzendorf	1946	1949	Rex von Hohenneuffen	Draga von Kunzendorf

BITCHES

Name	Born	Made Champion	Sire	Dam
Ch. Panfield Serenade	1945	1947	Juniper of Bramblings	Alma von der Frankenwarte
Ch. Thornick Beta of Oidar	1944	1947	Stainburndorf Minesweeper	Stainburndorf Prudence
Ch. Cuckmere Krinetta	1945	1947	Cuckmere Krin	Bluemountains Lottery
Ch. Florri of Breakstones	1947	1948	Champus von der Fischerhutte	Maragay of Maspound
Ch. Asphodel of Knowlecrest	1947	1948	Stainburndorf Jaguar	Ch. Thornick Beta of Oidar
Ch. Cuckmere Bomza Fiesta	1947	1948	Cuckmere Andrew	Bomza Revelmere Lulu
Ch. Annelie von Eddys-Gluck	1946	1948	Tom von der Sievershohe	Flamme von Vierlingen
Ch. Alrakim Orburn Akaboo	1947	1949	Ch. Holger von Germania	Magarethe of Maspound

188

Statistics Showing the Number of Boxers Exported

1947 Country	Number of Dogs	1948 Country	Number of Dogs
Australia	4	Australia	8
America	3	America	7
Canada	1	Malaya	5
		South Africa	3
		Southern Rhodesia	2
		Belgium	1
		British East Africa	1
		Canada	1
		Czechoslovakia	1
		China	1
		Kenya	1
		Sweden	1
Total	8	Total	32

Statistics Showing Distribution of Challenge Certificates

Year	Certificates Available	Won by..........Dogs	Qualified as Ch's
DOGS			
1939	5	3	1
1946	1	1	—
1947	12	10	—
1948	20	11	5

Year	Certificates Available	Won by..........Bitches	Qualified as Ch's
BITCHES			
1939	5	4	—
1946	1	1	—
1947	12	5	3
1948	20	11	4

OSTERREICHISCHER BOXERKLUB SITZ WIEN

Geschäfts und Zucktbuchstelle: Wien VII. Burggasse 88/10
OSTERREICHISCHER KYNOLOGEN-VERBAND

Wien, am (Vienna, Austria)
Minoritenplatz 3.

MR. MILO G. DENLINGER,
Silver Spring, Maryland

Dear Sir:

I am writing to inform you about the situation regarding Boxers in Austria, since 1945.

Registrations during the year, 1946   172   (Nos. 4198-4370)
    "   " " " 1947 230 (" 4371-4600)
    "   " " " 1948 225 (" 4601-4825)

The Boxer has won unquestioned popularity and is one of the best loved breeds in Austria but there are no large Boxer kennels in this country which bred more than two litters per year since 1945.

Boxer breeding in Austria directs its chief aim to working quality and the stabilization of head type. In the attainment of the latter, a uniform Boxer bite is of special importance. The Boxer bite is judged severely here. Boxers whose front teeth are visible when the mouth is closed, should not be used for breeding or only conditionally. Further details concerning the Boxer bite are given in a scientific discussion by E. Camus of Wiener Neustadt, Dr. Menzel of Linz and Dr. E. Hauck of Vienna.

Other items of interest for American breeders are: The Boxer stands in the front rank of all breeds of dogs in this country, regarding temperament.

White markings, such as blaze or spot on the chest are liked and meet with approval, although these spots should not be too large.

A book entitled "Our Boxer" was published by the Austrian Boxer Club on the occasion of its tenth anniversary in 1931. This booklet is unfortunately sold out and a second edition is not possible.

Very truly yours,

(Signed) Hans Huemer
Vorsitzender.

190

The Boxer in Hawaii

By Ernest S. Chang

KALAKAUA Kennels, owned by Lau Ah Chew, is advertised as the oldest Boxer kennels in the Territory of Hawaii and rightfully so, as it is believed that they imported the first boxers into the islands. It was in the year of 1935 when the initial Nora v. Dom who is by Ch. Sigurd v. Dom out of Prisma v. Dom arrived in Hawaii for the Kalakaua Kennels. Nora was bred by Frau v. Miram and was Best opposite sex winner under Anton Rost at a Hawaiian show on July 16th, 1939.

At this same show, the 1936 import, Czardas v.d. Sielwall-Fahre also owned by Kalakaua Kennels was Best of Breed Winner. Czardas was by Dago v. Rosenheim out of Afra v. Uracher Wasserfall and was bred by Herman Allermann.

Later in 1940, Mrs. Tony Guerrero imported into the islands from Mrs. Ed. A. Prinz, Jr., Zombi v.d. Prinzenburg, sired by Ch. Banner of Barmere out of Ch. Astrid v. Lew. Zombi was Best of Breed at the Hawaiian Kennel Club's show on July 14th, 1940, under the great dane breeder Vincent J. Garrity. It was in 1941 when the first John P. Wagner bred boxer, Cara v. Tal, was imported by Mrs. Guerrero. Cara is by Ch. Hermes v. Uracher Wasserfall out of Ch. Cynthia of Mazelaine. Meantime in that same year, Kalakaua Kennels imported the great Ch. Pitt v.d. Wurm, to head their now growing kennel of boxers, which are gradually taking a foothold in the Hawaiian fancy.

Then came the unforgettable incident of Pearl Harbor, which brought forth many restrictions for the inhabitants of the islands, one of which was the ban on importation of dogs into the territory and a setback for this up-and-coming breed.

191

However, when restrictions were gradually eased, the Hale Kai Kennels, owned by Harlan and Violet Nakai started things rolling again for the breed in the importation of True-Hart's Battle Maid, breeder, Richard E. Tank. She is a Ch. Frisco of Woodbarr daughter out of Leesa v.d. Belzig of Amerikeim and was purchased in early 1945. Later in that same year, Hale Kai again imported the very fine stud, Invader of Briarnole, a Ch. Schoolmaster of Mazelaine son out of Jando's Exotic Lady bred by Lewis E. Daniels. Invader was heading for a sure championship when his success in the Hawaiian show ring was cut short by a very untimely death, much to the loss of the breed, and to his owners.

It was in the year of 1946 when the first Dr. Dan Gordon bred dog was shipped into the islands consigned to Mrs. Owen Young, who was very much in the breed with numerous other imports. This was a Ch. Bladan's U-Chetnik son, Bladan's Anzac, out of Ch. Blue Smoke of Bladan, who ran a string of reserves to Emperor of Kesthal in island shows, besides a best opposite sex win under the all arounder, Selwyn Harris, plus a group win under Dan Shuttleworth in a match show. The bulk of the local youngsters today are Anzac sired gets and even at this writing, he is doing limited service, although he had been retired completely from ring competition. Mrs. Young later imported the first Sirrah Crest bred boxer, the bitch, Liberty Belle of Sirrah Crest, bred by the R. C. Harrises. Belle was sired by Ch. Endymion of Mazelaine out of Oracle of Sirrah Crest and her successes in the show ring were terminated by an accident of an undetermined nature whilst serving her required period of quarantine at Territorial controlled kennels. Wah Kei Young, who is related to Mrs. Owen Young, imported the good quality bitch, Bladan's Traveling Gypsy, a full sister to Bladan's Anzac out of a later litter, also from the Bladan's Kennels of Dr. Dan Gordon. To complete the Bladan importations for the Youngs in the year of 1946, Bladan's Snappy Girl, a Ch. Sir Galahad of Bladan daughter, was brought in, which was later sold to the Henry Lums as a foundation towards his pioneering kennel. Snappy Girl was out of the popular Dan Gordon bitch, Blue Glow of Bladan. In this same year Hale Kai Kennels increased their holdings

192

of Boxers with the importation of Emperor of Kesthal, a Ch. Brace of Briarnole son out of Barbel v. Kerspetal, which was bred by the John J. Klockes; plus a Ch. Fast Stepper of Barmere bitch out of Bravenhartz Yoldring in Princess Pat of Hytress, a breeding by the plans of Charles E. Newton. During this bubbling year, the Hokuloa Kennels owned by the Robert Browns, imported three boxers: Freeman's Ozark Jerry; Love Lyric of Mazelaine and Roselle of Amerikeim.

Ozark Jerry is sired by Ch. Lustig v. Dom out of Midi v. Kaye and bred by the Tom Freemans. Love Lyric is a Ch. Warlord of Mazelaine daughter out of M & M Victory Girl bred by the Mazelaine Kennels of the J. P. Wagners. Roselle is by Ch. Frisco of Woodbarr out of Frances of Amerikeim bred by Gordon W. Keim. Kalakaua Kennels revived themselves with two Tulgey Wood bred boxers in Illinoy and Illian of Tulgey Wood. Illinoy is an Eagle of Tulgey Wood son out of Rhumba of Tulgey Wood. Illian is a Ch. Lustig v. Dom daughter out of Ch. Xanta v. Germanenstolz and best opposite sex winner at the December 15, 1946 Hawaiian Kennel Club show under E. E. Ferguson of Hollywood, California.

Herbert Ching helped to swell the 1946 importations with two: Pandrake of Mel-Zoa and Melinda of Mel-Zoa both bred by John W. Smietana. Pandrake is by Zoa of Bladan out of Christina v. Heidescooper and Melinda is by Ch. Duke of Danboro out of Heida v. Roll.

To bring the year of 1946 to an end, Mrs. B. J. Jones imported the Mervin F. Rosenbaum bred bitch, Bettina of Emefar, a Pegeant of Mazelaine daughter out of Renown of Barmere; and the John Lunquists came into the islands with Bladan's Sir Gallant, a Sir Galahad son out of Blue Glow of Bladan, which incidentally was of identical mating to the Young's Bladan's Snappy Girl.

It was not too long after the initial month of the year of 1947 had passed, when the far reaching arms of Mrs. Owen Young's desires, secured from the Clinaude Kennels their young son of Ch. Carlo v. Wolfschult out of Clinaude's Hennessy. He was the rich red fawn, Clinaude's Yarlo, who attracted the whole local boxer fancy's attention due to his excellent qualities and superb manners. The shepherd fancier,

193

Arthur Zane, followed with a Mervin F. Rosenbaum bred dog, Bellboy of Emefar, a Ch. Applause of Emefar son out of Ch. Belfine of Brielyn. Mrs. Lenore V. Rogers, a fancier stepping into the boxer field brought over Baratone of Dellwood who was by Ch. Southdown's Errol out of Interlude of Dorick and bred by the C. B. Mortons. Almost at the footsteps of Mrs. Roger's import, the retired U.S. Navy officer, Frank M. Dillion, brought over Arrosel Coco, a quality daughter of Ch. Quixote of Mazelaine out of Arrosel Asta, bred by Mrs. H. H. Hager. Kevin and Cecelia Cochrane, who have a strong following of friends on the mainland in the boxer field, moved into the islands, together with their Gaylord v.d. Gudneau and offspring of Anton of Shinnecock out of Heidi v. Freidenheim bred by the Howard McCormicks.

Commander Jumping Joe Sir, owned by Lt. and Mrs. Paul R. Lewis, came forth into the islands to join his master's tour of duty here and gathered for himself in his first island ring show, a best opposite sex win under the California all arounder, Mr. Anton Korbel. He was bred by Dr. R. F. Jackson and sired by Lusty of Marienhof out of Anitra of Marienhof, thus bringing the 1947 imports to a close.

The Charlie Pells, who are mutual friends of Mrs. Miriam Z. Breed of the famous Barmere Kennels, brought over the brindle bitch, Zany of Barmere, to begin the year of 1948's imports. Zany is by Ch. Dawn Patrol of Barmere out of Honey of Barmere and bred by Barmere. Following the arrival of Zany, another Barmere bred boxer came forth in King Cole of Barmere, another son of Ch. Dawn Patrol of Barmere out of Wedding Bells of Barmere consigned to the family of the Lawrence R. Perrys. Another Perry import followed in K. K. Heide, who was out of Birbama Shock and sired by Ch. Kobang of Sirrah Crest and bred by Mary M. Plank.

Kalakaua Kennels bounced back into the picture when they brought over a total of three all at one time to strengthen their kennel holdings. They were: Baroness Panz of Zandu, a daughter of Ch. Vorspiel of Mazelaine out of Ch. Tanz of Danboro; the stud, Playboy v.d. Tim-Roc, is by Ch. By Request of Lilac Hedge out of Aristocratic Lady of Hytress, plus a Ch. Schoolmaster of Mazelaine daughter bred by the Sunwoods Kennels of Barberton, Ohio.

194

The Boxer in the Orient

By Michael J. Harkins

Bang Kapi,
Bangkok, Siam
23rd December, 1949

MR. MILO G. DENLINGER,
117 Hamilton Avenue,
Silver Spring, Maryland, U.S.A.

Dear Mr. Denlinger:

You mentioned in your recent letter that you were at the publishing stage of a new edition on the Boxer, and whilst my knowledge of conditions regarding this breed is limited to Hong Kong and this country, the attached remarks may be useful to some degree.

Regarding conditions in Hong Kong, I am quite conversant with both prewar and postwar developments of the various breeds and have all available statistics on the subject. As elsewhere, the most popular breeds are the German Shepherd and the English Cocker. The former, as has been the case for many years, is by far the most popular of all breeds and represents the greatest number of registrations of any single breed with the Hong Kong Kennel Club, with the English Cocker a close second. The Chinese, of course, as in China proper, are mainly interested in dogs as watchdogs, and their interest rarely extends beyond the purely utilitarian aspect. Hence, the fact that the Chinese almost invariably express their interest in terms of the German Shepherd, which is far more popular than all the other breeds put together.

It may surprise you to know that there are at least 700 registrations of various breeds in Hong Kong today, and, for a place with a population of some 6,000 Europeans and Americans, this represents a very high percentage.

In Hong Kong, the vast majority of pure-bred dogs have been imported from Australia since the war. During the war, those dogs of

195

English origin which were in the Colony registered practically 100 per cent mortality due to the lack of food. I myself possess two English Cockers which are the offspring of Australian parents. I have them here in Siam with me, although they are never permitted to leave the confines of my own grounds, except in the car, owing to the danger of infection in the shape of rabies or mange.

Boxers have become quite popular recently in Hong Kong due mainly to the efforts of a Mr. Cowie, the owner of a number bred by him under the kennel name of "Walpool." They are of British stock, and, of course, conform to the British standard as far as ears are concerned, *i.e.*, no cropping. I am familiar with conditions in Hong Kong as they exist today, although I doubt very much whether your American readers are aware of the fact that many hundreds of dogs of different breeds were shown at the annual dog show in Hong Kong early this year. The senior judge, also for your information, was Mr. Hunt, of British "Ottershaw" Kennels fame. Much of your cocker stock originated with his kennels, if I am not mistaken.

Unfortunately, the annual show which is held each February, will be somewhat handicapped in 1950, I understand, as there has been an outbreak of rabies on the mainland, and the Colonial Veterinary Surgeon will not issue permits for dogs to cross the harbour for exhibition in the show which is held on the island of Hong Kong itself. I brought two English Cocker puppies from Hong Kong to Siam last August, and fully intended showing them in the puppy class in February next, but unfortunately this is not now possible in view of the restrictions.

Finally, you have expressed interest in conditions regarding Australia. I think you will find that, as a result of conditions following the last war, breeding in England has been handicapped to a very great extent due mainly to lack of foodstuffs, and Australia has emerged into the limelight as far as breeding is concerned. Much of the better British stock has been exported to Australia, where extensive breeding now takes place. Much of this product finds its way into Far Eastern countries and more particularly into Malaya and Hong Kong.

I trust that you will find the enclosed remarks of some value to you in your forthcoming publication on the Boxer and I only regret that, since my allegiance is mainly to the English Cocker, I am unable to furnish you with more exhaustive details.

Sincerely yours,

(Signed) MICHAEL J. HARKINS

The Boxer, apart from the interest displayed by a small band of enthusiasts spread throughout the Orient, has never excited any widespread attention in the Orient, generally speaking. Efforts have been made from time to time to increase public interest, but they have never met with the success they have deserved.

Possibly one of the most important efforts to arouse general interest in the breed has taken place in the British Colony of Hong Kong during the years following the war. With the arrival of the Japanese in 1941, and the internment of almost all Americans and Europeans, the population of purebred dogs of all breeds gradually diminished until, by 1945, it had practically vanished. However, following the war, and due to the efforts of one or two enthusiasts, several Boxers were imported into Hong Kong, the first really serious attempt to introduce the breed into that British colony. It caused a minor sensation, more especially amongst the Chinese, many of whom had never seen one previously.

In all, up to the end of 1948, two dogs and four bitches had been imported and registered with the Hong Kong Kennel Club, of which two bitches, **Baroness Heidi v. Dorfli** (sire, Marshall of Wolf Trap; dam, Choice of Mossmount) and **Pretty Peggy** (sire, Whirl Blast of Jamaye; dam, Time Bomb of Barmere), were of American origin. The remainder, with the exception of one dog, **Alf v.d. Biburg** (bred in Austria), were of United Kingdom origin. Of those imported from the United Kingdom, probably the most important were **Stainburndorf Gareth,** a dog, and **Stainburndorf Jeanette,** a bitch, both of whom are largely responsible for the various Boxers at present in Hong Kong. It should perhaps be mentioned in passing that the practice of clipping ears renders Boxers ineligible for shows in Hong Kong, where the Kennel Club follows the rules laid down by the Kennel Club of Great Britain. Thus, the two bitches of American origin mentioned above, although placed on exhibition in the 1949 Hong Kong Kennel Club Show, were unfortunately ineligible for competition with other entrants of the breed.

From the modest beginnings outlined above, and by the end of January, 1949, there were in all 18 registrations of Boxers with the Hong Kong Kennel Club, although it is to be doubted whether this number represents the total bred during the postwar period to that date. In view of the efforts made to establish the Boxer in Hong Kong to date, and the results which have ensued, those individuals who have introduced the breed and who have made such efforts to increase the popularity of the Boxer are to be congratulated, and it is reasonable to suppose that their united efforts will eventually go far to establish the breed permanently in Hong Kong and adjoining areas. It may well be that, in course of time, the somewhat ferocious aspect of the Boxer, allied to the fact that he is adaptable and easily managed, will recommend him more strongly in a watchdog capacity, and will tend to oust the less reliable breeds from the favour of the Chinese.

In Siam, on the other hand, the writer has noted during his stay here, a remarkable apathy regarding dogs of all breeds, and whilst there are a few purebred dogs of various breeds, the Boxer is conspicuous by his complete absence. It must be remembered, however, that conditions in Siam do not lend themselves to the keeping of well-bred dogs of any description. There is no registration body resembling the American Kennel Club or the Kennel Club of Great Britain. No statistics as to the number of dogs, or the types thereof, are available in Siam, and there are no shows by which one can arrive at any estimate of the breeds or the numbers of the various breeds which have been imported into Siam or bred here.

It represents a deplorable state of affairs, more especially in a country where there is an abundance of skilled veterinarians to advise breeders and to attend to the various canine complaints which arise in even the best-organized kennels from time to time. Perhaps this may seem incredible to the average American reader and needs some explanation.

The Siamese, being mainly Buddhist by religion, are prohibited and in actual practice refrain from inflicting injury or pain on animals of all descriptions, but, at the same time, their religion does not require them to evince any particular interest in dogs. The resultant apathy is appalling to one who is accustomed to according his dogs the same degree of consideration he would accord himself. In Siam, dogs are permitted to wander anywhere, acquiring disease as they stray, and spreading it amongst their equally unfortunate fellows. Living on garbage, their main source of sustenance, they abound in the open market places where offal is more plentiful, squabbling in packs over any morsel which is in the slightest degree edible. Breeding is, of course, indiscriminate, and it is by no means uncommon to find a bitch nursing an equally mangy array of pups in a public thoroughfare.

The individual who keeps dogs of any breed, therefore, and who displays any consideration for them, confines them to his own premises, as does the writer. Fortunately, the average person keeping dogs under such conditions is also the fortunate possessor of extensive grounds, adequately fenced, in which his dogs may run freely and obtain all the exercise they require, at the same time remaining free from infection.

From the above it will be realized that the future of the Boxer in Siam, as well as the future of all other well-bred dogs, is a matter for conjecture, and the writer doubts whether that future can be considered particularly rosy. Advertisements appear from time to time in the Siamese press, offering Boxers, as well as dogs of other breeds, for sale in Siam, and more recently a Malayan kennel has offered such dogs for sale, delivered at destination in Siam, but, judging from the conditions existing in Siam, the response must be very discouraging.

CH. TERUDON'S KISS ME KATE

Sire: Ch. Barrage of Quality Hill
Dam: Canyonaire's Katrinka II

Breeder-Owners: Mr. and Mrs. Theodore Wurmser

CHAPTER IX

Blueprint of the Boxer

THE postwar popularity of the Boxer is a phenomenon for which there is small explanation. That popularity rests basically in the very merits of the breed.

It required a world war to make those merits known in America, just as the merits of the German Shepherd dog were brought home to us after the first World War. We should accept credit for the fact that our enmity with the Nazi government does not prejudice us against the worthy products of the German race, of which the Boxer is one.

The Boxer is the culmination of all that is excellent in German dog breeding—beauty, symmetry, strength, efficiency, and intelligence. He is in fact the super dog. Clean, short coated, of a comfortable size, big enough for most purposes and small enough not to be cumbersome in the car or in the house, level headed, neither vicious nor effusively friendly to strangers, distinctive and striking in his appearance, there can be no wonder that the Boxer has obtained such a hold upon the imagination that has brought him to his high status in the public esteem. The Boxer is fashion's favorite. Not everybody can afford a Boxer, which may have something to do with making everybody want one.

The triumph of Warlord of Mazelaine as best dog of any breed at the 1947 show of the Westminster Kennel Club at Madison Square Garden in New York served to further the cult of the Boxer, which, it appeared, had already reached the zenith of the breed's popularity.

The Boxer of the present time is far different from the Boxer of even twenty years ago. Breeds develop, evolve, change and improve, gradually and imperceptibly within the framework of their respective standards until at length it becomes necessary to change the standard adequately to describe the dog. The standards lag behind the growth of the breeds. The Boxer changes were more rapid than the changes of most breeds; they can almost be called abrupt.

The Boxer as he was first known was little more nor less than a colored Bull Terrier without any marked attributes of type. He lacked in elegance, distinction, beauty, and his type was but ill defined. All that, however, is now changed. The Boxer has been standardized within a very short while. This was brought about largely by the importation of Sigurd von Dom, which occurred in 1934. That great dog personified the ideals of the breed which had never before been realized. He combined strength, symmetry, elegance, style and type. He revolutionized the Boxer. From him and his progeny the Boxer breed was re-constructed, until now we have Boxers of a beauty and uniformity found in few other breeds of dogs.

Let us take our Boxer out into a flat, open space where we can examine him to best advantage. The lawn and walks in front of the house will suffice, or a park, even a quiet street. He should be equipped with a strong, light collar and lead, and should have a handler to control him.

We may assume that the dog has been bathed and brushed, that his nails have been cut back to neaten his feet, that any fringes have been trimmed from his ears, that his antennae hairs have been shortened, and that his teeth have been scoured. We may also assume that the dog is in hard, firm flesh, that he is free from worms, bright-eyed and eager. There is little to be gained from exhibiting a dog that is not in top condition, and it is discouraging to examine an ill-kempt and dirty dog *hors concours*. We may believe that we can make allowance for bad condition, but we survey the animal as we see him and bad condition or careless grooming detracts from the ensemble as much as does a light eye, a shallow chest, or a weak hindquarter. How often do we see a dog go down to defeat in a dog show, only in some subsequent show to come back in better condition and with better handling to win over dogs that had previously beaten him.

The first consideration in the evaluation of a Boxer is his symmetry, the suitability of every part to every other part. We should then first stand away from the dog to look at him whole, consider him standing and moving. Is his head too large or too small for his body? Is he coarse or overly refined? Do his ears stand erect and set off his head? Is he obviously short of neck? Is he giraffe-like in his station or too squat? Is he too long of loin? Does he wobble in action from one side to the other? Is he cow-hocked or bandy-legged?

We shall come back to consider all these details later, but if a defect is so marked as to be immediately apparent to the amateur, the Boxer is so inferior that it is a waste of time to complete the survey. The experienced eye will detect abnormalities instantly, although the novice may require considerable time to study the dog as a entirety before he undertakes to consider the individual parts. Short of absolute rejection, no final decision is to be made from this preliminary going over.

The head is by no means the most important part of the Boxer, but it is the key or index to the breed. Spectacular as the head may be, it is yet a study in logic, moderation and efficiency. The standard of the breed is very long and purports to describe the Boxer head in detail. While it can not be alleged that such a description of the Boxer head as the one in the standard is in any detail incorrect, it is to be doubted that a person unfamiliar with the Boxer would be able to identify a dog as a member of this breed from the perusal of the standard.

Indeed, the Boxer head is difficult to describe without the aid of pictures, which will convey more of what is wanted than all the words that can be written. The Boxer, especially in regard to its head properties, is different from any other dog, so different that in description it may appear preposterous to a person who has never seen one. It is like a jig saw puzzle in that the parts, taken separately, may appear meaningless and ill assorted; whereas, fitted together, the results are beautiful and logical in the extreme.

203

The Boxer is in part a descendant from the Bulldog and the bull baiting breeds, and it partakes in its head structure of many Bulldog features, but these features are so modified that nobody can accuse the elegant and alert Boxer of being a merely bad specimen of the Bulldog. The Boxer has a moderately broad skull; the muscles of the cheeks are visible; its stop is pronounced; it has a slight furrow; it has a turn-up and a suggestion of lay-back; it has distinct wrinkles on the sides of the muzzle and a suggestion of wrinkle over the forehead when its ears are erected and alert; it is somewhat undershot; and its chops are cushioned. These are all Bulldog characteristics, but so modified in the Boxer as never to appear extreme or in excess.

While the Bulldog is presumed to possess the attributes that best fit it for the baiting of bulls, the early Bulldog that was actually employed in that cruel and happily obsolete sport approached the Boxer in type more nearly than it approximated the modern Bulldog. The early Boxer was also employed in the baiting of bulls, and it is probably better constructed for that purpose than is the modern Bulldog. The Bulldog breeders are extremists who consider that if a little is good, a lot is better. The Boxer breeders were restrained to moderation; they sought as much of any attribute as would serve their purpose to the maximum, but stopped short of the grotesquery that characterizes the modern Bulldog. In short, then, the Boxer is, among other things, the German Bulldog.

The Boxer head is a series of curves and angles, and is symmetrical in the extreme.

The skull is of only moderate width and length, neither coarse nor showing any semblance of weakness. It is not absolutely flat, but is slightly arched and rounded to the cheeks. There is a slight furrow, but by no means as deep as that of the Bulldog. The occipital protuberance is hardly noticeable. A series of fine wrinkles crease the skull when the dog is at intense attention. This does not imply that the Boxer possesses the extreme wrinkle pattern of the Bulldog, however. Except when the dog is in an intense and alerted mood with ears erect and at attention, the top skull is smooth and free from wrinkle. (This does not apply to the indication of wrinkles at the sides of the muzzle, which are always apparent, whatever the dog's mood may be.)

The skull rounds to the cheeks, as we have said, and the cheeks, though not prominent, are apparent but only just noticeable. They are not rounded as in the Bulldog nor are they flat as in the terrier. The cheeks in turn round gradually to fit into the muzzle.

The eyes are set far apart, but within the planes of the cheek bones, and between them there is the distinct and deep stop between the skull and the top of the muzzle with some indentation in the stop which leads into the slight furrow. This indentation is not exaggerated; there is no depth into which to bury a large marble, as in the Bulldog, but it is apparent.

The muzzle, long, broad and deep, emerges gracefully from the top skull, as if it belonged to it and not as if it were affixed to it. The plane of the top of the muzzle is not quite parallel with the plane of the top of the skull, but slants slightly upward from that plane—a mere tendency to up-face or dish-face, as opposed to a down-faced formation. This is not a distinct lay-back such as is found in the Bulldog, but as the dog is seen in profile is very distinctly seen when looked for. There is not enough of it to appear grotesque and hardly noticeable if not sought.

From the stop to the corners of the mouth there are indications of wrinkles, mere folds of skin, not deep and obtrusive like those of the Pekingese or the Bulldog, but distinctly apparent. Here is the junction of the skull and muzzle.

The muzzle includes that part of the head from the stop to where the lips meet, which is beyond the tip of the nose, and this measurement should be approximately two-thirds as long as the top skull (from the occiput to the stop). If one is not considering the entire muzzle but only the distance from the stop to the tip of the nose, this length should be about one-half as long as the top skull. A well carried muzzle, balanced with width and depth, gives symmetry and balance to the head.

The under jaw is somewhat longer than the upper jaw and is turned up at the end, leaving the dog undershot. This turn-up is not the long and intense sweep upward of the jaw of the Bulldog, but is sufficient to provide a vise-like formation from which, once it is clamped, nothing can escape.

This formation of the mouth and teeth is very important in determining the merits of the Boxer's head. The jaw is wide; it is not too much to say as wide as possible. The teeth must be large and white and even and solidly implanted. The width between the canines has much to do with determining the character and strength of the jaw. The jaw is very distinctly undershot, although not enough to show when the mouth is closed. The lower incisors are in a straight row between the canines, whereas the upper incisors are somewhat convex. This gives width to the muzzle as the turn-up gives it depth. The importance of this formation can hardly be too strongly emphasized. Withal, there is nothing grotesque about this formation of jaw, nor about any other feature of Boxer anatomy. The jaw is just sufficiently prognathous to afford the dog a maximum of grasping power and holding power, but without the exaggeration that makes the dog a freak.

The sides of the Boxer muzzle are heavily padded with muscle—in the Bulldog, this is called the cushion. It fills out the contours of the muzzle and gives it character.

This "cushion" is elongated into lips, called flews in the Bulldog and in many other breeds. These lips are moderately thick and long enough to cover the edges of the under jaw and to determine the dog's profile. They are not so long, however, as to appear ponderous or to cause the animal to slobber. The lips rest upon the lower canine teeth, which are required to be large and long and wide apart. This gives an aspect of greater width to the muzzle than would be determined by the bony structure of the fore face.

The nostrils are large, wide apart, and open. The nose is always black.

Except for the white marked areas on the muzzle, the entire muzzle is black. This black mask should not extend beyond the muzzle, however, to give the dog a somber or forbidding expression.

The standard of the breed states that "the black mask is absolutely required." While this may be true of the exhibition specimen, it is not "absolutely" true of a dog or bitch used for breeding, since, if properly mated, a maskless specimen may produce masked puppies, or at least a certain proportion of the puppies should be masked.

There exists a misapprehension that white markings on the muzzle of the Boxer are undesirable. How it gained a foothold is impossible to say. The fact is that white markings are frequently interesting and serve to liven up the expression. So, far from being objectionable, they are actually desirable, although by no means are they essential.

Boxer eyes are wide apart, but within the planes of the cheeks. They are not spread to give the dog a "goldfish expression." They are of medium size and are set squarely in the skull. An oblique placement of eye gives the dog a sharp expression that is not characteristic of the breed. Small eyes, especially when placed too close together, produce a querulous, suspicious, petty and mean expression. Large eyes, on the other hand, result in a liquid, soft expression too much like that of the Boston Terrier.

The haw of the eyelid should not be visible. When the haw can be seen, it is usually the result of lips too heavy or too long, the weight of which drags on the lids of the eye and turns them out. Here we see wherein one part of a dog affects the appearance of other parts, and the whole animal is a unit and not to be judged as an assemblage of pieces. To the uninitiated, it may not be apparent or may make no difference that the weight of the lips should affect the expression of the eyes, but to the trained observer it is significant.

As a general rule, the eyes should be as dark as possible. Occasionally a dog is found with irises so black that there is no demarcation between them and the pupils of the eye. Such dogs may appear to be blind, although they are not. When it occurs, some judges will assess a minute penalty to the fault although most judges will consider it an added virtue. There is no doubt that it becomes an asset to the breeding animal, especially one to be mated to a consort with eyes that are too light.

While dark eyes in well nigh any breed are desirable, and the darker the better, a somewhat lighter eye is less offensive in a fawn than in a brindle Boxer, and a light fawn can carry a lighter eye than a red fawn. Sometimes a dark eye will be found in a very light fawn dog, and it is very gratifying. Light yellow eyes, what the Germans call "bird of prey eyes," are intolerable, and a dog that carries them is to be penalized to the very limit. They are not, however, an absolute disqualification.

The eye rims are black. Flesh colored or even partly flesh rims, spoil the expression, causing the eyes to appear weak and the dog to appear treacherous. It is a mere illusion, but one that it is impossible for us to escape.

The ears are set on the outer corners of the skull and are usually trimmed to stand upright. The cropping of the ears smartens the appearance of the dog and improves the expression, and it is almost impossible to win a high award in an American show with an uncropped Boxer. The cropping of a dog's ears is forbidden in England by a law which is taken seriously and enforced. It is a natural reaction for an American, who is used to trimmed ears in many breeds, to feel that a sudden stop in trimming would ruin the breed's popularity here; but in England where they are accustomed to long-eared Danes and other breeds, the breeders probably do not miss the smartness and elegance we feel trimming gives our Boxers.

There are also laws in some American states that forbid the cropping of ears, but these laws are evaded by the dog breeding public and, at any rate, are seldom enforced. It is usually possible to take the puppies into some adjacent state to have them cropped, if the laws of the state where they are whelped preclude their being cropped in that area.

Cropping is not a serious operation, but it is one for the expert. Inexperienced surgeons frequently spoil the expressions of otherwise good dogs with a bad job of cropping; and even good surgeons can not guarantee a successful cropping job. The texture of the ears or the erectile muscles of the ears may render it impossible to crop ears in such a fashion that they stand firmly erect without nicking inward. Cropping does not consist merely of slicing off a part of the ear. An expert cropper studies the dog's head in order to produce an ear crop to bring out the symmetry and expression to best advantage.

He leaves enough of the base of the ear to assure firmness of foundation, but no more than is necessary for that purpose. The ear in length should usually be as much as will stand firmly without wavering, but it should serve to balance the head. The ears should be exactly alike in form, length and carriage; they should stand quite erect without disposition to nick in or to lie across the skull. They should be alert and active, ready to catch any sound.

One should not, however, be too critical of a puppy's ears, since the carriage is subject to change up until the dog is seven or eight months old. Sometimes unfortunately carried ears can be subsequently remedied by having them retrimmed by an expert, that is, if too much of the shell has not been taken off.

However difficult it may be to win in the shows with defective ear carriage which results from a botched job of cropping, and however much bad cropping may affect a Boxer's appearance, an otherwise excellent Boxer is not harmed as a breeding animal by bad ear surgery.

A description of the correct head of a Boxer is bound to be misleading. However much efficiency of jaw power is implied in such a description, it appears to visualize little of symmetry and beauty. From a description, the reader is likely to gather that the Boxer is merely a bad Bulldog or a mongrel of more or less Bulldog type. There can be no doubt that the Boxer is indebted to the Bulldog for many features, but there can be no confusing the types of the respective breeds; the Boxer is a Boxer with a type of his own, whereas the Bulldog remains a Bulldog. Those Boxer features that are derived from the Bulldog are so modified as to make for an efficiency that the Bulldog is too exaggerated to possess. Taken together, Boxer features unite to form a head of symmetry and beauty that, to use a trite phrase, must be seen to be appreciated. And the appreciation grows. As the efficiency of the head structure is realized and studied, the more apparent will be the beauty of the head contours. The Boxer head embodies the adage that "Beauty is use; use, beauty."

Boxer type behind the head structure is more orthodox and easier to describe. The Boxer body embodies the utmost of power combined with a grace, agility, soundness, and above all an elegance that is to be found in no other breed of dogs. It is a dog of medium station, neither squat like the Bulldog or even the Bullterrier, nor high in the air like the Greyhound.

For a few recent years there has been a tendency toward high Boxers. This selection for highness is presumed to contribute toward an increased elegance, although there is some doubt that it does in fact. Sigurd von Dom of Barmere, Austrian Sieger of 1931, German Sieger of 1932 and 1933, and American Champion of 1934, the property of Mrs. William Z. Breed of Van Nuys, California, at the height of his career was considered to be the highwater mark of what up to that time had been produced either in Germany or in America, the veritable *beau ideal* of Boxerdom. Many of us believe that there has been no more recent improvement upon his type. Yet, compared to the great winners of the present year, Sigurd would appear somewhat low to the ground and thickset, not to say cloddy. The Boxer in his evolution appears to be growing in his comparative height at the shoulders. Whether the Boxer fancy believes that an added elegance and length of head is attainable through greater comparative height and a sacrifice of substance it is impossible to say, as it is impossible to prognosticate how far the movement toward taller Boxers may go. However, a glance at Sigurd's picture (the dog is no longer alive) will show that there is no necessity to turn the Boxer into a giraffe to attain elegance, a quality that was personified in the great old gladiator.

This quality was attained in the particular dog, and is attainable in breeding practices, by the comparative length of neck and layback of shoulder. The Boxer neck should be as long as possible, compatible with strength and symmetry. But it must needs be powerful, broad and deep withal. The Boxer head is comparatively large and the neck must be strong enough to support it with its musculature. It should

210

serve as a bridge between the body and the head and should support anything that the jaws can grasp.

The neck should taper from its set-in at the shoulders, and should show a crest in its profile, as it is sure to do if it is correctly knitted between well-laid shoulders. Any semblance of ewe neck or tendency toward concavity of neck implies that the shoulder formation is wrong and usually in such cases the shoulder blades will be found to be nearly upright. The crest is likely to be more marked in the male dog than in the bitch.

The throttle should be clean and free from dewlap. Theoretically at least, any surplusage of folds of skin under the throat or around the neck provides an objective upon which a competitor in combat may grab and fix his teeth; actually it is an impediment to the eyes of a judge as they sweep over and survey the whole dog. It is a superfluous appendage which serves no purpose and must be eliminated.

The neck and shoulders can not be divorced, because the correct formation of one rests upon the correct formation of the other. Indeed, all the parts of a dog are inter-dependent. The animal is a unit and can not be judged in parts. One famous judge, James Watson, once said that the most important part of a Greyhound was the neck—seeing the neck, he could visualize the whole dog. It is well known that an osteologist, given a single fossil bone of an extinct animal, will formulate the entire skeleton of that animal. So it is in dogs, one part is dependent upon every other part.

Boxer shoulders are as long as it is possible for them to be and as well laid back. The closer the approximation to a right angle their junction with the upper arm (or humerus), the better the shoulder formation. This is a normal shoulder structure for good dogs of well nigh every breed, but its necessity is especially stressed in breeds of German origin. It enables the shoulder to open freely to permit the dog to take long steps in front. Despite the fact that power is developed in the hindquarters and the forequarters provide mere points of suspension to prevent the dog from falling forward on its face, the long, well laid back shoulder provides a cushion that enables the dog to move with a minimum of fatigue. A like formation is found in good horses, and, in fact, in any well constructed quadruped. It contributes a good deal to the grace and symmetry of the animal.

The fore arms of the Boxer are perpendicular when the dog is standing at attention, and parallel from the elbows to the pastern joint. There is a suggestion, just a suggestion, of give at the pastern, to absorb the shock of running. If this turn is not present and the leg is absolutely straight, most judges will refuse to penalize the absence of spring, too little of which is certainly to be preferred to too much. The pasterns are short and the feet face absolutely forward; any tendency to truss or to turn outward from the pastern joint constitutes a serious fault.

The feet are short, tightly arched, deep, thick of pad, and cat-like, the toes well knuckled up and close together. No detail detracts more from a Boxer's merits than a thin, spreading foot. Most dogs that receive ample exercise wear their nails blunt, but long, sharp nails can spoil the appearance of a foot, and the artificial removal of the horny part of the nails—without injury to the quick—may transform an indifferent foot into a good one, or at least may turn a bad foot into a somewhat better one. The nails of a thoroughly good foot are big, thick, and blunt.

The Boxer stands well up on its shoulders, and is not hung between them. The front is of moderate width, neither with both legs coming out of the same hole, like a too narrow fronted terrier, nor spread out like a Bulldog. The elbows are tight against the chest, but are not turned inward. If they turn in, the feet will turn out; if the elbows turn out, the dog is likely to be pigeon-toed.

The shoulders are flat and free from bunchy muscles, it is true, but the play of the long hard muscles is visible under the skin of a well conditioned Boxer that has sufficient exercise. In the words of the standard as they pertain to the hindquarters: "strongly muscled, the musculation hard as a board and standing out very plastically through the skin." This hard musculation and plasticity of the muscles is equally applicable to the forequarters.

The torso of the Boxer is deep, extending at least as far as the elbow. Its depth defines the dog's station approximately, the vertical height of the dog at the shoulder being twice the depth of the body at its deepest point.

The rib cage is well sprung and capacious, adequately rounded and extended well back. The importance of this feature is to provide adequate space to accommodate a great heart and generous lungs. That should be self-evident. However, the chest should not be barrel-shaped or round, but the ribs should spring widely from the spine, and should then drop immediately with little bulge to meet the sternum. The old quest for barrel-shaped ribs on the dog has been abandoned; at best it has always been a mere figure of speech and was never really wanted. It is now recognized that a chest that approaches the circular, with its protruding ribs, impedes the dog's action and interferes with the play of the elbows.

The back line is absolutely level from the withers to the pelvis. The croup then slants ever so slightly to the set-on of the tail. It can well nigh be said that the less the slant of the croup the better, and some judges look for an absolutely level top line, which is almost unobtainable, even in the Fox Terrier. The tail is to be shortened to about an inch and a half or two inches on a grown dog, set on high, and carried erectly. The set of tail and its carriage can never be correct if set on a croup that slopes too much.

The back is as short as is practicable, and the ribs extend so far toward the rear that the loin is particularly short—just long enough to enable the animal to turn and manoeuvre with lissomeness and agility. The underline of the Boxer body shows a moderate tuck up of the loins, but no extreme, no Greyhound outline. The belly is not constricted, but is firmly under the control of its muscles.

The hindquarters are broad, with big muscular hams. The second thighs are long and the hocks well let down, the hocks short. Boxer angulation in the rear is considerable and distinct, but it can be overdone. There is a good turn at the stifle and hock, but not so much as in the German Shepherd dog. A little too much angulation is distinctly to be preferred over stiltiness. Too many Boxers (and many other dogs) have mere props for hind legs, from which no leverage can be developed.

Adequate angulation is important, since all the power of movement the dog may possess is developed by the series of levers in the hindquarters of the dog, manipulated as they are by the musculature. This power is transmitted through the spine to the forequarters. It is better that the Boxer possess somewhat too much angulation, rather than too little; although the greater the angulation, the greater must be the musculature to support and manipulate it.

Despite the difficulty in obtaining a perfect head upon the Boxer, the production of a perfect set of hindquarters is an even harder problem. So much attention has been paid to the attainment of perfect heads by the Germans that adequate hindquarters have been neglected.

Seen going away from the observer, the hindquarters must be true. That is, they must not be spraddled out, even less must they be too close together. The hocks must be upright and parallel, and the knee must turn neither in nor out. Cow hocks are the bane of the breed, as they are of most other breeds, but of the Boxer in particular. Cow hocks are recognized to be a heritable fault, which the amateur is prone to overlook, but no fault of a dog is more painful to the expert.

The turning of the hocks outward is only less reprehensible than their turning in. A bandy legged dog is likely to be pigeon-toed and to move with the awkwardness of the pigeon-toed person. Either formation of the quarters warrants a severe penalty.

The Boxer colors are fawn in any of its manifestations from light cream to rich red, plain or shot with brindle. White markings, preferably symmetrical ones, are permissible and even desirable, but the total area of white shall not occupy more than one third the surface color of the entire dog. White or black ground color is reason for disqualification. Why this should be true is not entirely clear, since in the earlier Boxers, white dogs were common.

The black mask is essential, but it must not extend far enough back on the head to give the dog a somber expression. White markings in this black mask are entirely permissible, a detail that is not too clearly understood. Many a good Boxer has been needlessly discarded as a puppy because of its having white markings in its black mask.

214

The standard is specific about the markings of brindle Boxers. "The brindle variety should have clearly-defined black stripes on fawn background." While in two otherwise absolutely equal dogs, the one with the better brindle markings should win, yet the brindling and its distribution is an unimportant detail and the less attention given to it at the expense of the consideration of correct structure, the better. Distinct brindling renders a Boxer neither more nor less efficient than mottled brindling, and, while it is well to have it if possible, few judges take any cognizance of it. There is no choice between a fawn and a brindle Boxer, either being equally acceptable.

The sizes of Boxers as defined in the new standard are now "Males—22½ to 25 inches at the withers. Females—21 to 23½ at the withers. Males should not go under and females should not go over.

While these heights may be accepted as approximately correct, it will be found that a big, upstanding dog will probably win over a dog of moderate size, other things being equal, and many times under judges who are not sure of themselves a big, impressive dog will win over a slightly better small one. This is likely to occur in bitches, although even here a 23 inch bitch will usually get the nod over an equally good one of 21 inches.

Despite what is said in the standard, it is impossible to test a Boxer's temperament in the show ring and it is unwise to try. Dogs that are overly aggressive and overt cowards are, of course, subject to penalty, for the simple reason that it is impossible to examine them. They fail to make the best of themselves. A vicious dog may behave well on one day and show treachery on another. There may be days when an utterly craven dog, in an environment exactly to his liking, may permit himself to be examined without cringing. The show ring is, therefore, no place to seek to ascertain the mental or temperamental qualities of a dog.

A dog that shows disposition to attack strangers or other dogs without provocation, one that is obstreperous and refuses to stand for examination, is better left at home; the dog show is no place for him until he is reconditioned to behave properly.

The same may be said of a dog that shivers and crawls on his belly, for he is sure to be defeated, whatever his excellent qualities may be.

Elegance is an absolute necessity for a top Boxer, probably more so than for a dog of any other breed, unless it be a Poodle. And, unfortunately, elegance is a term that can not be accurately defined as it applies to a dog. It is somewhat physical, in that it implies a refinement of structure, and the correct relation of part to part. A well arched, "dry," and gracefully long neck, fitting into flat and well laid back shoulders contributes much to this element of elegance.

Even more, however, elegance is a matter of the spirit. It manifests itself in a debonair jauntiness, a freedom and liberty of action, a high headed style that defies definition. A Boxer has it or has it not, and it requires no expert to recognize it when it is present.

The Boxer's character, his trustworthiness and loyalty, his "soul of honesty," can not be evaluated in the show ring. A description of that character is included in the standard of the breed, but it has no place there. Boxer character, like human character, is largely the result of conditioning. It results much from the way a dog has been treated from its puppyhood and it reflects the human characters with which the dog has been brought into contact. Winning dogs may, and sometimes do, violate every tenet of Boxer character as it is laid down in the standard.

For pet, protector and companion, the matter of character of a dog is of supreme importance; but what kind of character a dog may possess can only be ascertained by living with the dog, not merely by looking at it for a few minutes in the judging ring.

No scale of points is appended to the Boxer standard. This is fortunate, since it precludes judging of the dog in pieces. It leaves the judge to look at the animal as a unit. While the absence of a scale of points imposes an added responsibility upon a judge, it leaves him free to put the generally best dog at the top of the class.

216

BOXER SKELETON

1. Upper Jaw
2. Lower Jaw
3. Eye Socket
4. Frontal Bone
5. Occiput
6–14. Cervical vertebrae or neck.
15. Shoulder Blade
16. Upper Arm Bone
17. Radius, Meet at Upper
18. Ulna, End at Elbow
19. Wrist
20. Toes
21–32. Ribs.
33. Dorsal vertebrae
34. Lumbar veretbrae
35. Coccyx
36. Caudal vertebrae
37. Pelvis
38. Femur or thigh bone
39. Patella or knee
40. Fibula and tibia or shank
41. Hock Joint
42. Hock

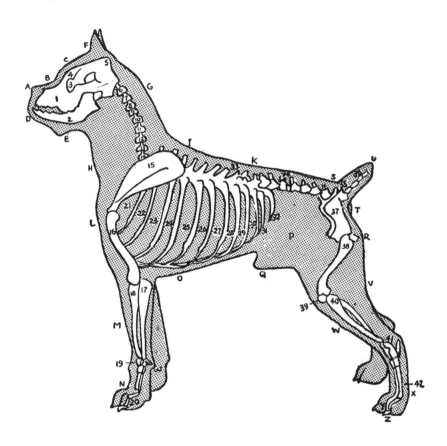

BOXER ANATOMY

A. Nose
B. Stop
C. Forehead
D. Chin
E. Flews or lips
F. Ear
G. Crest or nape of neck
H. Throat
I. Withers
K. Back
L. Chest
M. Forearm
N. Pastern
O. Brisket
P. Flank
Q. Penis
R. Ischial Tuberosity
S. Croup or rump
T. Anus
U. Tail
V. Upper thigh
W. Stifle
X. Hock
Y. Toes
Z. Claws

2. Good Head.   3. Down Faced, Skull Too Flat.   4. No Chin.   5. Too
Pronounced Falling Off of Brow.   6. Too Light A Muzzle.

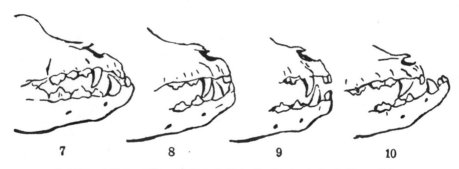

7. Normal Boxer Bite.   8. Not Sufficiently Undershot.   9. Even Bite.
10. Bulldog Bite.

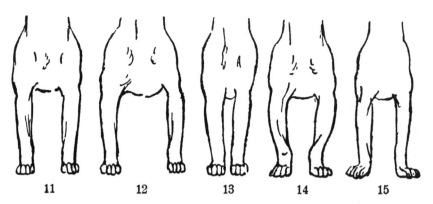

11. Correct Front. 12. Too Wide. 13. Too Narrow. 14. Rickety.
15. Feet Turned Out.

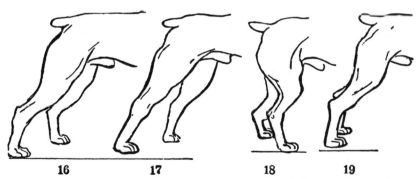

16. Good Hind—Quarters. 17. Too Steep. 18. Stands Under. 19. Stands Back.

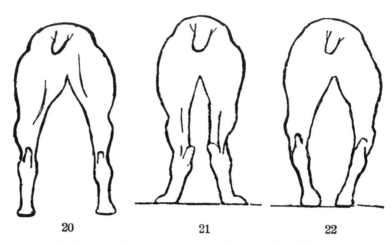

20. Correct Stance. 21. Cow—hocked. 22. Barrel-legged.

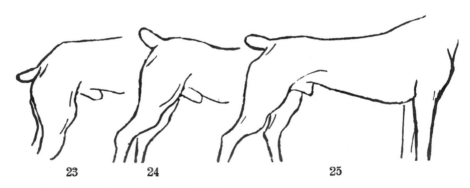

23. Sloping Croup, Too Low Tail Seat. 24. Overbuilt. 25. Too Long a Back.

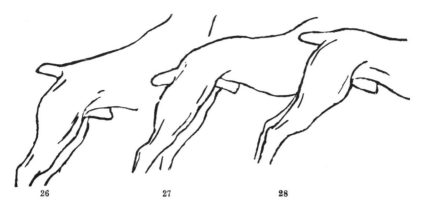

26. Shows Good Back. 27. Roach Back. 28. Sway—Back.

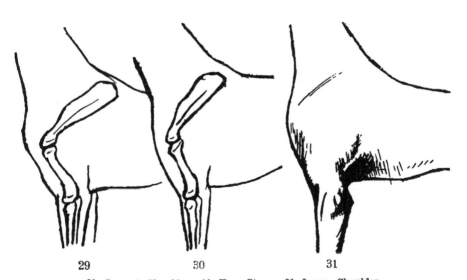

29. Correct Shoulder. 30. Too Steep. 31. Loose Shoulder.

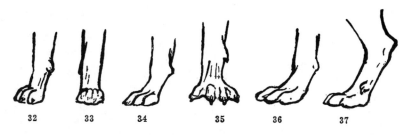

32. Good Foot From Side. 33. The Same Foot—Front. 34. Weak Pasterns.
35. Splay Foot. 36. Harefoot. 37. Hind Foot With Dew Claw.

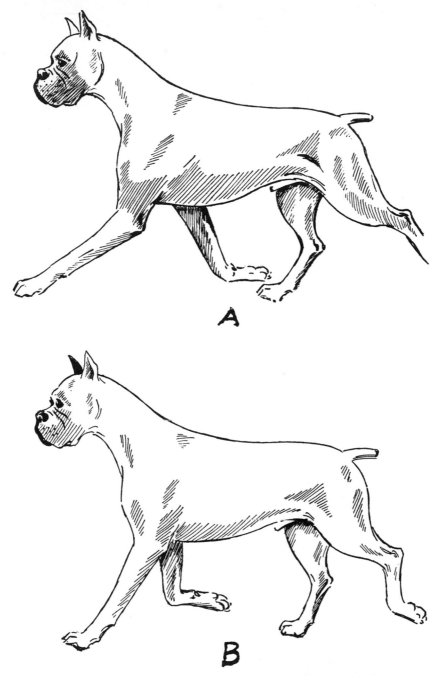

A. Good Gait.   B. Stilted Movement.

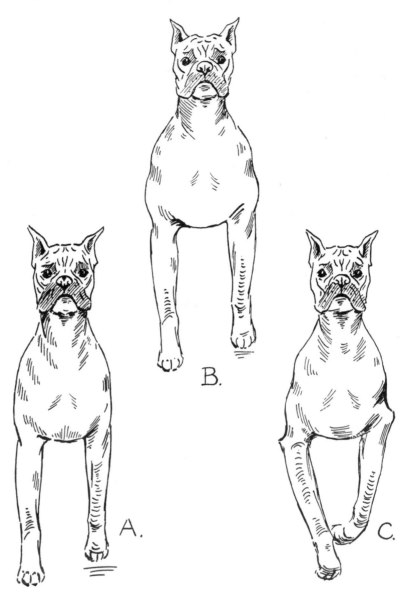

A. Correct Movement. B. Wide Shoulders. C. Out at Elbows, Front Paddling.

224

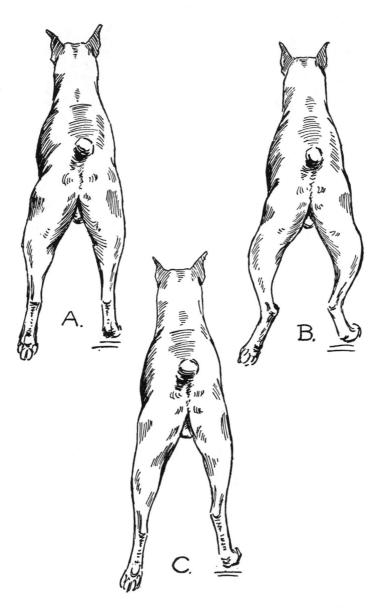

A. Correct Gait. B. Cow Hocks. C. Light Thighs, Stiff Gait.

STANDARD FOR BOXERS

The Board of Directors of The American Kennel Club has approved the following new Standard —January, 1968.

GENERAL APPEARANCE: The Boxer is a medium-sized, sturdy dog, of square build, with short back, strong limbs, and short, tight-fitting coat. His musculation, well developed, should be clean, hard and appear smooth (not bulging) under taut skin. His movements should denote energy. The gait is firm yet elastic (springy), the stride free and ground-covering, the carriage proud and noble. Developed to serve the multiple purposes of guard, working, and escort-dog, he must combine elegance with substance and ample power, not alone for beauty but to insure the speed, dexterity, and jumping ability essential to arduous hike, riding expedition, police or military duty. Only a body whose individual parts are built to withstand the most strenuous efforts, assembled as a complete and harmonious whole, can respond to these combined demands. Therefore, to be at his highest efficiency he must never be plump or heavy and, while equipped for great speed, he must never be racy.

The head imparts to the Boxer a unique individual stamp, peculiar to him alone. It must be in perfect proportion to the body, never small in comparison to the over-all picture. The muzzle is his most distinctive feature, and great value is to be placed on its being of correct form and in absolute proper proportion to the skull.

In judging the Boxer, first consideration should be given to general appearance; next, over-all balance, including the desired proportions of the individual parts of the body to each other, as well as the relation of substance to elegance—to which an attractive color or arresting style may contribute. Special attention is to be devoted to the head, after which the dog's individual components are to be examined for their correct construction and function, and efficiency of gait evaluated.

General Faults: Head not typical, plump bulldoggy appearance, light bone, lack of balance, bad condition, lack of noble bearing.

HEAD:. The beauty of the head depends upon the harmonious proportion of the muzzle to the skull. The muzzle should always appear powerful, never small in its relationship to the skull. The head should be clean, not showing deep wrinkles. Folds will normally appear upon the forehead when the ears are erect, and they are always indicated from the lower edge of the stop running downward on both sides of the muzzle. The dark mask is confined to the muzzle and is in distinct contrast to the color of the head. Any extension of the mask to the skull, other than dark shading around the eyes, creates a sombre, undesirable expression. When white replaces any of the black mask, the path of any upward extension should be between the eyes. The muzzle is powerfully developed in length, width and depth. It is not pointed, narrow, short or shallow. Its shape is influenced first through the formation of both jawbones, second through the placement of the teeth, and third through the texture of the lips.

The Boxer is normally undershot. Therefore, the lower jaw protrudes beyond the upper and curves slightly upward. The upper jaw is broad where attached to the skull and maintains this breadth except for a very slight tapering to the front. The incisor teeth of the lower jaw are in a straight line, the canines preferably up front in the same line to give the jaw the greatest possible width. The line of incisors in the upper jaw is slightly convex toward the front. The upper corner incisors should fit snugly back of the lower canine teeth on each side, reflecting the symmetry essential to the creation of a sound, non-slip bite.

The lips, which complete the formation of the muzzle, should meet evenly. The upper lip is thick and padded, filling out the frontal space created by the projection of the lower jaw. It rests on the edge of

227

the lower lip and, laterally, is supported by the fangs (canines) of the lower jaw. Therefore, these fangs must stand far apart and be of good length so that the front surface of the muzzle is broad and squarish and, when viewed from the side, forms an obtuse angle with the topline of the muzzle. Over-protrusion of the overlip or underlip is undesirable. The chin should be perceptible when viewed from the side as well as from the front without being over-repandous (rising above the bite line) as in the Bulldog. The Boxer must not show teeth or tongue when the mouth is closed. Excessive flews are not desirable.

The top of the skull is slightly arched, not rotund, flat, or noticeably broad, and the occiput not too pronounced. The forehead forms a distinct stop with the topline of the muzzle, which must not be forced back into the forehead like that of a Bulldog. It should not slant down (down-faced), nor should it be dished, although the tip of the nose should lie somewhat higher than the root of the muzzle. The forehead shows just a slight furrow between the eyes. The cheeks, though covering powerful masseter muscles compatible with the strong set of teeth, should be relatively flat and not bulge, maintaining the clean lines of the skull. They taper into the muzzle in a slight, graceful curve. The ears are set at the highest points of the sides of the skull, cut rather long without too broad a shell, and are carried erect. The dark-brown eyes, not too small, protruding or deep-set, and encircled by dark hair, should impart an alert, intelligent expression. Their mood-mirroring quality combined with the mobile skin furrowing of the forehead gives the Boxer head its unique degree of expressiveness. The nose is broad and black, very slightly turned up; the nostrils broad with the naso-labial line running between them down through the upper lip which, however, must not be split.

Faults: Lack of nobility and expression, sombre face, unserviceable bite. Pinscher or Bulldog head, sloping top line of muzzle, muzzle too light for skull, too pointed a bite (snipy). Teeth or tongue showing with mouth closed, driveling, split upper lip. Poor

228

ear carriage, light ("Bird of Prey") eyes.

NECK: Round, of ample length, not too short; strong, muscular and clean throughout without dewlap; distinctly marked nape with an elegant arch running down to the back.
Faults: Dewlap.

BODY: In profile, the build is of square proportions in that a horizontal line from the front of the forechest to the rear projection of the upper thigh should equal a vertical line dropped from the top of the withers to the ground.

CHEST AND FOREQUARTERS: The brisket is deep, reaching down to the elbows; the depth of the body at the lowest point of the brisket equals half the height of the dog at the withers. The ribs, extending far to the rear, are well arched but not barrel-shaped. Chest of fair width and forechest well defined, being easily visible from the side. The loins are short and muscular; the lower stomach line, lightly tucked up, blends into a graceful curve to the rear. The shoulders are long and sloping, close-lying, and not excessively covered with muscle. The upper arm is long, closely approaching a right angle to the shoulder blade. The forelegs, viewed from the front, are straight, stand parallel to each other, and have strong, firmly-joined bones. The elbows should not press too closely to the chest wall or stand off visibly from it. The forearm is straight, long, and firmly muscled. The pastern joint is clearly defined but not distended. The pastern is strong and distinct, slightly slanting, but standing almost perpendicular to the ground. The dewclaws may be removed as a safety precaution. Feet should be compact, turning neither in nor out, with tightly arched toes (cat feet) and tough pads.

Faults: Chest too broad, too shallow or too deep in front, loose or over-muscled shoulders, chest hanging between shoulders, tied-in or bowed-out elbows, turned feet, hare feet, hollow flanks, hanging stomach.

BACK: The withers should be clearly defined as the highest point of the back; the whole back short, straight and muscular with a firm topline.
Faults: Roach back, sway back, thin lean back, long

229

narrow loins, weak union with croup.

HINDQUARTERS: Strongly muscled with angulation in balance with that of forequarters. The thighs broad and curved, the breech musculature hard and strongly developed. Croup slightly sloped, flat and broad. Tail attachment high rather than low. Tail clipped, carried upward. Pelvis long and, in females especially, broad. Upper and lower thigh long, leg well angulated with a clearly defined, well-let-down hock joint. In standing position, the leg below the hock joint (metatarsus) should be practically perpendicular to the ground with a slight rearward slope permissible. Viewed from behind, the hind legs should be straight with the hock joints leaning neither in nor out. The metatarsus should be short, clean and strong, supported by powerful rear pads. The rear toes just a little longer than the front toes, but similar in all other respects.
Dewclaws, if any, may be removed.

Faults: Too rounded, too narrow, or falling off of croup, low-set tail, higher in back than in front; steep, stiff, or too-slightly-angulated hindquarters, light thighs, bowed or crooked legs, cowhocks, over-angulated hock joint (sickle hocks), long metatarsus (high hocks), hare feet, hindquarters too far under or too far behind.

GAIT: Viewed from the side, proper front and rear angulation is manifested in a smoothly-efficient, level-backed, ground-covering stride with powerful drive emanating from a freely operating rear. Although the front legs do not contribute impelling power, adequate "reach" should be evident to prevent interference, overlap or "side-winding" (crabbing). Viewed from the front, the shoulders should remain trim and the elbows not flare out. The legs are parallel until gaiting narrows the track in proportion to increasing speed, then the legs come in under the body but should never cross. The line from the shoulder down through the leg should remain straight, although not necessarily perpendicular to the ground. Viewed from the rear, a Boxer's breech should not roll. The hind feet should "dig in" and track relatively true with the front. Again, as speed increases, the normally broad rear track will become narrower.

Faults: Stilted or inefficient gait, pounding, padding or flailing out of front legs, rolling or waddling gait, tottering hock joints, crossing over or interference—front or rear, lack of smoothness.

HEIGHT: Adult males—22½ to 25 inches: females—21 to 23½ inches at the withers. Males should not go under the minimum nor females over the maximum.

COAT: Short, shiny, lying smooth and tight to the body.

COLOR: The colors are fawn and brindle. Fawn in various shades from light tan to dark deer red or mahogany, the deeper colors preferred. The brindle variety should have clearly-defined black stripes on fawn background. White markings on fawn or brindle dogs are not to be rejected and are often very attractive, but must be limited to one-third of the ground color and are not desirable on the back of the torso proper. On the face, white may replace a part or all of the otherwise essential black mask. However, these white markings should be of such distribution as to enhance and not detract from true Boxer expression.

CHARACTER AND TEMPERAMENT: These are of paramount importance in the Boxer. Instinctively a "hearing" guard dog, his bearing is alert, dignified and self-assured even at rest. In the show ring, his behavior should exhibit constrained animation. With family and friends, his temperament is fundamentally playful, yet patient and stoical with children. Deliberate and wary with strangers, he will exhibit curiosity but, most importantly, fearless courage and tenacity if threatened. However, he responds promptly to friendly overtures when honestly rendered. His intelligence, loyal affection and tractability to discipline make him a highly desirable companion.

Faults: Lack of dignity and alertness, shyness, cowardice, treachery and viciousness (belligerency toward other dogs should not be considered viciousness).

DISQUALIFICATIONS: Boxers with white or black ground color, or entirely white or black, or any color other than fawn or brindle. (White markings, when present, must not exceed one-third of the ground color.)

231

The Boxer in a Nutshell

Look For:	Avoid:
A sturdy, short, square dog.	A leggy, squat, or long loined dog.
Weight of male dogs 60 to 70 pounds; bitches, a few pounds less.	A weedy small dog or an excessively large and gross one.
Slightly arched top-skull, moderately long and narrow.	Skull absolutely flat or much rounded, wide and gross.
Muzzle powerfully developed in length, breadth, and height.	Muzzle pointed or narrow, short or shallow.
Protrusion of lower jaw beyond upper jaw, with slight upward protrusion of lower jaw.	Absolutely vertical truncation of jaws.
Mouth moderately undershot with large, sound teeth. Incisors in even, very slightly curved line, between canines widely spaced.	Even or overshot bite. Crooked, unsound or overshot teeth. Canine teeth close together. Teeth showing when mouth is closed.
Tip of nose slightly higher than base of muzzle.	Top of skull parallel with plane of top-skull, or down-faced.
Distinct but moderate stop between skull and muzzle, with very shallow furrow.	Absence of stop, or bulldog-like indentation.
High set ears, clipped to a point and carried upright.	Low set, flopping ears, carried at side of head.

232

Look For:	Avoid:
Dark eyes with dark rims. Eyes moderate in size, neither small and stingy nor large and protruding.	Light eyes or flesh-colored rims. Overly small or overly large eyes.
Expression of energy and intelligence, neither aggressive nor shy.	Gloomy, threatening, or piercing expression; fierce or cowardly.
Neck long and muscular, crested and clean in throat.	Short, stubby, or concave neck, with dewlap.
Body short, deep and well ribbed back.	Long back, with shallow or narrow thorax.
Back line straight and short from withers to pelvis, with slight backward slope.	Long, sway-back; camel back. Overbuilt.
Long shoulder blades, well laid back to high withers.	Short, upright s h o u l d e r blades.
Heavy boned forearms, straight and dropping perpendicularly from elbows.	Light or shelly bone structure. Forearm bent or bowed.
Small, deep, closely knuckled feet.	Large, sloppy, thin or splayed feet.
Hindquarters with large hams, well bent stifles, and short hocks.	Scrawny, straight hindquarters with long hocks.
Smooth, short coat, lying tight to body.	Rough, staring or ragged coat.
Color, the various shades of fawn to rufous, or rich brindle, with or without white markings, which must not exceed one third of surface. Black mask on muzzle, which may be broken with white marking.	White or black ground color, gray or gray-brindle. Absence of black mask.
Sound, straight forward action, without fanning or weaving.	Action in front too loose or too tight. Cow hocks or bandy legs.
B o l d, confident behavior, without unprovoked aggressiveness.	Viciousness or shyness, sluggishness or lack of style.

Miss Penelope Rae Harris shown with the two Boxers which Frau Phillip Stockmann chose from the Sirrah Crest Kennels, owned by Dr. and Mrs. R. C. Harris, to take back to Germany with her, when she visited the United States in 1949.

On the left is GOODY GOODY OF SIRRAH CREST; on the right, ABRA DABRA OF SIRRAH CREST.

CHAPTER X

Brain and Temperament

REEDING for brains and temperament has been much less consistently carried on among fanciers than breeding for show type. Often it has been completely ignored. In other cases a show and bench type have developed side by side which are almost as different in appearance as different breeds and are of quite distinct bloodlines. This has happened in many if not most of the so-called working breeds. Originally bred for use, these breeds were selected in pre-show days almost wholly on the basis of performance. The pups of an exceptional worker were in demand, regardless of their appearance. But when a breed began to be shown and to acquire popularity in the ring the pendulum generally swung to the other extreme. No matter how carefully the standard might be drawn up with a view to perpetuating working characteristics, show wins and championships soon became the principal aim of nearly all breeders. And for the most part there was little opportunity to correct this mistake by a corresponding test of working qualities. Efforts were made in Germany before the War, when it was declared that all champions must have passed at least the most elementary training test in order to obtain the title. Later, for at least some breeds, it was ordained that one, and later both parents should have passed such a test before a litter could be registered. In this country, however, training was much less frequent and no such regimentation of dog clubs and fanciers as obtained under Hitler has ever been maintained. Some breeds have suffered severely from the emphasis on show type at the expense of brains. A partial corrective is to be found in the Obedience training and tests developed in the last dozen years, but to be truly effective this work must be greatly extended.

The value of breeding from trained stock lies not in any direct effect upon the puppies but in the check provided regarding the quality of the parents. Similarly, dairy herds are tested for production. No one believes that the calf of a tested cow will give more milk because her dam was tested, but by breeding only from tested parents a positive check is provided which is not a matter of opinion. In like manner the puppies of trained parents will be no more intelligent than if those same parents were untrained. However, if only trained stock is used for breeding a certain level of intelligence is automatically maintained. Any dog or bitch which lacks the intelligence to take training is discarded.

The Boxer has been lucky in several respects. First, the breed standard set for the show ring is favorable to the preservation of intelligence. While the size of the skull which contains the brain is not proportional to intelligence, the weight of the brain itself does have a fairly direct bearing. Consequently, the brain must have adequate space in which to grow and develop. A breed standard which calls for an extremely long, narrow skull will sooner or later have an unfavorable effect upon a breed's intelligence. The Boxer standard calls for a good width of skull and a brain case which could allow for plenty of development. Not every breed has been so fortunate.

The old-time Bullenbeisser was prized for his intelligence and the ease with which he could be trained. These qualities continued to be valued after he ceased to be bred at court for hunting. They were part of the inheritance of the Boxer when he developed into his modern form.

Finally, the breed today is the result of strong inbreeding and line-breeding to a few individuals of exceptional quality. The München strain, which eventually absorbed all others, was primarily house dogs fifty to sixty years ago. So far as showing was concerned the breed was still in its infancy.

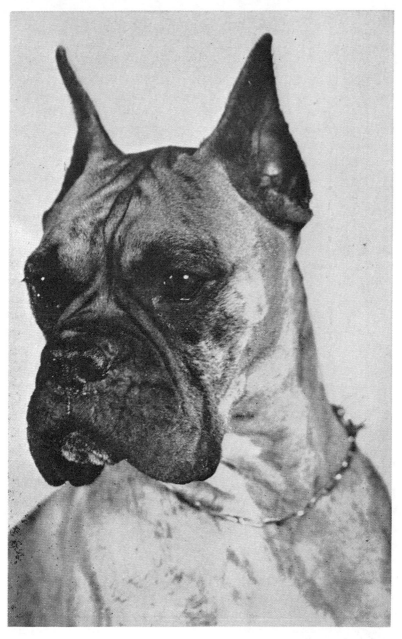

CH. COUNTRY GIRL OF TRECEDER
Sire: Ch. Mahderf's El Chico.   Dam: Rosanna von Neuffen
Owner: Mrs. H. C. Stewart, Treceder Kennels, Bryan, Texas

No one could foresee that from this little group would descend thousands of Boxers who would make the breed one of the leaders in a country thousands of miles from their native Germany. But the personalities of those foundation dogs and bitches—Meta v.d. Passage, Mirzl, Flock St. Salvator, Wotan and Bosco Immergrun—were well known. They spent their lives in a small community where dogs were important and the outstanding ones were remembered. Stories of their intelligence, character and virtues became legendary and were remembered and retold forty or more years later. With due allowance for exaggeration, they bequeathed their descendants an invaluable heritage of brains and character.

This inheritance was concentrated a few generations later in the great Ch. Rolf v. Vogelsberg Sch. H. Rolf, who appears repeatedly at the back of all modern pedigrees, was not only a great show dog and sire but a trained worker as well. He won first in competition for working dogs and served all through the first World War, returning home at the age of eleven to win his fifth Sieger title. And he handed down to his get his brains as well as his show qualities.

When attempts were first made to have the Boxer recognized in Germany as a breed suitable for police work they met with determined opposition from the breeds already established in this field. Despite the excellent service rendered by Boxers during the War it was not until 1925 that they were officially classified as police dogs. At least as early as 1926 Boxers were in service in Germany as blind guides. While few trained dogs seem to have reached America, a number of successful show dogs and sires attained training degrees. Among them may be mentioned Sieger Alex v.d. Magdalenenquelle P.H., Ch. Egon v. Gumbertusbrunnen P.H., Austrian and Swiss Sieger Buko v. Biederstein Sch. H., Siegerin Cora v. Tredintafu P.H., Ch. Rolf Walhall P.H., all of whom have American descendants.

In this country Boxer fanciers were rather slow in taking up Obedience training, but recently there has been a great advance. The first Boxer awarded a C.D. was Indra se Sumbula owned by C. Kenneth Quinn, on June 10, 1939. The first to win the more advanced degree of C.D.X. was Coquet v.d.

Stuttgarter, owned by Mr. and Mrs. Glenn W. Studebaker, on September 9, 1939. The following year Harry of Hinshenfelde, owned by J. A. Brownell, won the first U.D.

Up to the end of 1947 Boxers had won 85 C.D. titles, of which 38 were granted during the year 1947 alone. Three out of 15 C.D.X. and one out of four U.D. titles were acquired during the same year. Among the Obedience winners are several bench champions. Ch. Christl of Kernia is a U.D. The outstanding American-bred sire Sir Galahad of Bladan made his C.D. in 1940, the same year in which he completed his championship. Others are: Ch. Ode of Mazelaine C.D., Ch. Beatrix v. Jansu C.D., Ch. Blason Dell-Ray C.D., Ch. Chriss of Treceder C.D., Ch. Heigh Ho As You Were C.D., Ch. Heigh Ho Carry On C.D., Ch. High Spot Trigger C.D., Ch. Sir Royal of Bladan C.D. and Ch. Officer of Tulgey Wood C.D.X. Ch. Dauber's Debutante C.D. and Ch. Clinaude's O'Flap Jack C.D. both finished their championships in 1947, making a total of thirteen. Whirlaway of Mazelaine C.D., sire of Ch. Apollo of San Joaquin, deserves mention also, though he died without finishing his title. It is interesting to observe that there are two pairs of litter-mates on the list— Sir Galahad and Sir Royal of Bladan, and Heigh Ho As You Were and Heigh Ho Carry On. Ch. Dauber of Tulgey Wood has the distinction of being the only Boxer sire credited with three champions who are also Obedience title holders. Dauber's sire, Lustig, also has two to his credit, indicating that this line combines show type and temperament to a high degree.

The growing interest in Obedience training and tests is clearly shown by the fact that while in 1945 Boxers received only 10 degrees, in 1947 they received 42. This places them sixth on the list of all breeds for the year and only two behind the poodles.

As early as 1941 the specialty show held by the New England Boxer Club at Great Barrington, Mass. on August 29th had Obedience classes with a total of thirteen entries. A special tracking exhibition was given at this time by Harry of Hinshenfelde U.D. and Ch. Christl of Kernia U.D. This show, with 101 Boxers entered, was the first separate specialty. The Pacific Coast Boxer Club claims to be the first club in America to sponsor an all-Boxer training class, under the leadership of Carl Spitz. The Mid-West Boxer Club has also promoted Obedience work. And in August, 1945, the Maine Boxer Club opened an Obedience Training Class at Scarboro with ten members.

On February 9, 1947, Obedience Trials judged by Jack Baird were held in connection with the fourth annual specialty show of the American Boxer Club. Mrs. Evelyn S. Rawcliffe's Alma of Skole Gate, U.D. made a perfect score in the Utility class and 249½ in Open B. The combined scores of 449½ in these two classes were the highest ever made in an Obedience class in this country by any breed.

In March, 1947, the Metropolitan New York Boxer Training Club was established under the direction of Ed Schachte, and by the end of the year five Boxers in the New York area had already earned C.D. degrees.

During the late war a comparatively small number of Boxers was accepted by Dogs for Defense and utilized by the armed services. Those which were made available generally performed very well indeed, but their number should have been far greater. The slowness with which Obedience work took hold is unquestionably responsible to a large extent and the progress made during the past couple of years, had it occurred earlier, would undoubtedly have made a difference. Among those who did serve was Rudy, owned by Mr. J. Howard Davis of Bakersfield, Calif. Rudy served as a sentry and guard dog at the Sierra Ordnance Depot for a year and a half and was highly praised for his work there. Other Boxers served in the Canal Zone and on the Eastern seaboard. Owing to the fact that the Dogs for Defense records are filed under the owner's name and not by breeds it has proved impossible to obtain full information concerning the Boxer's war service.

Thousands of Boxers are said to have been used by Germans for guards, patrols, messengers, wire stringers and in rescue work. In 1945 an American soldier severely wounded behind the German lines near Anzio, wrote to the editor of *Dog News* that his life had been saved by a fawn Boxer with the Red Cross insignia on his saddle. After discovering the soldier, the

240

dog dashed away and returned two hours later with stretcher bearers. It was a three hour trip out of the mountains, and the Germans reported that this Boxer had done rescue work in every area where the Germans had fought and saved the lives of over a hundred wounded.

Boxers have done well in Seeing Eye work and a considerable number are in service. The story of a Seeing Eye Boxer appeared in the *Elks' Magazine* for April, 1946. The best known Seeing Eye Boxer, however, is undoubtedly Wizard, owned by Hector Chevigny of New York City. Bravenhartz The Wizard is royally bred, by Ch. Kniff v.d. Blutenau out of Ch. Mazelaine Miranda, and is a litter brother to Ch. Meritaire's Bravenhartz Wish. He figures prominently in "My Eyes have a Cold Nose," a very stimulating and thought-provoking account of Mr. Chevigny's experiences when he lost his sight. In reply to a request for Wizard's picture his owner wrote, "Wiz's attitude toward most of the show dogs has been, I fear, that of the practical business man for the leisure class, and at times this has led to an exchange of canine remarks on the street which I would do better not to repeat. But I'm sure he would be secretly pleased to have his picture in the book." Having appeared in the pages of *Fortune* and the *Reader's Digest,* Wizard is unquestionably known to a large public which never attends dog shows. Another Seeing Eye Boxer, owned by Milton Jacobs of Brooklyn, had his photograph in *Picture Parade* of September 16, 1945. Breeders with intelligent young stock to dispose of should bear in mind the outstanding success of Boxers in Seeing Eye work. The demand for suitable dogs is likely to increase rather than diminish in the future, since replacements are required at intervals of eight or ten years in addition to new requirements.

Here is Mr. Chevigny's description of his "eyes". "We attract a great deal of attention when we are together, but Wizard is a ham and loves it. He weighs a little over eighty pounds, has a sort of brindle coat—they tell me—and a curiously black, wrinkled face, and when he walks with me he has a habit of keeping his tongue lolled out and exposing his bull-dog teeth in a way that quickly clears the path for us. His ferocious

Mr. HECTOR CHEVIGNY and his Seeing Eye Dog—
BRAVENHARTZ THE WIZARD

appearance belies his character, though. I have never heard him bark. He is a sensitive creature, susceptible to moods, and I have to be careful to be bright and cheerful with him or he gets worried about me. When *he* isn't cheerful I worry about *him,* so between us we do a great deal of worrying and are well matched. While we were training at Seeing Eye, Wizard had a brief period of illness during which I worked with another dog—a German Shepherd bitch—who was much cleverer than Wizard but who, I am sure, would never have understood me. For they have an apt phrase at Seeing Eye: the dog doesn't belong to you, you belong to the dog."

The great majority of dogs which served during the war were trained as sentry dogs. Out of a total of 10,452 assigned to service 9,298 were sentry dogs, 595 were scouts, 268 sledge and pack dogs, 151 messengers and 140 mine detectors. It is therefore likely that most if not all the Boxers served as sentry dogs. Thomas Young's *Dogs for Democracy,* published in 1944, mentions that "a Boxer on sentry duty near a defense plant in Boston attacked and caught a saboteur carrying complete plans for the plant's destruction," but he does not mention the name of the alert guardian. Doubtless military secrecy forbade identification at that date.

I have not come across any record of the use of Boxers on active service. However, a War Department report states that short-haired dogs are considered undesirable for jungle warfare and probably for any use in the tropics (although Dobermans were used considerably by the Marines in the Pacific). Hence it is probable that few if any Boxers were sent to the Pacific.

Two Boxers, "Porky" and "Tina," owned in New Jersey, appeared on the cover of *Life* magazine for November 17, 1947. They had the distinction of being photographed by Ylla, the fashionable New York canine photographer, at the request of a lady whose pet collie's life they had saved. Further information about this incident has not been forthcoming.

Alfred Putnam of Puttenham Kennels
with Ch. Puttenham's Brigadier and Ch. Puttenham's Bandmaster

CHAPTER XI

Boxer Character

By Alfred Putnam

THE real reason why most of us own a Boxer is because he is what he is and not because he looks like what he ought to be. So, let's check over some of the characteristics to which he can properly lay claim. He is kind to Aunt Minnie. He won't put his paw on the face of a sleeping baby. His idea of a proper comfort station is out-doors. A tree is more aesthetically satisfying to him than the Oriental rug grandpa gave you for a wedding present. Unlike a hound, he doesn't roll in horrible and smelly things that he may find in the woods. He doesn't yap like a Poodle or a Dachshund. Nor does he gather burrs and a miscellaneous collection of filth like the long haired dogs. He doesn't have to have his own special edition of Charles of the Ritz to barber him. If you don't feel like giving him a bath it doesn't seem to make much difference because he washes himself like a cat. He pays small attention to the passing of years, retaining many puppy traits until the day he dies: he can be fascinated by a ball, by anything that makes a queer noise, and takes genuine delight in being pushed, mauled, or good humoredly teased. He never loses his temper, but on the contrary likes people best who have also retained enough childishness to temper their maturity. But, on the other hand, the Boxer acquires dignity at an early age. If he has torn up one cushion and been admonished, the chances are that he won't tear up another one. If his master is the tired business man type who wants to go to sleep over his newspaper, the Boxer, young or

245

old, decides that an outstretched foot is the best pillow ever manufactured and tears off a long winter's nap with gusto. Of course, you get out of any dog what you put in him, but it is safe to say that if you want a Boxer to be a watch dog, he will be; if for some strange, thoroughly unsound reason, anyone wants him to be a fighting dog, he will be; and if, being sensible, you don't want him to fight, he won't. He isn't like a Terrier; he won't bite before he thinks. But when he has made up his mind that the thing to do is to defend, it is very doubtful whether he has any superior. And here is a funny thing; he can talk. I don't mean that he can speak the English language or that he can articulate in exactly the same way that human beings do. But anyone who has ever owned a Boxer for any length of time certainly can carry on a conversation with him. That's ridiculously easy. The majority of readers will understand this and agree with it. The ones who don't understand it and agree with it ought to swap their Boxers in for Staffordshire and Crown Derby dogs and put them on the mantlepiece. Conversing with dogs has always interested me. I have no trouble with Boxers or Weimaraners and I have been on a good heart to heart conversational basis with a Keeshond, with several smooth haired Fox Terriers, and with a Collie. But I haven't the slightest idea of how to talk to a Doberman, a Shepherd, a Bull Terrier, or a Bull Dog, and I am not sure that I want to learn. Some dogs, like Spaniels, have a conversation all their own, but most of it consists of just one word which is "gimme". The Boxer, certainly the most fluent, can tell you all sorts of things. He is sorry for you if you are sad. He is delighted with you when you are gay. He knows hours in advance when you are going away and if you start to pack a bag he says very plainly that it is an offensive pastime as far as he is concerned. With no more than a lift of his eyebrow he can tell you that it is time for his lamp post duty or that he is annoyed because supper isn't ready. And if he thinks it is time you pulled yourself together and took a little more notice of man's best friend, which he undoubtedly is, he can do various things that tell you so, much more plainly than humans talk together.

A few years ago I read in one of the sporting magazines that

CH. SALGRAY'S FASHION PLATE

Sire: Ch. Salgray's Battle Chief
Dam: Ch. Marquam Hill's Flamingo

Bred and owned by Mr. and Mrs. Daniel M. Hamilburg

the Boxer had been used for bear hunting. I don't know whether it is true or not. But I know that he would try. Several people have used him for duck hunting.   Perhaps a Chesapeake Retriever could teach him a lot about how to bring back a bird from the water; and I feel perfectly certain that the Boxer would listen to the Chesapeake. But if there isn't any canine professor around he will go after the birds on his own hook. Puttenham's Amaranth, an Utz daughter, was used successfully in Utah by Sam Rudd for pheasant hunting. Sam's best bird dog had an accident just before the three day pheasant season opened and Amaranth was used as a pinch hitter. Sam got his limit every day. He said Amaranth went up a little too close. No, she didn't point. But using the powers of conversation and pantomime she somehow or other conveyed to Sam where the birds were. The late Pete Widener, Shepherd judge, told me a year or so ago that a Boxer had won a Field Trial. The competition was probably strictly fourth class. The point is that the Boxer was in there pitching. He will try anything—obedience work, war work, guard work, or leading the blind. There is some dispute as to whether the Shepherd or the Boxer was the first dog used by blind people. When I asked the Seeing Eye about this they said that they had used the Shepherd first but that they had had fine success with Boxers. Frau Friederun Stockmann, owner of the Von Dom Kennels, which possesses the fancy address of Reichschmitt, Post: Pleiskirchen uber Muhldorf, Oberbayern, wrote to me in 1946 and said that "As far as I know the Boxer has been used as a guide for the blind for a long time. In our records the Boxer has been shown as such since 1926. Since the year 1914 the Boxer has been found as a service dog and probably as a guide for the blind, too." It doesn't make much difference which breed did this magnificent work first. I am only trying to show that the Boxer will bend his brains and his back to anything that is remotely within reason. You can ask him to be serious and solemn and he will try his best to act like The Gloomy Dean. But if you want the funny papers to come to life he will raise pluperfect cane with a rubber bone, or play hunt the slipper, or chase a grasshopper, just to please you. The end of his existence is, in

CH. DEMPSEY'S COPPER GENTLEMAN

Sire: Ch. Jered's Spellbinder
Dam: Fontana's Crimson Mist

Breeder: Robert Dempsey
Owners: Don and Mary Smith

point of fact, to please. He isn't a sulker and, unlike the Dalmatian, isn't ordinarily a one man dog, that annoying canine snob who picks out one person as the object of his affections and turns up his nose at society in general. But don't kid yourself that the Boxer loves everybody that walks on two legs instead of four. As an example, my five and a half year old house dog, who rejoices in the name of Zilch, who has faults enough to fill an encyclopedia, and who I wouldn't sell for any amount of money, is as soft hearted as a bowl of mush. Once a year I talk to a boys' school about dogs and last week was my annual appointment and I turned Zilch loose among 270 boys. His hind end made a bowl of jelly look like a fixed and immovable object and if he didn't apply his large red tongue to every one of 270 shining school-boy faces, my bet is that it was 269. Yet during the war we had a new maid at our house and, although Zilch had been properly introduced, he would have none of her and he actually growled deep in his stomach, seeming perfectly willing to carve a piece out of her leg. I was amazed. But two days later this creature left without notice and stole every gasoline rationing stamp in the house. You can't tell me Zilch didn't know what kind of a person she was.

All of us know the dumb questions that inexperienced puppy buyers ask. How do you housebreak a Boxer? Will a Boxer run away? Lots of people won't believe you when you tell them that the answer to the first question is to let the puppy out often enough for a short period of time and simply tell him that you prefer to have him go out for certain necessities rather than stay in, and that the answer to the second question is that the Boxer won't run away if, this provided he has some maturity, you take him around your place several times, explaining the limits, and tell him where he can go and where he can't go. It has been my experience that most Boxers learn these simple lessons by just that method. I think that in training a Boxer, tone of voice is far more important than a slap. People who beat dogs ought to be chloroformed anyhow.

I go to many shows and expect to continue the practice as long as I live. At the show ring I am entirely susceptible to the epidemic of criticism that flourishes for a day. I saw a ten months old puppy at a show recently that I don't think I will ever forget. He was about as close to perfection as I have ever seen a Boxer of his age and if he doesn't coarsen he will be a stand out. I saw a beautiful brindle bitch at another show. She made the show worth seeing all by herself. Some of the Specials that I have seen before impress me each time I see them and comparing the entries point for point always has a definite fascination. But when I get home, although I am proud indeed to own two champions that were bred at Puttenham, I must confess that Zilch, who never won a point in his life, seems to be The Best Boxer in Existence. As I have said, you own a Boxer for what he is and not because he looks what he ought to be.

Alfred Putnam

May 4, 1948.

CH. BARON TREVOR OF TREDEGAR
Sire: Ch. Mahderf's El Chico
Dam: Queen of Bethlehem
Breeder: Sally Morrissey, Chester, N. Y.
Owner: Keith Merrill, Herndon, Virginia

THREE PUPPIES FROM A LITTER OF SIX
Sired by Ch. Barmere's Trouble Shooter
ex Ch. Grand Romance of Barmere
Whelped February 2, 1952   Photograph taken at eight weeks

CHAPTER XII

Boxer Breeding

IT is generally agreed that like begets like. This belief has a measure of truth but it is not to be taken literally. The more uniform the inheritance of two individuals, the more likely they are to resemble each other, but even litter brothers and sisters carry such a variety of chromosomes that they may be completely unlike each other. While it is of course true that the mating of two Boxers will not produce a whippet, for instance, within the range of a given breed the results are sometimes unexpected. Recessive characteristics, which do not appear on the surface, may be carried unseen for generations, only to reappear when the same or supplementary factors are combined from both sides of a mating. Not only may two brindles produce fawns, but two champions may on occasion produce quite atypical puppies. In like manner, two rather ordinary individuals may have puppies much better than either parent. There is a definite tendency for the progeny of any mating with a given breed to fluctuate about an average. There is a regular distribution curb, with the largest number at the middle, some toward the higher limit and some toward the lower. If the parents are average, the puppies are likely to be of about the same quality, for they tend to approach the average in any case. If the parents are below average, the puppies still tend to resemble the average for the breed and strain. Consequently they may be better than their parents. If the parents are unusually good individuals, it is quite likely that none of the puppies will be as good, since they still tend to approach the normal average in a majority of cases. However, by careful selection and line breeding the average for a given strain can be raised above the average for the breed as a whole.

So many interacting factors go into the makeup of any dog that it is impossible to select for all desired characteristics at once. While a breeder is concentrating on color or feet or jaws or some other point, another group of faults appears. There is consequently a tendency to breed to the best individuals available and trust to luck, instead of attempting to work out the exact transmission of characteristics in detail. To breed champion to champion regardless of type or bloodlines is a gamble which may lead to many disappointments. The dog and bitch should be suitable as individuals. Do not mate two extremes, expecting to obtain results somewhere between the two. It is, for instance, better to mate a medium or small bitch to a dog of correct size and substance, not to the biggest stud available. Avoid the mating of a dog and bitch with the same faults, especially if they are faults which commonly occur in the near ancestors or collateral relations of both. Inbreeding is a valuable tool, since it tends to fix the type, but inbreeding to a common fault will fix the fault just as quickly as the desired characteristics.

There have been many different theories of breeding. Often they are derived from a lack of knowledge of the way characteristics are transmitted and from a desire for some short cut or rule of thumb which would infallibly produce the results wanted. Before the chromosome theory was worked out no one understood the reasons for many of the results which are clear today, and even now there are still gaps in our knowledge.

One of the early theories was that a dog derived half of his inheritance from his parents (25% from each), half of the remainder from his grandparents (6.25% from each), etc. The great grandparents would each contribute 1.5625%, the fourth generation .390625% and the fifth generation .09765625%. The chromosome theory nullifies this belief. A dominant characteristic can be completely bred out in one generation if the chromosome make-ups of the mating pair

254

are known. A character is either present or not present and has nothing to do with the percentage of the "blood" of any individual which appears in a pedigree. However, it remains true that the influence exerted by any single dog in the pedigree becomes very rapidly less, unless it is heavily reinforced by inbreeding or linebreeding. A dog which traces repeatedly to a notable producer within three or four or five generations is much more likely to carry chromosomes derived from him than from an ancestor appearing only once over a like period.

A study of the pedigrees of Boxer champions over a period of years indicates that the majority of breeders do not apply the knowledge of scientific principle which is available. Out of nearly 8,000 puppies registered during 1946, only .333% (one out of three hundred) came from matings in which both parents were champions, yet in the past 2% of champion Boxers have had both parents champions. This is about six times as many champions as should be produced by chance alone. However, it is well to bear in mind that the parents of some of these puppies may still finish their titles, so that a survey five or ten years from now should show a somewhat larger proportion of puppies belonging to the group with both parents champions. The same is true for the groups of puppies with champion dams (2% of the year's registrations) and champion sires (31% of the year's registrations). Some of them will eventually be transferred to the two-champion group, while some from the 67% of matings with neither parent champions will eventually transfer to one of the other three groups. Hence, this largest group will certainly become somewhat smaller in the course of time.

A very interesting study, if it could be made, would be a comparison of the matings at the time they were actually made, with the results after ten or fifteen years. To do this would, however, involve either a long wait or an exhaustive amount of checking back to discover the champion status at the time of mating the parents of dogs which have already finished their titles. It would certainly be of value, however, to know how many matings of champions made before the parents finished, resulted in champion get, as compared

255

to the general run of non-champion matings. For only 2% of earlier champions came from non-champion parents and this is a poor outlook for the 67% of puppies whelped from sires and dames neither of whom is a champion.

A recent analysis of Boston Terrier pedigrees (*The Mathematics of Breeding*, by Robert Schelling, in *Gaines Dog Research Progress, Winter 1946-47*) states that during the last twenty years 401 Boston males made championships in the United States, yet only 82 of them ever sired a champion. It was found that of these 82 champion sires 64 had pedigrees which contained at least 12 individuals out of the 30 ancestors in a four-generation pedigree who had produced champions, even though they were not champions themselves. Out of the 82 there were 11 male champions who had less than the required number of producers in their first four generations, but in these cases the bitches to which they were mated carried well over the minimum. Only seven of the 82 male champions produced a champion where the potential producing power of both sire and dam was definitely below the minimum of 12.

In breeding for champions by this formula Mr. Schelling recommends at least 15 out of 30 champion producers in four generations of a given mating, and at least 60 champions produced by them as a total. He cites, apparently as a typical example, a stud with 18 champion producers out of the 30 ancestors in four generations, the said 18 producing a total of 78 champions. This gives what he calls a producing index of 60%-78.

When attempting to apply this formula to Boxers it quickly becomes apparent that the situation is somewhat different. Under the German system of awarding Sieger titles there were many less titles granted each year than in the United States. Moreover, complete records as to title winners are not available. Hence, when a four generation pedigree goes back to imported stock the record is likely to be incomplete. Then the Big Four—Sigurd, Dorian, Lustig, and Utz—have so many champions to their credit that the figures are at once thrown out of balance. Crediting Sigurd, for instance, with only the 55 dogs and bitches sired by him which made American championships, any dog or bitch who has Sigurd within four generations will at once receive a credit of 55. Every appearance of Dorian gives 63, of Lustig 67 and of Utz 51. A rough check of eight of the outstanding sires and winners among American-breds of the past few years gives results which vary from 12 to 19 in the number of champions appearing in four generations, and from 321 to 481 in the total of points assigned for producers of champions. This is from four to seven times the 78 points assigned by Mr. Schelling to the Boston with 18 champions. And in a few cases imported dogs may not have been credited with all the points to which they were properly entitled. The results of this tabulation are as follows:

Ch. Yobang of Sirrah Crest	15 chs.	481 points
Ch. Schoolmaster of Mazelaine	17 chs.	480 points
Ch. Archduke of Valcar	14 chs.	426 points
Ch. Warlord of Mazelaine	13 chs.	420 points
Ch. Apollo of San Joaquin	18 chs.	400 points
Ch. Dauber of Tulgey Wood	11 chs.	397 points
Ch. Sir Galahad of Bladan	16 chs.	366 points
Ch. Mahderf's El Chico	13 chs.	321 points

How useful this type of tabulation may prove to be I do not know. It gives equal value to all the individuals in a litter until they have actually proved themselves as breeders. Even then the point rating would be only five points higher for the sire of five champions than it would be for his litter brother who had sired nothing. Yet any breeder knows that litter brothers may vary enormously in their success at stud. It also seems to me to allow too little credit to the parents of non-champion producers. Sigurd's dam, for instance, rates only one point so far as I can discover, and Kavalier of Mazelaine, sire of ten producers and grandsire of both Schoolmaster and Apollo, receives no points at all. Also, Sigurd or Dorian in the fourth generation gives as high credit as in the first, although the influence exerted would certainly be much less. By way of contrast to the foregoing dogs I checked the pedigree of a 1947 champion selected because he had only one champion in the first two generations. This dog nevertheless shows 11 champions in four generations and a total of 306 points, even though the bottom quarter of his pedigree has no champions at all for the entire four generations.

Such formulas as the above may be useful as a general guide but it appears that the selection of a mating pair which are suited in type, are both of high quality, and carry enough common ancestors to carry on line breeding remains the method most likely to be successful.

If I were starting a Boxer kennel and economy was not a prime necessity I would purchase several of the best bitches available. They should be not only individuals of quality but should be as near as possible to my idea of the ideal type and resemble each other as closely as possible. Then I should select the most suitable stud I could find and breed to him. Starting in this way, with stock as uniform as possible in type and breeding, and mated to the most suitable dog I could find, I should hope to build a strain which would soon become recognizable. I should breed as many litters as I could care for adequately, and cull them rigorously, retaining only the best for future breeding operations. And I hope I should never breed to a stud, regardless of his show reputation, who was not suitable in type and breeding for my particular bitches. And never, never, choose a stud because he belonged to my own kennel or was more conveniently located than some dog which I knew was actually better. And having established my type by careful selection I should endeavor to retain it by careful inbreeding. Also, most important of all, I should never breed a really shy or nervous animal, no matter how good its physical qualities. For once acquired, shyness is one of the most difficult faults to eliminate. The Boxer's typical breed disposition combines great intelligence with the sweetness of temperament and amenability which are found in practically all the breeds of the bulldog family. This is a tremendous asset and one of the best guarantees of continued popularity. It should be valued accordingly and retained at all costs.

CHAPTER XIII
Boxers in Vaudeville

Reprinted from *American Kennel Gazette,* January, 1950
By Albert W. Seaman

THERE was a vaudeville act of basketball-playing Boxers appearing at a local theater last month.

The act is owned and trained by one Rudy Docky, a native of Kitzbuhel, Austria. Mr. Docky is 37 years old and single. He has been an acrobatic comedian and clown for most of his early life, having played in just about all of the principal cities in Europe and South America.

During the recent war, he served with the United States Army in Germany and Austria, and it was on the basis of his military service that he migrated to the United States and became a citizen of our country. Like most owners of Boxers, he is a "real gone guy on the breed." In Europe, he had an act of soccer-playing Boxers. When he decided to come to the United States, he realized that soccer was not a popular game here so he sold the act and decided he would start a new one upon arrival in America.

He witnessed a few basketball games, observed the spectators' enthusiasm and frenzy and decided basketball was the game for his Boxers. He organized his act by first purchasing in Seattle, Wash., Carlo von Dom, an Austrian import, brought over by a U. S. Army major. Rudy added to his string from time to time, and now has a troupe of 14 Boxers. All he could say pertaining to their pedigrees was that most of his Boxers are of Mazelaine bloodlines. He stated that he knew the breed as a fancier in Europe and that he tried to choose Boxers of good type.

Docky said he could take any Boxer between the ages of six months and two years and train him for his act. Also, that he personally found that a Boxer reaches maturity between two and two and one-half years of age. After he assembled his cast, he trained them every day for one year, then he was ready for the road.

Last year, during the spring, summer, and fall months, he played 35 weeks for Polack Brothers, Shrine Circus; during the winter months, he played vaudeville and estimated the act traveled at least 80,000 miles in two years' time. He found the Boxer a real trouper, unbothered by climatic changes. He alleges that if a Boxer "goes off his feed" for a week, the dog will show a willingness for work and give a good performance. He believes that the Boxer should be kept busy because he is a substantial, energetic dog who likes and endures lots of action.

Rudy chose Boxers because to him they possess the greatest intelligence in dogs. He feels so strongly about it that he claims other breeds do not possess one per cent of Boxer intelligence. Wow!

Rudy starts the act when he comes tumbling out onto the stage to the accompaniment of a blaring, blasting musical fanfare. After performing a variety of somersaults, spins, turns, etc., he blows a policeman's, or referee's whistle and from both sides of the stage on come the players, five on a team, dressed in appropriate colors. Rudy takes a blown-up balloon from a cluster which is suspended from the ceiling, blows the whistle, tosses the balloon into the players' midst and they butt or paw the ball toward the baskets which stand at either end of the stage about four feet off the floor. The game is closely contested and play moves back and forth across the stage. Needless to say, quite a few of the balloons are broken but each time Rudy tosses in a new one.

When I asked Rudy whether he taught the dogs zone, or man to man, defense and if he believed that the small Boxer in basketball was a thing of the past, he registered a complete blank.

Play continues until a basket is made, whereupon the game ends. Rudy reaches up for the cluster of blown-up balloons, pulls them down to floor level and the ten Boxers jump all over

260

Rudy to get at the balloons and amid the noise of the bursting balloons, the curtain comes down and the act is over. At curtain call, they all line up and Rudy takes a bow. You say, "So what?" Ah, but there is more than meets the eye! Not once during the hotly contested game did any of the performers register any mean temper toward his playmates.

Rudy says that in his circus experience, lions and tigers will fight and claw each other to death over greed or jealousy and that a wrought-up Boxer will fight with an intensity which makes lions and tigers, kittens. The trick of the act is to train the Boxers to forget their possessive instinct and to teach them to live, play, and work together. Almost sounds like "one-world" philosophy! Rudy was quick to add that he believes the Boxer is the best kid's dog in the world, has good judgment, and sense which is unequaled in other breeds. He told me that his dogs show him things which he has never taught them. For instance, if an armed man comes within their midst, the dogs will lay back their ears, sniff out the concealed gun and indicate where it is on the person.

When Rudy exercised the dogs, between acts, on a vacant lot adjacent to the theater, the older dogs corralled the younger pups traveling with the troupe, to keep them from going on the sidewalk, curb, and road. When a strange dog came sauntering down the street, the older ones corralled the younger ones and turned, standing at attention toward the intruder. Something must have been communicated between the Boxers and the intruder, for the outsider made a wide berth around them and went about his business. I personally witnessed this display.

For the breeders reading this: Rudy has bred and raised four litters on the road. I asked how he disposed of the pups and he said that he gave most of them to his Shrine friends. Incidentally, when the girls in the group become indisposed, substitutes take their places in the line-up.

In a seven-act bill, Rudy's act rates the last spot, which I understand is top billing. I asked Rudy what he thought of vaudeville's chances for a comeback and he dismally answered, "No good—there are no performers today. Everything is sing and tap." I guess he could sum up by saying vaudeville suffers from "hoof-and-mouth disease."

FLIP OF BEROLINA
Sire: Lucky of Marienhof (by Int. Ch. Lustig v. Dom)
Breeder and Owner: Mr. and Mrs. Herbert A. Brauer, Berolina Kennels

CHAPTER XIV

Ear Cropping

THE cropping of ears is a delicate subject and I realize that by giving instructions to the novice, I am treading on dangerous ground. It may cause the displeasure of veterinarians who find this operation a lucrative addition to their profession. Also there are states that have laws governing ear cropping. In some cities the S. P. C. A. has demanded a health certificate at dog shows. Therefore, the amateur breeder may find that he will run into difficulties when exhibiting his dog.

Like most of our laws, the law governing ear cropping has loopholes. It was pushed through the State Legislature but at the same time, a clause was included which in substance states that in the case of a dog whose ears have become badly lacerated or ulcerated, if removal of a large portion of the flap should be necessary to promote healing, and if this operation was performed by a licensed veterinarian, it would be considered necessary to the dog's health to crop his ears. In my opinion, the only occasion where cropping would be required would be in the case of a dog fight where one of the animals received a rip or tear of the ear, that refused to heal.

It has been the custom in states where anti-cropping laws exist for veterinarians to give a health certificate certifying that ear cropping was necessary on account of a dog's health and armed with such a certificate, exhibitors will not experience embarrassment at a dog show.

However, it has been my personal experience that although

263

New York and Pennsylvania have ear cropping laws, no demand for a certificate has ever been made at the larger shows such as New York City or Philadelphia, although there are smaller shows in towns like Pittsburgh where the S. P. C. A. has been more active and health certificates have been demanded.

While I feel that the majority of the readers of this book will be one-dog owners who may breed an occasional litter, and from lack of experience would consider no other procedure than to take their dog to the veterinarian for ear and tail cropping, I do feel that a chapter of instructions on cropping forms an important part of this book inasmuch as there are also many who intend to turn out several litters a year.

As it is almost impossible to sell an uncropped puppy except at a very early age, if you intend to enter upon an extensive breeding program, the amount of money spent for veterinarian fees will wipe out practically all the profits from breeding. The average price up until recently has been $10.00 for each dog cropped but it is my understanding that this rate has been doubled.

While I agree that it is better to pay $20.00 and be sure of a good job and that the ears will stand and are cut uniformly than to take a chance and do your own work, we must also consider the personal element and realize that all veterinarians are not designers and do not know what is essential in the way of correct ear cropping.

Human nature is not the same and while each veterinarian has graduated from his studies at college, one man may be more handy with the tools of the profession and may have given more attention to what constitutes a show type dog than another, whose main livelihood is derived from the large animal practice.

Before selecting your veterinarian to do the cropping, it is well to inquire of the various breeders and one-dog owners as to the satisfaction they have obtained. Some veterinarians make a specialty of ear cropping and by practice, become perfect. It is therefore wise to select a man who has had ample experience in this line.

264

HOME CROPPING

Hobday, who was a member of the Royal Academy of Veterinary Surgeons, tells us that previous to the revision of the rules of the Kennel Club in Great Britain on July 1, 1903 when ear cropping was abolished, the method used was to cut a piece of cardboard the required shape and lay it on the flap of the ear after the dog had been put under a complete anaesthetic. Strong scissors were then used to crop the right ear along the margins of the cardboard. When cropping the other ear the cardboard was reversed. Care must be taken to reverse the cardboard or the result will be very far from what is desired. Schmidt in his second edition of The Doberman Pinscher in America, advises the use of ear clamps. These clamps are supposed to give the correct shape to the trimmed ear and at the same time, shut off the circulation and prevent bleeding. Clamps are all very well if they are correctly placed. Otherwise the result is no better than the use of the cardboard pattern.

As the width of skull and length of head differ not only in breeds but in individuals of the same breed, a stereotyped pattern of cropping should not be used and the operator should learn from experience the type of cropping that will bring out the individual's expression. Dogs with short heads or thick skulls should have a longer ear crop, accentuating the length of head. This gives the over-all perspective of greater length.

I write the following from personal experience and while I do not claim to be ultra perfect in ear cropping, I did attain a semblance of perfection from experience as the result of numerous operations. The reader can take my suggestions for whatever they are worth and while I am aware that a very small percentage of the readers of this book will ever attempt to do their own ear cropping, if they are to make a financial success of raising a breed of dogs that require cropped ears by the dictates of fashion, they must curtail their overhead and thereby eliminate the expense of cropping. My experience was acquired on Standard, Miniature and Giant Schnauzers but cropping the ears of any breed is essentially the same.

My first litter of Schnauzers consisting of eight puppies cost me $10 apiece and the work was done by our leading veterinary surgeon, since deceased. One puppy out of the eight was a success. His ears stood beautifully. The balance either drooped or went over the head. Our surgeon was accustomed to cropping the ears of Boston Terriers and he cropped my Schnauzers on the same style, the ears being brought to needle points.

On the second litter, I sold the puppies uncropped at an early age and retained two males which were never cropped.

In the third litter, two sales hinged upon the delivery of the puppies with cropped ears and something had to be done. A friend of mine, who was a paperhanger, and raised a few Dobermans for pleasure, had done some successful cropping with ear clamps on his own dogs. He offered to crop the ears of my two puppies and, having more confidence in him than in the veterinarian, I gave him the job.

The result was all that could be desired and a few weeks later, I asked him to come to the kennel and crop a few of my older dogs, including a nine-months old Great Dane. This second try was not so successful. The dogs were of various ages and sizes and the use of ear clamps did not give a uniform effect. The Dane with large floppy ears was the worst of the lot. The right ear looked like a soup plate and the left ear although correct in design, was too long and did not stand.

I realized that if I were to continue raising Schnauzers or any breed that required cropped ears, I must do the work myself and I must learn to do it correctly or not at all.

As I did not believe in clamps or patterns, I wanted to learn the free-hand method. I therefore took cardboard cut in the shape of an uncropped ear and proceeded to cut the cardboard as I would cut the dog's ear. I did this hundreds of times and became so proficient that I could actually cut out a perfect ear blind-folded.

I was then ready for the next exercise. I obtained a cloth sack about the size of a dog's head, stuffed it tightly with sawdust and pinned onto the dummy head, flexible cardboard the shape of an uncropped ear. I then proceeded to cut the cardboard and found that it was an entirely different matter when it was attached to the dummy head than when I could turn the cardboard around in my hands. Being right-handed,

266

the left ear came easy but the right ear was a different matter: the shape was never the same. I seemed to get a narrower trim on the right ear than on the left. I overcame this difficulty by cropping the right ear first and then the left ear to match it.

After I had satisfied myself that I had gone as far as I could with the dummy, I took advantage of every dog that died at my kennel and before he was buried, his ears were cropped. Naturally as rigor mortis had set in, the ears would stand and the operation was not complicated by incorrect healing that sometimes occurs in live animals. However in several months I had become proficient in cropping free-hand and more than that, I had worked up a confidence in my own ability, which is the greater part of the battle.

My first endeavor was on a litter of Standard Schnauzers, most of which had ears like airplane wings, carrying them off to the side. I knew that with this type of ear carriage, the ears would be carried erect after cropping. First I put one puppy to sleep, using Abbott's Nembutal by hypodermic in the abdomen. The dosage is 1 c.c. to five pounds of body weight and the dog should go completely "out" within 15 minutes.

I did not crop the entire litter as a case of nerves on my part might have caused considerable damage. The next day I operated on two puppies and the following day, on four which was the balance of the litter. All operations were a success and the ears of each puppy stood by the time the tape was taken off.

Since that date which goes back to 1934, I have cropped many dogs and can perform the operation with practically no loss of blood.

Care should be taken as to the amount of nembutal to be injected. The dosage is 1 c.c. for each five pounds of body weight, administered hypodermically for a dog of normal condition and correct weight. Should the dog be underweight or emaciated, it is far better to let the cropping go until it is put back into condition. However if the operation must be done immediately, a dosage of one c.c. to each 7 pounds of body weight is advisable and if the animal does not go completely "out", finish it up with an ether cone.

On an extra fat dog, do not attempt to give an additional dose of nembutal. It is better to give the correct amount and if insufficient to put it to sleep, finish up with an ether cone.

Should your hypodermic needle strike the bladder or the liver, the dog may not go to sleep but will merely stagger and wobble around, in which case under no consideration give it a second injection. Let it come out of the effects of the injection and a few days later try again.

The dosage of nembutal given in capsules by mouth is 2 c.c. for 5 pounds of body weight but I do not advise this method as the time required is too prolonged.

After you have had considerable experience you might try to give the nembutal intravenously. Shave the front leg above the first joint, put a tourniquet above the elbow and feel for the artery. Have the correct amount of nembutal in your syringe and when you are successful in puncturing the artery with the needle, a slight amount of blood will enter the syringe. Now inject the nembutal very slowly, and I mean very slowly, a fraction of a c.c. at a time, waiting a few seconds after each pressure of the plunger. Almost at the same moment when you have a sufficient quantity in the artery, the dog will go completely "out" and become limp. Any additional nembutal injected may cause death. The advantage of this method is that sleep is instantaneous. You do not inject too much or too little. There are no delays and no chance of the animal not going to sleep and the operation being delayed.

You should have in readiness a pair of sharp serrated scissors, to prevent slipping and at least two hemostats. These should have straight blades from two to three inches in length. Shorter blades or curved blades are not desirable. You may place these forceps on the ear about one-half inch back of where you intend to make the cut and thereby stop practically all bleeding. Now cut the ear and remove the lower hemostat near the base of the ear. Tie a knot in the cat-gut and start to sew, using the lace stitch pictured on an adjoining page. After you have stitched up as far as you can, remove a second forcep and continue sewing to the tip of the ear.

Do not pull your stitches too tightly, only enough to stop bleeding as otherwise you may cause the ear to pucker when healed. When you reach the tip of the ear, pull the cat-gut tight and tie a couple of knots in the end, about one-half inch from the ear. When released the slack will be taken up and the knot will hold the stitches from coming loose. If you do not pull the stitch tight before tying the knot, there will be too much slack in the cat-gut and the ear will bleed.

The use of the serrated scissors is necessary as otherwise the skin with hair on the outside of the ear which is loose and not attached to the cartilage, may either slip back or forward and you will have difficulty in sewing it evenly.

When ears are too heavy and inclined to flop, it is sometimes advisable to trim the skin that is covered with hair slightly back from the cartilage and draw it up to the edge of the cartilage when sewing. This tends to hold the cartilage erect.

There are just two arteries in the ear: one near the base and one about two-thirds of the way up, toward the tip. If you do not mind working in the blood, you may crop the ear before putting on the artery forcep and then merely clamp off these two arteries.

It is advisable to use cat-gut rather than surgeon's silk for the stitching as cat-gut will sluff off while silk has to be picked out and when left in too long, the ear will heal over the silk.

While I have always made a practice of sterilizing my instruments, I do not believe that it is necessary to go to extremes as the ear is bound to become infected, no matter what you can do. This is entirely different from an abdominal operation, the same care need not be exercised.

TAPING

There are many methods used to assist the cartilage to stand erect. With a dog that flies his ears out to the side, you need feel no alarm. The ears will stand of their own accord. But in the case of a dog where his ears flop like a hound, assistance should be given.

Tape must not be placed over the raw edges as this causes infection and a discharge of pus, retarding the healing. The ears can be taped over the head, the raw edges exposed to the air and dusted with BFI powder. If this method is used, the tape must extend not only over the ears but under the neck as well, otherwise it will not stay on. The dog will lose the hair where the tape has adhered. This of course is not a permanent injury as the hair will grow back in a few weeks but is unsightly until nature takes it course.

Another method is the use of collodion in conjunction with the tape, to insure adhesion and plaster many layers of tape on the outside of the hair part of the ear with the view to obtaining a stiff board-like effect which is rigid enough to hold the ear erect.

You could also insert a small piece of orangewood similar to a tongue depressor between the layers of tape to give more rigidity.

Another method is to place one layer of adhesive on the hair side of the ear and then coat the tape with water glass such as grandmother used to use to put her eggs down for the winter, only do not dilute the water glass with water. Use it as it comes from the can. This will become very rigid and the ears cannot possibly droop.

Each day grease the raw edges and pick off the surplus scabs. If there is any indication of puckering, stretch the edge and break the pucker. This is painful to the dog but it is unavoidable for if the edge heals in a pucker, the ear will never stand.

After the operation, put the dog in a small cage. While recovering from the effects of the anaesthetic, he will throw himself from side to side and unless confined in small quarters, may not only damage his ears but may do himself bodily harm.

It is well to be prepared and have on hand strychnine tablets of 1/120 grain. Should you through some error have administered an overdose of nembutal, you may be able to correct the damage and save your dog by the use of strychnine, a stimulant which counteracts the effects of the nembutal.

Dissolve 1/120 grain of strychnine in several teaspoonfuls of sterile water. Draw it into the hypodermic and administer half the contents of the syringe into the neck. If the dog does not show signs of recovering from the anaesthetic within 30 minutes, the remainder of the solution in the syringe may be administered.   Be sure the water has been boiled and is sterile.

I want to warn the readers that while it is perfectly lawful to operate upon your own animals, under no conditions, practice on those belonging to a friend, either for a fee or gratis, as you are not a licensed veterinarian and if anything should go wrong, you can be held liable for damages for practicing without a license.

TAIL CROPPING

This is a minor operation when performed on puppies of from four to ten days of age.   There is little pain and the wound is soon healed.

Have someone hold the puppy for you; push the skin of the tail back toward the body as far as it will go and cut off the tail with a pair of scissors to the proper length.

When released, the skin should cover the stump and if it does not, then cut off a small portion of the stump or bone so that the skin may be drawn over the end and stitched.

It is not necessary to use cat-gut or surgeon's silk, just borrow a piece of your wife's sewing cotton and one of her needles.   It might be more convenient and would facilitate sewing if you could procure a curved surgical needle.   Use two cross-stitches.   This usually is sufficient but in severe cases of hemorrhage, put in as many stitches as are required to stop bleeding.

Some authorities advise the use of a tourniquet of cord at the base of the tail to shut off circulation.   However this is not at all necessary or desirable, if you will squeeze the tail between the thumb and index finger, shutting off the circulation while you are making the cut and putting in the stitches.

The practice of using a tourniquet is, in my estimation, the wrong procedure.   Should you forget to take off the tourniquet soon enough, the lack of circulation will kill the flesh between the tourniquet and the end of the tail and then a second operation will be necessary in order to remove the dead stump and you will have ruined your dog by causing him to have too short a tail.

Another reason for advocating sewing rather than a tourniquet is that it is always the liveliest pup that does the most moving around and consequently loses the most blood. He is more liable to break off a scab and start a fresh hemorrhage than a less active puppy. When tails are properly sewed, there is no danger of weakening an extra good puppy from excessive loss of blood.

It is well to touch the raw stumps with a little iodine but other than that, no medication is needed as the mother will lick the stump and keep it clean.

CROPPED EAR
LOOP STITCH

CH. CAPRIANA'S STEP ASIDE
(with handler Stan Flowers)

Sire: Ch. Capriana's Renegade
Dam: Ch. Leskay's Ginger

Breeders: Charles J. and Isolde Stofko
Owners: Don and Mary Smith

HEAD STUDY OF CHAMPION YOBANG OF SIRRAH CREST
Breeder and Owner: Dr. and Mrs. R. C. Harris
Sire: Ch. Duke Cronian; Dam: Madeira of Sirrah Crest

CHAPTER XV

The Boxer on the West Coast

By Robert W. Leach

NOWHERE in America has the Boxer made greater strides than on the West Coast. He has found an enthusiastic welcome in the movie stars' homes of Southern California; he has adapted himself to the city apartments of busy San Francisco; and he has fitted perfectly into the vigorous, progressive life of the Pacific Northwest. So widespread has been his acceptance that he easily tops all other working dogs in show entries. In fact, it is a rare show in which the Boxer entry does not top all other breeds.

This tremendous popular acceptance by Westerners is the sparkplug that has created a breed and exhibiting fancy that is not exceeded, on a population basis, anywhere else in the country. Some of Boxerdom's best-known kennel names and several of the American Boxer Club's most active member clubs are on the West Coast.

These clubs include: The San Diego County Boxer Club, The Pacific Coast Boxer Club (Los Angeles), The Boxer Club of Southern California (Los Angeles County), The California Boxer Club (San Francisco Bay Area), The Oregon Boxer Club and The Pacific Northwest Boxer Club (Washington). All of these clubs hold specialty shows, puppy matches and obedience trials, some of them as separate events and others in connection with all-breed shows.

CH. SALAL'S SURE CONCEIT

Sire: Ch. Adonidin v. U-Chetnik   Dam: Bladan's Hellcat

Breeder-Owner: Salal Kennels, Mr. and Mrs. O. M. Orton

Their sponsorship of entries and offering of fine premiums has contributed a great deal toward making the Western Boxer owner show-conscious, and the competition for championship points and best-of-breed awards is especially keen.

Nor have these clubs ignored obedience training. On the contrary, most of them actively sponsor training classes or otherwise encourage their membership to train their dogs. The Boxer Club of Southern California has, for six years, held regular training classes for C.D. work as well as the more advanced work required for C.D.X. and U.D. degrees. Nearly a thousand Boxers have been trained by this one club's classes thus far and many of them have won their C.D. degrees with correspondingly smaller percentages going on to win C.D.X. and U.D. degrees. As a result the Boxer is a familiar sight in all obedience rings on the West Coast. At the 1949 Harbor Cities all-breed show (Long Beach, California), there were 73 Boxers entered in the obedience trials, far more than any other breed and nearly half of the total entries.

Behind this great popular acceptance of Boxers and the accompanying show and obedience activity are the breeders. On the West Coast they are numerous, many with national and international reputations, and they are producing specimens whose quality and influence on the breed generally are on a par with other sections of the country. Not that West Coast breeders have attempted to develop bloodlines by sole use of local studs or otherwise maintained a provincial attitude in their breed. Before the war, of course, rail transportation of bitches to Eastern studs was an expensive, time-consuming proposition and consequently many breeders used local studs who would have preferred to have a wider choice. But since the war, air transportation has brought the Western breeder into close contact with the rest of the country and now nearly every worthwhile stud is no more than 24 hours away from any West Coast kennel. And this has been advantageous to Eastern breeders, too, as evidenced by the ever-increasing number of bitches that are air-shipped to the West Coast to be bred to top local studs.

INT. CH. HIGH SPOT REQUESTED, C.D.

Sire: High Spot Hot Shot   Dam: Ch. Lady Jill of Marmac
Breeder-Owner: High Spot Kennels

CH. MAZELAINE'S MASTERPIECE

Sire: Ch. Bubbling Over of Lilac Hedge   Dam: Omen of Mazelaine

Breeder: Mazelaine Kennels

Owners: Mr. and Mrs. Keith Rider, Northridge, California

CH. MARQUAM HILLS COMANCHE

Sire: Ch. Bang Away of Sirrah Crest
Dam: Legacy of Clover Downs

Bred and owned by Dr. and Mrs. Robert Burke

Before the war, Boxer bloodlines in the West were identical to those of other sections—that is, Sigurd, Lustig, Dorian and Utz sons and daughters. However, the first California-bred litter was bred by Dr. and Mrs. Clark James Burnham, Jr., of Berkeley in 1935. The sire was Bimbo I v. Preussenadler and the dam Elmi v.d. Hohen Schrott. It is interesting to note, in this connection, that Mr. Keith Rider of Northridge, California, brought the first registered Boxer to California. This Boxer was Kolbs von Graudenz, 97079, whose sire, Arnulf Graudenz, was the first Boxer ever registered by the A.K.C., in 1904. Kolbs' dam was also the dam of Arnulf, Rose v. Graudenz, who was out of Flora Fuhr, a Flock St. Salvator daughter. Kolbs, a brindle, was purchased in Chicago in 1906 as a puppy by Mr. Rider's father as a present for his son. Mr. Rider brought the dog with him to California and he died in Los Angeles in 1916.

Although this early beginning was without issue, it none-the-less prophesied that Southern California was to later become the center of Boxer activities on the West Coast. Probably the first Southern California breeder, and who is still active, was Paul M. Streib of Los Angeles. He bred the third litter ever registered from California. From this litter came his Adeline of Pacific who was bred to the Check son, Gomo se Sumbula, and produced Ch. Astrid v. Lew.

Another early Boxer breeder in Southern California was Dr. Blake Watson of Hollywood, who established the von Tal kennels. He imported or purchased from the East several fine dogs, including Ch. Jod v. Neu Drosedow and Ch. Ingo v. Heger se Sumbula. Ingo, a son of Sieger Fachinger v. Neu Drosedow and a double Sigurd grandson, became the first important sire on the West Coast. He died in 1945, leaving seven champions and two additional producers. Although not now as active as formerly in breeding and exhibiting, Dr. Watson maintains a real interest in the breed and his services as a judge of the breed are widely sought.

In the fall of 1935, the first of several well-known

281

Eastern Boxer kennels moved to Southern California. This was the High Spot kennel of Paul and Helen Beck Ladin. With them they brought three promising dogs: High Spot Dotti, High Spot Major and High Spot Boots. All three were by the imported stud, Armin v. Hanseatenhof Stoeckersburg, and all three became champions. Dotti was, in fact, the first Boxer to be shown to the title on the Pacific coast, in 1937. Major was sold to George Zimmerman of Los Angeles, who, in addition to finishing him, put him through obedience training and earned a C.D. degree. It is believed that Major was the first Boxer champion to win an obedience degree.

Paul Ladin died in 1940 but Helen (now Mrs. Glenn Dodrer) carried on the High Spot breeding program. She purchased the imported Lustig son, Ch. Eros v. Luisenblick, and Lady Jill of Marmac, which she showed to her championship, a splendid fawn daughter of Ch. Sir Gallahad of Bladan, C.D. From these two came several fine progeny, including High Spot Lady Be Good, who was forced into retirement after earning 9 points. The outstanding male from this breeding is High Spot Jill's Sir Eros, C.D., owned by Mr. and Mrs. Robert W. Leach of North Hollywood, who has already sired a number of promising puppies. Another product of Eros-Jill breeding was High Spot Jennifer, an excellent producer. She was bred to Mrs. William Z. Breed's Ch. Dawn Patrol of Barmere, a Ch. Edel of Barmere son, and produced High Spot Hot Shot. This splendid young red fawn with 15 points died before he could be finished but several breedings were obtained from him that indicated he would have been a terrific producer. One such breeding was back to Lady Jill from which came Int. Ch. High Spot Requested, C.D. Requested already has produced a number of excellent match-winning puppies and gives every indication of becoming an outstanding sire.

The High Spot breeding program before the war showed a strong tendency to line-breed through the Armin get. But during the war and immediately thereafter, High Spot invested heavily in Lustig blood (through Eros), Sigurd blood through the purchase of Ch. Buko v.d. Sommerau of

INT. CH. MONARCH'S EGO OF GARAKONTI
Sire: Ch. Merry Monarch   Dam: Ch. Pansy of Sierralair
Breeder: H. C. and Isabel Rublee
Owner: Valley Grove Kennels, Dr. and Mrs. Kenneth G. Ruedy

Marenore, one of Sigurd's finest sons, and through Dorian by breeding Ch. High Spot Dotti to him.

The importance of High Spot in the growth of Boxerdom on the Pacific coast cannot be measured by breeding activities alone. Paul and Helen Ladin showed their dogs everywhere, doing a magnificent job of public relations for the breed. As a consequence, many breeders and exhibitors now in the forefront of the Fancy got their start by the acquisition of a High Spot Boxer.

One of this group is Dr. and Mrs. R. C. Harris of Santa Ana, California, whose Sirrah Crest kennel, since its founding in 1940, has been one of the most successful in the history of the breed. Their two foundation studs were Dorian sons, the first being Ch. Duke Cronian who was out of a Lustig daughter. The second was Ch. Endymion of Mazelaine who was out of a Sigurd daughter.

With this beginning Dr. and Mrs. Harris repeatedly bred back to these two sires and their offspring, producing an unbroken string of champions now approaching thirty in number, many of which have done tremendous group and best-in-show winning. Duke Cronian's first title-winning son was Ch. Kobang of Sirrah Crest who was out of Kantatrix of Mazelaine, a Lustig-Nocturn daughter. Kobang has proved himself to be a pillar of the Sirrah Crest breeding program. Bred to a Ch. Kavalier of Mazelaine daughter, he produced Madcap of Sirrah Crest. She was, in turn, bred to Nightcap of Sirrah Crest, who was by Endymion and a Kobang daughter. This breeding produced Ch. Xebony of Sirrah Crest, an extremely dark brindle, who compiled a remarkable show record and is undoubtedly one of the most striking and eye-catching Boxers ever seen in the breed ring.

Xebony has proved himself also to be a potent sire. He was bred to Ch. Questa of Sirrah Crest, a Kobang daughter, and this breeding produced the golden brindle, Ch. Vick Wick of Sirrah Crest, a best-in-show winner.

Another successful example of the Sirrah Crest line breeding is Ch. Yobang of Sirrah Crest. He is by Duke Cronian and out of the Utz daughter, Madeira of Sirrah Crest, who

HIGH SPOT JILL'S SIR EROS

Sire: Ch. Eros v. Luisenblick   Dam: Ch. Lady Jill of Marmac

Breeder: High Spot Kennels

Owners: Mr. and Mrs. Robert W. Leach, North Hollywood, California

285

is herself a Duke Cronian granddaughter. Yobang climaxed a successful show career by going best Boxer and topping the group at Westminster in 1948.

But Yobang was, perhaps, even more successful as a sire. He was bred to Umbra of Sirrah Crest, a Whirlaway of Mazelaine daughter out of Ch. Oracle of Sirrah Crest, and produced Ch. Ursa Major of Sirrah Crest. Ursa was then bred to Verily Verily of Sirrah Crest, a litter sister to Vick Wick, and on February 17, 1949, produced a litter containing a puppy that was destined to become the greatest show-winning dog of all time—for all breeds.

This was Ch. Bang Away of Sirrah Crest, who, just past his third birthday, has amassed an incredible total of more than sixty best-in-show wins. His greatest feat occurred in February of 1951 when he won the American Boxer Club specialty and then, two days later, took best-in-show at Westminster. No other Boxer has ever been able to score this double triumph.

The perfect Boxer hasn't been bred and possibly never will be. But in Bang Away, Dr. and Mrs. Harris have arrived at a combination of qualities that has proved unbeatable. Bang Away is a handsome fawn, beautifully marked with four white feet, white chest and a white blaze on his black muzzle. The over-all impression created by the dog in the ring is best characterized by the word, "elegance." In addition to this, Bang Away possesses a quality all too rarely seen in Boxers—a quality that is indispensable for the dog that wants to win regularly in group and best-in-show competition. That quality is showmanship. It is probable that no Boxer has ever stepped into the ring that could top Bang Away in this respect. He struts, he gaits beautifully and with a magnificent assurance and he seems to glory in the applause of the gallery. One experienced observer commented that Bang Away seemed to be *daring* the judge to put up any other dog.

As a sire of the breed, Bang Away has only begun his career, and there is no way of predicting how he will fare in this respect. Certainly he will have ample opportunity

286

CH. RUDA RIVER'S EBONY BELLE

Sire: Ch. Vick Wick of Sirrah Crest
Dam: Ardaranda of Ruda River

Breeders: Mr. and Mrs. Arthur Davidson
Owner: Lynn Barkow

CH. APOLLO OF SAN JOAQUIN
Sire: Whirlaway of Mazelaine C. D.
Dam: Gay Lady Inga of San Joaquin
Breeder and Owner: Mr. and Mrs. J. Howard Davis, Bakersfield, Calif.
BEST BOXER at the 1948 Specialty Show of the American Boxer Club

to prove himself but because of the tremendous number of Boxers being whelped in the country, it has been asserted that the day when any one stud can dominate the breed as did Sigurd or his three famous grandsons, is forever past.

About the time Sirrah Crest was getting its start, Mr. and Mrs. J. Howard Davis of Bakersfield, California, became interested in Boxers. Their foundation bitch, acquired from Dr. Blake Watson, was Folly von Tal, by the Lustig son, Ch. Jod v. Neu Drosedow and out of the Sigurd granddaughter, Ch. Yanna von Marienhof se Sumbula. Though not of show quality, Folly proved a sound investment for when she was bred to Ch. Ingo von Tal, a son of Ch. Ingo v. Heger, she produced Gay Lady Ingo of San Joaquin. Although not a champion, Gay Lady proved herself to be one of the important producing bitches of the breed. By Furore Falcon, a grandson of champions Draper and Dauber of Tulgey Wood, she produced the bitch Ch. Falcon's Folly. When bred to the ill-fated Whirlaway of Mazelaine, a Lustig and Dorian grandson and producer of six champions, she whelped Ch. Apollo of San Joaquin.

The advent of Apollo served notice to the Boxer world that the West Coast had "arrived"; that breeding efforts there were beginning to bear fruit; and that henceforth campaigners from the West would be a factor in show rings of the East. Apollo won all up and down the Pacific coast including what was then very rare—groups and best-in-shows. A handsome fawn, Apollo proved himself a wonderful ambassador of the breed and did much to make the public Boxer-conscious. He climaxed his show career by going to New York in 1948 and winning the American Boxer Club specialty—the first Western dog ever to do so.

Apollo was thereafter retired from the show ring—to a career as a stud which is still going strong and successfully. To date he has produced seven champions: El Camino's Antonia, Inclinta del Rey, Jembox's Debonair, Bar None of San Joaquin, El Molino Schone Kristina,

Rulaine's Ballerina and Fancy's Pleez Wynne. With the exception of Bar None, none of these were campaigned by the Davises and all of them are out of different bitches. A number of other Apollo get are point winners and most of them seem certain of finishing. Thus far Apollo is the West Coast's most widely used stud and it is likely that he is making a lasting impression on the breed.

Another prominent Southern California kennel which got its start during the years immediately preceding the war was the Valley Grove kennels of Dr. and Mrs. Kenneth G. Ruedy in Tarzana, California. Their first Boxer was acquired from High Spot and as a six-months-old puppy it won its class the first time shown. This was enough to give the Ruedys the fever and they immediately plunged into Boxers. Their first champion was High Spot Gold Girl, which also was acquired from High Spot. This bitch was out of High Spot Letti by Ch. Magnet se Sumbula, one of Dr. Blake Watson's studs.

When the war came, the Ruedys disposed of their rapidly growing kennel but immediately afterward began rebuilding. They acquired three bitches from Dr. Harris: the Utz daughter, Madeira of Sirrah Crest, who was the dam of Yobang; Sirrah Crest Petty Girl, a Duke Cronian daughter out of an Ingo v. Heger daughter; and Quinkle of Sirrah Crest, a Ch. Kavalier of Mazelaine daughter out of a Ouida of Mazelaine daughter.

The results of the Valley Grove breeding program showed its greatest success after the purchase of a young golden brindle named Monarch's Ego of Garakonti. This handsome youngster was bred by H. C. Rublee. The dam was Ch. Pansy of Sierralair, a Yardbird of Barmere daughter. The sire was Ch. Merry Monarch, one of the leading sires of the breed. Ego was an immediate sensation in Western show rings. He completed his American and Canadian championships easily and then settled down to establishing a show record which has been topped by no other West Coast dog except Bang Away.

He was the leading sire on the West Coast for 1951.

CH. AIR MINDED MISS OF AIREALM
Sire: Ch. Ingo Von Tal
Dam: Duchess of Emlu (a double Dorian granddaughter)
Breeder-Owner: Keith Rider, Northridge, California

Nationally he was the third highest ranking in group wins for Boxers in 1951, being beaten only by Bang Away and Ch. Duke of Highwinds. During the peak of his showing activity he put together a string of 23 consecutive victories in the breed.

In addition Ego gives every indication of becoming one of the important sires of the breed. By early 1952 he had already sired five champions and a dozen or more of his get are point winners and many of them will undoubtedly finish. Valley Grove breeding plans call for intensive breeding in the Ego line and results seem to indicate that this strain will be very successful in the show ring and establish a potent influence in the breed generally.

The year 1943 saw the removal to California of the Barmere kennels of Mrs. William Z. Breed. And with the establishment of this great name on the Pacific coast, the Fancy could now boast that Boxers were truly a breed of nationwide importance with the very best bloodlines and breeding establishments evenly spread across the country.

Mrs. Breed brought most of her grown stock with her and immediately set about using the same technique that had brought such tremendous success to Barmere in the East. That is, she always bred her bitches to the stud she considered most suitable. Barmere never has held to the method of concentrating on studs held in the Barmere runs. Since the death of Sigurd, it is literally true that Barmere bitches have travelled to the court of nearly every important stud in the country.

In this connection it is interesting to note that Barmere's fifty Boxer champions fall into the following groups: 13 were either imported or bred in Germany; 10 were purchased here of which only one was already a champion, Ch. Dodi v.d. Stoeckersburg; and the other 27 were Barmere bred.

The top Barmere production of recent years undoubtedly is Ch. Barmere's Locket, an exceptionally stylish and beautifully moving fawn by Ch. Yachtsman of Barmere out of Ch. New Deal of Barmere. Her most notable win was

CH. CANYONAIR'S TALKED ABOUT
Sire: Ch. Canyonair Hickory Dick, C.D.   Dam: Canyonair Honey Chile
Breeder: Mrs. Paul Newhall Davis
Owners: Coleman B. Cook and H. J. Bremkamp, Columbus, Ohio

capturing best at the 1952 American Boxer Club specialty. And two days later she was best opposite to Bang Away at Westminster.

This makes the third time since 1948 that a Western-bred Boxer has taken this top Boxer show, Apollo having turned the trick in 1948 and Bang Away in 1951.

Mrs. Breed's latest champion is Barmere's Trouble Shooter. Out of Yolanda of Barmere, Trouble Shooter is a son of Bang Away—one of that great winner's first sons to reach the show ring.

Mr. Keith Rider, whom we mentioned earlier as bringing the first registered Boxer to California, revived his interest in Boxers some years later and now maintains the Skyrealm kennels in Northridge, California. Like many other Southern Californians, Mr. Rider used Dr. Blake Watson's Ch. Ingo von Tal in a breeding with Duchess of Emlu (a double Dorian granddaughter) and from this litter came his homebred Ch. Air Minded Miss of Airealm. In addition, he acquired Ch. Mazelaine's Masterpiece.

Masterpiece has proved himself to be an excellent stud. His sire was out of the famous "B" litter of Lilac Hedge, Ch. Bubbling Over. His dam was the Utz daughter, Omen of Mazelaine. Masterpiece first came to fame as a stud when he was bred to Canyonair Diamond Lil, C.D., producing Ch. Canyonair Hickory Dick and Ch. Canyonair Honey Chile. Because of the success of this breeding it was repeated and produced two more champions: Canyonair Lightnin' and Canyonair Lucidor. In addition, Masterpiece was bred to Frank and Virginia Lober's Gretchen von Lober which produced Int. Ch. Lober's Razzle Dazzle. This husky young fawn went through to his championship in four straight shows and won his Canadian title in the same fashion. Razzle Dazzle, in turn, shows every prospect of becoming a first-rate stud, and his puppies, from a variety of bitches, are just beginning to show their worth in the show ring.

Masterpiece's sixth champion is Ch. Skyrealm's Master Key out of Milchrista's Deborah. Several more are in

AM. & BRAZ. CH. EVO WEN'S IMPRESARIO

Sire: Ch. Evo-Wen's Big Story
Dam: Evo-Wen's Mecque Mecque

Breeder: R. R. Owen
Owner: Mrs. George M. Cowie

prospect. Mrs. Madeline Stapleton bred her Stapleton's Beau Allure to him and got Stapleton's Cover Girl and Whizz Bang. Cover Girl won the 1952 Boxer Club of Southern California Futurity and went to best opposite in the 1952 Specialty of the same club. She should be Masterpiece's seventh champion before long. Other point winners by this stud include Mr. and Mrs. Carl Hanson's Farmdale's Miss Talk of the Town which is out of their Farmdale's High Spot Duchess, C.D.X., and Canyonair O My Goodness, which is out of the Masterpiece daughter, Ch. Canyonair Honey Chile.

One of the most successful kennels established in Southern California since the war is the Canyonair Kennels of Mr. and Mrs. Paul Newhall Davis. They started by purchasing, from Dr. Harris, Ornadoon of Sirrah Crest, a daughter of Ch. Kavalier of Mazelaine. Ornadoon was bred to Endymion and produced two bitches that gave the Davises a great start. One was Bianca of Canyonair which completed her championship. The other, Diamond Lil, C.D., while not finishing, proved to be even more important for she turned out to be a remarkable producer.

In two breedings to Masterpiece she produced the four champions mentioned earlier. Canyonair's sixth champion is the beautiful young bitch, Canyonair's Talked About. She is the product of a breeding between litter mates, Ch. Canyonair Hickory Dick, C.D., and Ch. Canyonair Honey Chile. Talked About won the 1951 Boxer Club of Southern California Futurity and thereafter won her championship in short order. She has been campaigned in the Middle West and has been a consistent winner. Her sire, Canyonair Hickory Dick, C.D., has won several best-in-shows and numerous groups being campaigned both on the West Coast and in the Middle West.

Hickory Dick sired Canyonair Zickory Dick out of a Karlo von Wolffschlucht daughter. Zickory Dick in turn was bred to Canyonair Southern Belle which is by Ch. Baron Trevor of Tredegar out of Diamond Lil. From this breeding have come a beautifully matched pair of golden brindle

CH. NONITA OF CROSS ACRES

Sire: Ch. Schoolmaster of Mazelaine   Dam: Ch. Bonita of Cross Acres

Breeder: Mrs. Cecil Cross

Owned and shown to championship by Mrs. William Z. Breed,

Barmere Kennels, Van Nuys, California

puppies that should ably carry on the great reputation of their grandsires. In addition there are several other young dogs that are expected to enhance the Canyonair name. Two of them are out of Honey Chile as a result of a breeding to Mazelaine's Kappellmeister, and a third is Canyonair's Twice Told, a litter sister to Ch. Canyonair's Talked About.

Several other Southern Californians not previously mentioned are gradually working up kennels which show a great deal of promise for the future. Among these are Mr. and Mrs. Glenn Fancy. They bred their High Spot Heiress, C.D. (an Int. Ch. High Spot Requested daughter out of Ch. High Spot Classic) to Apollo and got Ch. Fancy's Pleez Wynne. This lovely young bitch was winner for five points at the 1952 ABC Specialty and finished soon thereafter.

Mr. and Mrs. Harry Singer are producing some excellent litters out of their High Spot Juliette, C.D.X., and High Spot Junior Miss. Both of these brindle bitches are strongly bred in the Lustig line. Mr. and Mrs. Mike Bird's Gay Holly kennel is rapidly coming to the fore based on Canyonair and Masterpiece bloodlines and Mr. and Mrs. Glen E. McDorman have already produced a number of outstanding puppies from their High Spot bloodlines.

In central California the Bonneville kennels of Darrel L. Hicken of Richmond has laid out a breeding program based on strong Sirrah Crest bloodlines. To date their outstanding production is the young Ch. Viking of Bonneville. He is by Ch. Vick Wick of Sirrah Crest. The dam is Venice of Bonneville who was by Ch. Riot of Sirrah Crest, an Utz son, and out of Yum Yum of Sirrah Crest who is a Duke Cronian daughter.

Farther north, in Washington state, a number of enthusiastic breeders have established Boxer kennels which seem to assure that the future of the breed in that area is safe.

The oldest active breeders and exhibitors in the area are Mr. and Mrs. O. M. Orton of Raymond, Washington, who have the Salal kennels. Their first venture into the

SAN JOAQUIN BOXERS
Owned by Mr. and Mrs. J. Howard Davis of Cayucos, California
Ch. Apollo of San Joaquin—in center; His son, Ch. Bar None of San
Joaquin—in background, and Bar None's son, Tip Topper of San
Joaquin—in foreground

breed was with the purchase of Ch. Vassal of Mazelaine, by Utz out of Nocturne. The Orton's sold Vassal and later purchased and campaigned to her championship, Bladan's Burning Flame. Flame was out of Ch. Bladan's U-Chetnik and by Binnie v. Kerspetal. This beautiful bitch was never defeated in the classes finishing in four straight shows. She was retired for breeding but died when her first litter was three days old—by Ch. Adonidin v. U-Chetnik. Another brood bitch, Bladan's Hellcat, died at the same time soon after whelping a litter by the same stud. This tragedy, caused by encephalitis, nearly wiped out the Salal kennels. However, the Ortons stuck it out and eventually finished two of Hellcat's orphaned puppies: Ch. Salal's Sure Conceit and Ch. Salal's Saucy Cherie. Both of these bitches live at Salal and are expected to carry on with their concentration of Bladan bloodlines.

The Sky Lane kennels of Mr. and Mrs. Lauren H. Enloe of Seattle, Washington, have their homebred Ch. Sky Lane's My Buddy, C.D., as their foundation. Buddy is by Int. Ch. Udandie of Sirrah Crest out of the Lustig daughter, My Gal Sal of Marienhof.

Eveleen Wedekind of the von Wedekind kennel, Vancouver, Washington, has the bitch Ch. Roulette of Barmere, a Ch. Linnay's Conquest daughter out of Yo Yo of Barmere. It is planned to breed her to the Bang Away son, Ch. Barmere's Trouble Shooter, in the summer of 1952. The kennel has at stud Grand Climax of Barmere, a Ch. Merry Monarch son out of Quick Scandal of Barmere. Climax needs but a few points to complete his championship.

The Meridian kennels of Mr. and Mrs. S. L. Pomeroy are located at Puyallup, Washington. This young kennel has gotten off to a promising start. Breeding their bitch, Unser Schonen Medchan, to Ch. Ursa Major of Sirrah Crest, they got a splendid bitch, Maychn of Meridian, which they promptly campaigned to her American and Canadian championships. Two others from this litter, the bitch Magic of Meridian and a young male Major of Meridian, are being shown and will probably be finished soon.

300

Meanwhile, show entries throughout the Northwest are increasing and more and more people are buying and breeding Boxers. It shouldn't be too long before some really outstanding dogs come from that area.

CH. DAWN PATROL OF BARMERE
Sire: Ch. Edel of Barmere   Dam: Juliet of Barmere
Breeder-Owner: Mrs. William Z. Breed of Barmere
Kennels, Van Nuys, California

CH. STAPLETON'S SHOW GIRL

Sire: Ch. Barrage of Quality Hill
Dam: Stapleton's Beau Allure

Breeders: Madeleine B. Stapleton and Phyllis King
Owner: Mrs. George M. Cowie

BLADAN'S ANZAC

Sire: Ch. Bladan's Chetnik   Dam: Ch. Blue Smoke of Bladan
Breeder: Dr. Dan M. Gordon, Bladan Kennels, New York City
Owner: Mrs. Owen Young, Alani Drive, Honolulu, Hawaii

Penelope Rae Harris, daughter of Dr. and Mrs. R. C. Harris, handling
Champion Mazelaine's Blond Bombshell

304